Issues in Media

Issues in Media

SECOND EDITION

CQ PRESS

A Division of SAGE
Washington, D.C.

SELECTIONS FROM CQ RESEARCHER

CQ Press
2300 N Street, NW, Suite 800
Washington, DC 20037

Phone: 202–729–1900; toll-free, 1–866–4CQ-PRESS (1–866–427–7737)

Web: www.cqpress.com

Cover design: Judy Myers, Graphic Design
Cover photo: AP Photo/Ross D. Franklin
Composition: C&M Digitals (P) Ltd.

⊗ The paper used in this publication exceeds the requirements of the American National Standard for Information Sciences—Permanence of Paper for Printed Library Materials, ANSI Z39.48–1992.

Printed and bound in the United States of America

14 13 12 11 10   1 2 3 4 5

A CQ Press College Division Publication

Director	Brenda Carter
Editorial Director	Charisse Kiino
Marketing manager	Christopher O'Brien
Managing editor	Stephen Pazdan
Production editor	Sarah Fell
Electronic production manager	Paul Pressau

Library of Congress Cataloging-in-Publication Data

Issues in media: selections from CQ researcher. — 2nd ed.
    p. cm.
    Includes bibliographical references.
    ISBN 978-1-60871-720-0 (pbk.: alk. paper) 1. Mass media—Social aspects. 2. Mass media and culture.
3. Mass media and public opinion. 4. Digital media—Social aspects. I. CQ Press.

HM1206.I77 2010
302.23—dc22

2010038352

Contents

Annotated Contents

good Summary

Future of Journalism

Thomas Jefferson once famously remarked that if he had to choose between government without newspapers or newspapers without government, he wouldn't hesitate to preserve newspapers. Today, however, newspapers across the country are declining in circulation, advertising and profitability. Some have ceased publication. Others are reducing or closing Washington and state capital bureaus, laying off staff and cutting back the news coverage they provide. Many journalists, scholars, political activists and government officials worry that government without newspapers could be on the horizon and that citizens may soon be unable to obtain sufficient information for effective self-government. As more Americans turn to the Internet and cable television for news, however, there is hope that new forms of journalism will fill the gaps. Meanwhile, newspapers are attempting to give themselves new birth online.

Media Ownership

Media companies are expanding rapidly, integrating broadcast television, cable, radio, newspapers, books, magazines and the Internet under their roofs. Five conglomerates control most prime-time TV programming, and one company—Clear Channel—dominates radio. Yet, in the paradox of today's media landscape, consumers have more choices than ever, although critics say too many of those choices are low-brow offerings like "reality" TV. Meanwhile, newcomers—such as satellite radio and bloggers—keep entering the arena. Now, as media companies push to grow ever bigger, a nationwide debate rages over whether there's enough diversity of content and ownership. In June 2003, the Federal Communications Commission relaxed its media-ownership rules, but subsequent resistance from lawmakers threatened to roll back the sweeping changes.

Future of Books

The migration of books to electronic screens has been accelerating with the introduction of mobile reading on Kindles, iPhones and Sony Readers and the growing power of Google's Book Search engine. Even the book's form is mutating as innovators experiment with adding video, sound and computer graphics to text. Some fear a loss of literary writing and reading; others worry for the world's storehouse of knowledge if it all goes digital. A recent settlement among Google, authors and publishers would make more out-of-print books accessible online, but there is concern about putting such a vast trove of literature into the hands of a private company. So far, barely 1 percent of books sold in the United States are electronic. Still, the economically strapped publishing industry is under pressure to do more marketing and publishing online as younger, screen-oriented readers replace today's core buyers—middle-aged women.

Blog Explosion

The term "blog" was coined only in 1997, but 13 years later the blogging phenomenon is sweeping across the United States and around the world. Millions of bloggers are filling the blogosphere with everything from personal journals and family photographs to political advocacy and journalistic commentary. Blogophiles say the blogging revolution is changing politics, business and popular culture for the better by reducing the influence of elites and institutions and allowing for wider public participation and greater interactivity. Some skeptics, however, question whether blogging is anything more than an Internet fad. And some critics say public-policy blogs spew too much unconfirmed information and overhyped rhetoric into the political process. But with easy-to-use software and a growing interest among individuals as well as businesses and government, the blogging phenomenon appears unlikely to peak any time soon.

Online Privacy

The Internet has become not only a primary means of communication but also a place where millions of Americans store important personal data—from credit-card numbers and bank account information to family photos and histories of their online purchases. But data stored online are not given the same legal protection as data that Americans store in their homes. What's more, powerful new technologies are creating unexpected challenges to privacy online. Advertisers, for example, can now track the websites you visit, and the actions you take on those sites, to analyze how to more effectively sell products to you. And they may sell the information they collect to others. Privacy advocates, and some lawmakers in Congress, say the growing threats to online privacy point to the need for stronger laws to protect users' data. But Republicans in Congress warn that overregulation may cripple the economic foundation of the Internet.

Press Freedom

Wrenching changes in the news business are starting to alter the legal landscape for journalists. The federal Freedom of Information Act and "shield" laws in many states give reporters access to official documents and offer some protections against prosecutors who demand to know journalists' confidential sources or information that reporters have gathered. Amid catastrophic revenue declines, however, media companies struggling to stay afloat have less money to throw into court fights to enforce their journalistic rights. An increasing number of online bloggers—including those who call themselves independent journalists—have even fewer resources. Moreover, politicians have been arguing over which kinds of bloggers—if any—should be defined as journalists entitled to free-press protections. The debate on that issue has stalled progress on a proposed federal shield law in the Senate, though backers were hopeful of reaching a compromise.

Preface

W ill traditional print books disappear from the market-place? Can the Internet fill the reporting gaps caused by the decline of newspapers? Should partisan bloggers get free-press protections? These questions—and many more—are at the heart of today's media landscape. How can instructors best engage students with these crucial issues? We feel that students need objective, yet provocative examinations of these issues to understand how they affect citizens today and will for years to come. This collection aims to promote in-depth discussion, facilitate further research and help readers formulate their own positions on crucial issues. Get your students talking both inside and outside the classroom about *Issues in Media*.

This second edition text includes six up-to-date reports by *CQ Researcher*, an award-winning weekly policy brief that brings complicated issues down to earth. Each report chronicles and analyzes the background, current situation and future outlook of a policy discussion or societal topic. This collection covers a range of issues found in most mass communication and media literacy courses.

CQ RESEARCHER

CQ Researcher was founded in 1923 as *Editorial Research Reports* and was sold primarily to newspapers as a research tool. The magazine was renamed and redesigned in 1991 as *CQ Researcher*. Today, students are its primary audience. While still used by hundreds of journalists and newspapers, many of which reprint portions of the reports, the *Researcher*'s main subscribers are now high school, college and public libraries. In 2002, *Researcher* won the American Bar Association's coveted Silver Gavel award for magazine excellence for a series of nine reports on civil liberties and other legal issues.

Researcher staff writers—all highly experienced journalists—sometimes compare the experience of writing a *Researcher* report to drafting a college term paper. Indeed, there are many similarities. Each report is as long as many term papers—about 11,000 words—and is written by one person without any significant outside help. One of the key differences is that writers interview leading experts, scholars and government officials for each issue.

Like students, staff writers begin the creative process by choosing a topic. Working with the *Researcher*'s editors, the writer identifies a controversial subject that has important public policy implications. After a topic is selected, the writer embarks on one to two weeks of intense research. Newspaper and magazine articles are clipped or downloaded, books are ordered and information is gathered from a wide variety of sources, including interest groups, universities and the government. Once the writers are well informed, they develop a detailed outline, and begin the interview process. Each report requires a minimum of ten to fifteen interviews with academics, officials, lobbyists and people working in the field. Only after all interviews are completed does the writing begin.

CHAPTER FORMAT

Each issue of *CQ Researcher*, and therefore each selection in this book, is structured in the same way. Each begins with an overview, which briefly summarizes the areas that will be explored in greater detail in the rest of the chapter. The next section chronicles important and current debates on the topic under discussion and is structured around a number of key questions, such as "Do federal privacy policies regarding the Internet need to be updated?" and "Is the U.S. media industry too consolidated?" These questions are usually the subject of much debate among practitioners and scholars in the field. Hence, the answers presented are never conclusive but rather detail the range of opinion on the topic.

Next, the "Background" section provides a history of the issue being examined. This retrospective covers important legislative measures, executive actions and court decisions that illustrate how current policy has evolved. Then the "Current Situation" section examines contemporary policy issues, legislation under consideration and legal action being taken. Each selection concludes with an "Outlook" section, which addresses possible regulation, court rulings, and initiatives from Capitol Hill and the White House over the next five to ten years.

Each report contains features that augment the main text: two to three sidebars that examine issues related to the topic at hand, a pro versus con debate between two experts, a chronology of key dates and events and an annotated bibliography detailing major sources used by the writer.

ACKNOWLEDGMENTS

We wish to thank many people for helping to make this collection a reality. Tom Colin, managing editor of *CQ Researcher,* gave us his enthusiastic support and cooperation as we developed this edition. He and his talented staff of editors and writers have amassed a first-class library of *Researcher* reports, and we are fortunate to have access to that rich cache. We also thankfully acknowledge the advice and feedback from current readers and are gratified by their satisfaction with the book.

Some readers may be learning about *CQ Researcher* for the first time. We expect that many readers will want regular access to this excellent weekly research tool. For subscription information or a no-obligation free trial of *Researcher,* please contact CQ Press at www .cqpress.com or toll-free at 1–866–4CQ-PRESS (1–866–427–7737).

We hope that you will be pleased by the second edition of *Issues in Media.* We welcome your feedback and suggestions for future editions. Please direct comments to Charisse Kiino, Editorial Director, College Publishing Group, CQ Press, 2300 N Street, N.W., Suite 800, Washington, D.C. 20037, or *ckiino@cqpress.com.*

—The Editors of CQ Press

Contributors

Charles S. Clark is a veteran Washington freelancer who writes for *The Washington Post, National Journal* and other publications. He previously served as a staff writer at the *CQ Researcher* and writer-researcher at Time-Life Books. He graduated in political science from McGill University.

Sarah Glazer, a London-based freelancer, is a regular contributor to the *CQ Researcher.* Her articles on health, education and social-policy issues have appeared in *The New York Times, The Washington Post, The Public Interest* and *Gender and Work,* a book of essays. Her recent *CQ Researcher* reports include "Increase in Autism" and "Gender and Learning." She graduated from the University of Chicago with a BA in American history.

David Hatch is a longtime Washington reporter and editor who specializes in telecommunications, media issues and international trade who has written for a number of publications, including *Congress Daily, National Journal, Crain's New York Business* and *Advertising Age.*

Melissa J. Hipolit is a reporter at WJHL-TV, the CBS affiliate in Johnson City, Tenn. She formerly served as a desk assistant at "The NewsHour with Jim Lehrer" and an assistant editor at *CQ Researcher.* She holds a master's degree in journalism from Syracuse University and a bachelor's degree in English from Hobart and William Smith Colleges.

Kenneth Jost, associate editor of *CQ Researcher,* graduated from Harvard College and Georgetown University Law Center. He is the author of the *Supreme Court Yearbook* and editor of *The Supreme Court from A to Z* (both from CQ Press). He was a member of the *CQ Researcher* team that won the American Bar Association's 2002 Silver Gavel Award. His previous reports include "Bilingual Education vs. English Immersion" and "Testing in Schools." He is also author of the blog *Jost on Justice* (http://jostonjustice.blogspot.com).

Peter Katel is a *CQ Researcher* staff writer who previously reported on Haiti and Latin America for *Time* and *Newsweek* and covered the Southwest for newspapers in New Mexico. He has received several journalism awards, including the Bartolomé Mitre Award from the Inter-American Press Association for coverage of drug trafficking. He holds an AB in university studies from the University of New Mexico. His recent reports include "New Strategy in Iraq," "Rise in Counterinsurgency" and "Wounded Veterans."

Patrick Marshall is a freelance writer in Seattle, Wash., and contributing writer for *CQ Researcher* who writes about public policy and technology issues. He is a computer columnist for *The Seattle Times* and holds a BA in anthropology from the University of California at Santa Cruz and an MA in international studies from the Fletcher School of Law & Diplomacy at Tufts University.

Tom Price, a contributing writer for *CQ Researcher,* is a Washington-based freelance journalist. Previously he was a correspondent in the Cox Newspapers Washington Bureau and chief politics writer for the *Dayton Daily News* and *The Journal Herald.* He is author, with Tony Hall, of *Changing the Face of Hunger: One Man's Story of How Liberals, Conservatives, Democrats, Republicans and People of Faith Are Joining Forces to Help the Hungry, the Poor and the Oppressed.* He also writes two Washington guidebooks, *Washington, D.C., for Dummies,* and the *Irreverent Guide to Washington, D.C.* His work has appeared in *The New York Times, Time, Rolling Stone* and other periodicals. He earned a bachelor of science degree in journalism at Ohio University.

1

Future of Journalism

Tom Price and Patrick Marshall

The last copies of the *Seattle Post-Intelligencer* roll off the press on March 17. After 146 years, the PI is becoming an online-only news operation. More than 450 daily newspapers have disappeared in the United States since 1940. While many Americans worry that democracy will suffer if citizens cannot obtain sufficient information for effective self-government, others are hopeful that online journalism — perhaps supported by philanthropy or even government itself — will fill the gaps.

From *CQ Researcher*,
March 27, 2009.
Updated September 3, 2010.

Forty-three years ago, *Time* magazine posed a provocative question on its cover: "Is God Dead?" The answer turned out to be: "not so much."

This February, the magazine's cover pondered ways to stave off the death of newspapers. With the industry copiously bleeding red ink, reporters and editors losing jobs by the thousands and online news becoming increasingly popular — and controversial — *Time's* editors aren't the only people wondering about journalism's future. Certainly the recent news has been grim:

- The *Rocky Mountain News* shut down on Feb. 27 after reporting about the Denver region for 150 years.[1]   2010

- The 146-year-old *Seattle Post-Intelligencer* turned off its presses on March 17, becoming a Web-only publication.[2]   2010

- *The Christian Science Monitor*, a highly regarded national daily newspaper since 1908, plans in April to become a Web and e-mail publication, offering only a weekly, magazine-like, printed edition.[3]

- Thirty-three newspapers — including the *Los Angeles Times*, *Chicago Tribune* and *Philadelphia Inquirer* — sought Chapter 11 bankruptcy protection from December through February.[4]

- Even the mighty *New York Times*, heavily in debt, in early 2009 borrowed an additional $250 million at 14 percent interest from Mexican billionaire Carlos Slim Helu, once described by *The Times* itself as having a "robber baron reputation."[5]

Newspapers across the country are declining in circulation, advertising and profitability. In 2008 alone, publicly traded newspaper *danger of reading only what reinforces opinion already held*

Newspaper Industry Numbers Falling

The number of daily newspapers in the United States declined by more than 450 from 1940 to 2007 (top graph). During the same period, circulation increased to its highest point in 1984, then declined by nearly 20 percent (bottom graph).

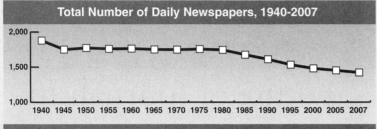

Total Number of Daily Newspapers, 1940-2007

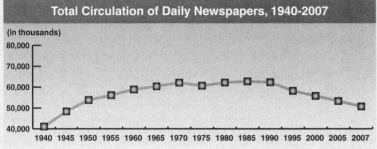

Total Circulation of Daily Newspapers, 1940-2007

(in thousands)

Source: Newspaper Association of America

Many journalists, scholars, lobbyists and government officials worry that the decline of newspapers will leave citizens without sufficient information for effective self-government. They also worry that the fragmented nature of Internet and cable television audiences could turn the clock back to the late-18th and early-19th centuries, when a large number of partisan newspapers printed more opinion than news, and many readers read only publications with which they agreed.

As more Americans turn to the Internet and cable television for news, however, others are hopeful that new forms of journalism will fill the gaps. They envision cable news channels, bloggers, other online content providers and newspapers' own Web sites picking up the slack.[10]

Ironically, newspapers' readership appears to be higher now than ever before as more and more readers access their papers online. *2009* U.S. daily

stock prices fell 83 percent.[6] The Fitch credit-rating service forecasts more newspaper closures this year and next, which could leave a growing number of cities with no newspaper at all.[7]

The collapse of newspapers threatens to leave "a dramatically diminished version of democracy in its wake," John Nichols and Robert McChesney warned.

"Journalism is collapsing, and with it comes the most serious threat in our lifetimes to self-government," wrote Nichols, *The Nation*'s Washington correspondent, and McChesney, a University of Illinois communications professor. "As journalists are laid off and newspapers cut back or shut down, whole sectors of our civic life go dark."[8]

Thomas Jefferson once famously remarked that, if he had to choose between government without newspapers or newspapers without government, he wouldn't hesitate to preserve newspapers.[9] In the subsequent 222 years, Americans have had both, and newspapers have been citizens' primary source of information about government at all levels.

newspapers sell about 51 million copies a day,[11] while hosting nearly 75 million unique visitors on their Web sites each month.[12] *The New York Times* sells about a million newspapers daily and about 1.4 million on Sunday, while its Web site attracts 20 million unique visitors monthly.[13]

Circulation and advertising revenues have been in a steady decline, however, and newspapers have not figured out how to profit from their Web sites. Only about 10 percent of newspaper advertising revenues are earned on the Internet.[14]

Journalists, scholars, entrepreneurs and philanthropists are looking for ways to finance high-quality, comprehensive reporting online. In addition to the traditional for-profit model, they are experimenting with nonprofit news organizations and philanthropic support of journalistic enterprises. Some are discussing government funding.

No less an Internet luminary than Google CEO Eric Schmidt views the loss of newspapers as "a real tragedy."

"Journalism is a central part of democracy," he said. "I don't think bloggers make up the difference."[15]

In fact, most news online is produced by newspapers or by organizations that are funded substantially by newspapers, such as The Associated Press. Many television organizations field significant newsgathering operations. But most lag far behind their newspaper counterparts — particularly at the local, regional and state levels — and they often follow newspapers' reporting leads.

"The decline of newspapers has a big ripple effect," says Peter Shane, executive director of the Knight Commission on the Information Needs of Communities in a Democracy, "because to a substantial extent television and radio news always has been based on local newspapers' reporting."

Yet, nearly across the board, newspapers are shrinking the government coverage that's most important to informing citizens in a democracy. Papers that remain in business are cutting staff, closing bureaus and reducing the number of reporters who cover public affairs full time.

Even as the United States is involved in an ever more globalized world — fighting wars in Iraq and Afghanistan, guarding against far-flung terrorist organizations, competing in a globalized economy — U.S. news organizations are bringing their foreign correspondents home.

And with a new administration shaking up Washington and the troubled global economy looking to Washington for leadership, newspapers are shrinking or closing their Washington bureaus.[16] More than 40 regional correspondents — those who cover a particular community's interests in the nation's capital — lost their jobs over the last three years.[17] Even major papers — including the *Los Angeles Times*, *Chicago Tribune* and *Baltimore Sun* — have cut the size of their Washington bureaus.[18] Other publications have eliminated their Washington staffs entirely — notably *The San Diego Union* whose D.C. reporters won a 2006 Pulitzer Prize for exposing corrupt U.S. Rep. Randy "Duke" Cunningham, who

[handwritten left margin: Parachute journalism]

Newspapers Getting More Online Traffic

Nearly 75 million people visited a newspaper Web site in January 2009, an increase of more than 80 percent from the same month five years earlier.

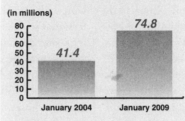

Unique Visitors to Newspaper Web Sites

(in millions)

January 2004: 41.4
January 2009: 74.8

Source: Newspaper Association of America

now sits in jail.[19] Newspapers in half the states now have no congressional correspondent.[20]

Associated Press Senior Vice President Sue Cross lamented declining coverage of city, county and state governments as well — not just the number of reporters but their expertise. "Seasoned beat reporters are, in many cases, leaving the industry," she said.[21]

Virginia's capital press corps shrank by half during the last decade, according to AP Richmond Correspondent Bob Lewis.[22] Maryland media are sending half as many correspondents to Annapolis to cover state government as they did just two years ago, former AP reporter Tom Stukey said.[23] In Broward County, Fla. (Fort Lauderdale), Commissioner John Rodstrom said, local newspapers have cut their county government coverage in half in a year.[24]

"So who's watching out for the interests of the public?" former *Boston Globe* investigative reporter Walter Robinson asks. "The answer is darn fewer people than used to be."

The reduction in regional correspondents has generated particular concern in Washington. Regional reporters' importance goes beyond uncovering wrongdoing, according to Michael Gessel, a longtime congressional aide who now works as a Washington lobbyist for the Dayton Development Corp. in Ohio. "At least equally important is the day-to-day — and sometimes mundane — coverage of what our elected officials do that isn't scandalous," Gessel says. *[handwritten: reason regional report decline]*

Members of Congress often work hardest on matters that get the most coverage by news media in their districts, Gessel explains. Without a hometown reporter tracking the districts' interests in Washington, he says, those interests are likely to get less congressional attention. *[handwritten: affects decreasing funding]*

Citizens also need to know when government does things well, he adds. "All democracies require consent of the governed. If people only hear about scandals, then that consent is withdrawn. Practically speaking, that means less willingness to have their tax dollars support government."

Political Science Professor Gary Jacobson, of the University of California, San Diego, is among those who discount the loss of local newspapers' Washington-based reporting. "You don't have to be in D.C. to find out what [members of Congress] are doing," Jacobson said. Reporters can interview lawmakers on their frequent visits home, he said, and citizens can track legislators' activity by accessing government documents online.[25]

disagrees

Journalists, lobbyists and government officials said Jacobson's comments reflect a misunderstanding of how governments really work. "When you're walking the halls of Congress and you are going into members' offices every day and you're developing sources, over time those people tell you things the public needs to know but lawmakers want to keep away from the public," says Andrew Alexander, chief of the recently closed Cox Newspapers Washington Bureau and now ombudsman for *The Washington Post*. "That's what's being lost."

ombudsman

A Washington correspondent must know the actors and understand the processes of the federal government, Gessel says. "You can't get that by phone, by Internet or by e-mail."

As journalists, scholars and politicians try to navigate the new media environment, here are some of the questions they are asking about the future of democracy:

Can the Internet fill the reporting gaps caused by the decline of newspapers?

News-reporting sites are popping up on the Internet even faster than newspapers are losing circulation.

On Jan. 12, for instance, *GlobalPost* went online in an ambitious effort to do the kind of international journalism that newspapers and television networks have scaled back. Led by news veterans, the site promises comprehensive, frontline reporting by more than 60 freelance correspondents in more than 40 countries.[26] The new operation hopes to turn a profit by selling advertising, syndicating its reporting to other news organizations and selling $199-a-year subscriptions to a premium service.[27]

research

Two years earlier, other news veterans launched *Politico*, which quickly became a popular source of political news during the long campaign that carried Barack Obama to the White House. *Politico* — a Web site and a newspaper

distributed free in Washington — is performing ahead of its business plan and expects to turn a profit this year, says Editor-in-Chief John Harris, a 21-year veteran of *The Washington Post*.

Across the country, countless sites have been created to cover local and regional communities. They range from highly professional organizations covering major metropolitan areas to primarily volunteer operations serving small communities to professional-amateur collaborations of all sizes.

MinnPost in Minnesota and *Voice of San Diego* have won widespread praise for practicing high-quality, professional journalism, for instance. Smaller, mostly amateur, sites contain little more than announcements from community organizations. *The New York Times* and the *Chicago Tribune* have assigned professionals to oversee networks of volunteers who report for Web sites operated by those papers, focusing on news about specific neighborhoods.

The Internet surpassed newspapers as Americans' favorite source of national and international news in late 2008. Both trailed television by a substantial margin among the population at large. But Americans younger than 30 turned to the Internet as often as to television — and twice as often as to newspapers.[28] Readers still turn to newspapers more than to the Internet for local news.[29]

Most of the news Americans obtain on the Web is not produced by online news organizations, however. On Election Day 2008, for instance, seven of the 10 most-popular Internet news sites belonged to CNN, MSNBC, Fox News, *The New York Times*, Tribune Newspapers, *The Washington Post* and *USA Today*. The others — Yahoo! News, AOL News and Google News — simply aggregate content produced by newsgathering organizations such as newspapers and television networks.[30] Many other Web sites also link to reports produced by traditional news organizations.

"Very interesting and hopeful things are happening on the Web," says Geneva Overholser, director of the University of Southern California's journalism school. However, she adds, "many people think the only thing that will work online will be niche publications," not replacements for comprehensive newspapers.

Politico and *GlobalPost* are promising examples of niche sites that might succeed by attracting national or

ombudsman
Politico

aggregate

international audiences that advertisers want to reach. *Politico*, for instance, sells most of its ads to organizations that want to influence the federal government, and many of those ads appear in the printed edition, which targets an elite Washington audience.

Another is Joshua Micah Marshall's "Talking Points Memo," which won the prestigious George Polk Award for Legal Reporting in 2007 for "tenacious investigative reporting" of the Bush administration's questionable firings of U.S. attorneys. TPM "connected the dots and found a pattern of federal prosecutors being forced from office for failing to do the Bush administration's bidding," which "sparked interest by the traditional news media and led to the resignation of Attorney General Alberto Gonzales," the Polk judges said.[31]

Started by Marshall as a one-man blog in 2000, TPM now has a staff of 17.

National niche sites can succeed because of economies of scale, says Henry Heilbrunn, a new-media management consultant and former Associated Press executive. Such sites might need smaller staffs than those providing comprehensive coverage to a metropolitan area, but they could still sell to a large national advertising base, he contends.

"There's no sign anywhere of anything replacing the comprehensive metropolitan newspaper, replacing the kind of watchfulness that even a mediocre city newspaper might offer," says Tom Rosenstiel, director of the Project for Excellence in Journalism.

Journalists should stop wringing their hands about the Internet's shortcomings and focus on what creative things they can do online, says New York University journalism Professor Jay Rosen.

"I think the kind of check that newspapers can provide — if they're run well and if they are big and strong — is very hard to get any other way, so I do not look forward to newspapers' decline," Rosen says. "But what I think about it is irrelevant to the market mechanisms and technological changes that are hollowing out the newspapers' business model."

Others worry that online news sites can't serve Americans who don't have Internet access, a group that tends to be older and poorer than the general public. While nearly all young Americans go online, nearly three-quarters of Americans older than 75 do not. That also is true for a majority between 70 and 75, more than a third

between 60 and 69, a quarter between 50 and 59 and a fifth between 45 and 49.[32]

Business consultant James Moore — who advises newspapers to shut down their presses and become online-only operations — argues that publications can't afford to worry about those lost readers. "They are not the people advertisers reach out to," Moore says. "The people they're going after are people in the 35-to-45 category. You have to look to the future, and the future is the young."

Are the new media bad for democracy?

On Oct. 3, 2008, CNN's *iReport* Internet site reported, incorrectly, that Apple CEO Steve Jobs had been rushed to the hospital after a heart attack. The account quickly was repeated on other Web sites, and Apple stock fell more than 9 percent in 12 minutes — a total loss of $9 billion in the company's value.[33]

A month earlier, the Bloomberg financial Web site mistakenly posted a six-year-old report about United Airlines' 2002 bankruptcy filing. Thinking the airline was going bankrupt again, investors dumped the stock, which lost three-quarters of its value before the NASDAQ stock exchange halted trading. A financial newsletter had found the old newspaper story while doing a Google search and passed it on to Bloomberg believing it was current.[34]

The credibility of the erroneous reports was enhanced by CNN's and Bloomberg's reputations as legitimate news organizations. But in both cases the reports appeared on the organizations' Web sites without being vetted.

The incidents illustrate some criticisms of Internet-based news operations.

Many bloggers — and even some traditional media — are cavalier about accuracy on the Web, critics complain. Moreover, they say, Internet public-affairs sites tend to publish more opinion than fact, much of it vicious, mean-spirited and profane. And they worry that fragmentation of the online audience can lead many Web surfers to experience a narrow, distorted view of the world in what some call the Internet "echo chamber."

Indeed, the Jobs story was repeated by blogger Henry Blodget on the widely read *Silicon Alley Insider* Web site. Blodget later unapologetically proclaimed he would do it again, noting he had warned readers he didn't know if the report was true.

"vetted"   cavalier

"journalism of assertion" vs "factchecking"

"You, our readers, are smart enough to know the difference between rumors and facts, and you are smart enough to evaluate what we tell you," Blodget said. Posting unverified information "flushes out the truth," he argued. "We wouldn't want you to not tell us what everyone was talking about because you couldn't verify it."[35]

That's an example of what Rosenstiel and Bill Kovach — former Washington bureau chief of *The New York Times* and former editor of *The Atlanta Journal-Constitution* — have termed "the journalism of assertion." Traditional journalistic ethics require that facts be confirmed before they're published, Rosenstiel and Kovach said. Many figures on talk radio, cable news and the Internet are "less interested in substantiating whether something is true and more interested in getting it into the public discussion."[36] While they coined the phrase a decade ago, Rosenstiel says, it's even more true today.

CNN also defended its unverified *iReports* by noting the Web site carries a disclaimer that "the stories submitted by users are not edited, fact-checked or screened before they post."[37]

CNN says it created *iReports* to extend CNN's news-gathering reach and to increase viewers' personal attachment to the cable network. It checks the accuracy of *iReporters*' contributions only before using them in its telecasts.

A growing number of news organizations are recruiting volunteer, "citizen" journalists, especially online, as a way to compensate for cutbacks in their professional reporting staffs.

"News organizations are really getting squeezed, and so it's incumbent on them to be looking for ways to engage citizens in the process," William Grueskin, academic-affairs dean at the Columbia University journalism school, noted. Citizen involvement "can be a very powerful influence when harnessed the right way," he added, "but sometimes it goes awry."[38]

At the *Chicago Tribune*'s *Triblocal* Web site, for example, which recruits amateurs to contribute community news, most stories about the 2008 Third Congressional District Democratic primary turned out to have been written by one candidate's publicist.[39]

Journalism historian Anthony Fellow at California State University, Fullerton, is among those who worry about the fragmentation of the Internet audience among ideologically oriented sites. "We're back to the party press era" after the Revolutionary War, he says, "the viciousness that went on between the two camps, the name-calling."

Matthew Hindman, an assistant professor of political science at Arizona State University, sees such partisanship as a natural outcome of the decline of monopoly newspapers.

"cutting thru the clutter"

"The local newspapers, as monopolies, have been inclined to neutrality, to alienating as few of their potential readers as they can," he says. "The more news outlets there are, the greater need to differentiate outlets from each other. Ideology is an effective way to do that. Conservative sites share very little traffic with liberal sites."

Fully 80 percent of talk-radio host Rush Limbaugh's listeners describe themselves as conservative, for instance.[40] During the 2008 campaign, Fox News Channel viewers were most likely to be Republicans while MSNBC viewers tended to be Democrats.[41]

City University of New York journalism Professor Jeff Jarvis rejects the echo-chamber charge. "We have more arguments than ever," he says. "The echo chamber was when there was one newspaper in town."

Similarly, the Knight commission's Shane says, "It would be surprising, in the most networked environment in human history, if people actually come across fewer things that are new to them than they did in the last half of the 20th century."

Most Americans aren't limiting themselves to partisan sites. Just 5 percent of the general public and 10 percent of conservatives say they listen to Limbaugh regularly, for instance.[42] According to the Project for Excellence in Journalism's 2007 report on the "State of the News Media," two-thirds of Americans prefer to get their news from neutral sources, while just a quarter want sources that share their point of view.[43]

Can philanthropy save journalism?

David Swensen, who manages Yale University's $17 billion endowment, thinks he knows how to save America's newspapers: Turn them into nonprofit institutions supported by charitable endowments just like Yale's.

"Endowments would enhance newspapers' autonomy while shielding them from the economic forces that are now tearing them down," he wrote with Yale financial analyst Michael Schmidt. "Endowments would transform newspapers into unshakable fixtures of American

"party press era after the Revolutionary War"

life, with greater stability and enhanced independence that would allow them to serve the public good more effectively."[44]

A $5 billion endowment, for example, would support *The New York Times'* newsgathering operation, which is the largest in the newspaper business, they wrote. The paper could continue to earn income from advertising and subscriptions to pay other expenses.

The proposal quickly was endorsed by Steve Coll, a *New Yorker* writer and former *Washington Post* managing editor, who estimated a $2 billion endowment could support *The Post*.[45]

Those are huge numbers, but not unheard of in the endowment world. Yale's endowment is nearly five times what *The Times* would need, according to Swensen and Schmidt's calculations. Harvard's is more than seven times larger. Eighteen universities' endowments exceed $5 billion.[46] Multibillionaire Warren Buffet could fund *The Post*'s endowment with about 5 percent of his fortune, Coll said.[47]

The idea has attracted critics as well as supporters.

Media analyst Alan Mutter and Zachary Seward, an assistant editor at Harvard University's Nieman Journalism Lab, calculated it would cost $114 billion to endow every newspaper in America. Their number skews high, however, because they used the highest newspaper employment in U.S. history — 56,900 journalists in 1990 — and assumed it would cost an average $100,000 to support each employee's wage, fringe benefits and business expenses. The Bureau of Labor Statistics says the average newspaper reporter earns less than $40,000 a year.[48]

Others attacked the very concept of nonprofit newspapers. "They declare surrender, that there's not a market demand for journalism," complains Jarvis at the City University of New York. "I believe there is market demand, and the hard work now is to find the new business model that will work."

Market discipline produces better journalism, according to Jonathan Weber, whose for-profit *New West* Web site covers the Rocky Mountain region from Missoula,

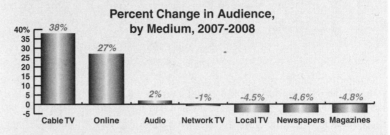

Audience Grew for Cable and Online News

Cable TV and online news were the only two forms of media exhibiting significant audience growth from 2007 to 2008. Audiences for more traditional forms of media had noticeable declines, with newspapers and magazines declining the most.

Percent Change in Audience, by Medium, 2007-2008

Cable TV	38%
Online	27%
Audio	2%
Network TV	-1%
Local TV	-4.5%
Newspapers	-4.6%
Magazines	-4.8%

Source: Pew Project for Excellence in Journalism

Mont. "The core problem that nonprofit journalism will never be able to solve properly is deciding what is worthy," Weber argued. "In a business, the customers ultimately decide what is worthy, for better and for worse."

New West earns income from running conferences as well as from online advertising, he said, "and we have some more new business angles up our sleeve."[49]

Philanthropy-supported and nonprofit journalism are growing phenomena, however. *MinnPost* and *Voice of San Diego* raise funds from foundations, wealthy individuals and businesses. They also recruit dues-paying members, following the model of public broadcasting.

The Knight Foundation, built on the wealth of the now-defunct Knight Newspapers chain, awards millions of dollars in grants to scores of journalism projects every year and encourages other philanthropies to do the same. "We're trying to convince foundations that a core need is not just health, education and welfare but also information," Gary Kebbel, the foundation's journalism program director, explained.[50] The Kaiser Family Foundation, known for its support of health care, has created a news service to cover health policy. The foundation hired two veteran journalists to run the organization, and they plan to hire a half-dozen reporters and several editors and to contract for projects by freelance journalists. Their work will appear on the Kaiser Health News Web site, and other media will be encouraged to republish it. The organization also will conduct projects in partnership with other news media, something the foundation has done on a selective basis since the mid 1990s.

In Hard Times, Papers Turn to Cooperation

Broader coverage offsets loss of journalistic competition.

Hard-driving newsmen Ben Hecht and Charles MacArthur have to be spinning in their graves. Their celebrated 1928 play, *The Front Page*, depicted the cutthroat competition they experienced as Chicago newspaper reporters, when numerous dailies fought to break the news first.

Today Chicago has just two dailies, both facing severe financial challenges. Most cities have one, and many could lose that newspaper as well. And a growing number of surviving papers are looking to cooperate rather than compete in order to cut costs.

The eight largest newspapers in Ohio have agreed to share their staffs' work. So have Florida's *Miami Herald*, *St. Petersburg Times*, *Palm Beach Post* and (Fort Lauderdale) *Sun Sentinel*. Even *The Washington Post*, one of America's very best — and most competitive — papers, has begun to cooperate with the neighboring *Baltimore Sun*.

The Ohio papers share each other's stories and coordinate their state government coverage. During the 2008 political campaign, the papers conducted a joint polling project. The papers are scattered around the state and don't have a great deal of overlapping readership, their editors say.

The arrangement enables each newspaper to provide more information to its readers than it could on its own, *Dayton Daily News* Editor Kevin Riley says.

"We could have sat around and complained that none of us could afford to have any polling," he explains. "Instead, we got a statewide poll that cost us more than any one paper would have been able to pay."

The Daily News no longer covers Ohio State football, using *Columbus Dispatch* reporting instead. *The Dispatch* carries *Daily News* coverage of the Cincinnati Reds.

In Florida, *The Herald* and *Times* have created a joint, six-reporter state capital bureau. *The Herald, Post* and *Sun Sentinel* have entered an agreement to share routine coverage in order to free reporters for more enterprise reporting. With Florida International University, they created the South Florida News Service, through which journalism students will produce video and audio content for the three newspapers as well as stories.[1]

The Washington-Baltimore agreement covers routine reporting about Maryland, but not state government or University of Maryland sports, where *The Post* and *Sun* continue to compete.[2]

The agreements have raised concerns about loss of journalistic competition.

The foundation started the news service because "news organizations are every year becoming less capable of producing coverage of these complex issues as their budgets are being slashed," foundation President Drew Altman said.

Other philanthropies are bankrolling health news organizations in California, Florida and Kansas.[51]

Charlotte Hall, president of the American Society of Newspaper Editors, said she could envision philanthropies supporting specific newspaper projects — "investigative reporting or an important local beat, for example. But a new kind of firewall would be needed to assure independent reporting and unencumbered editing."[52]

" New kind of firewall "
needed

Richard Tofel, general manager of *ProPublica*, says his nonprofit investigative reporting organization has established the same protections for its newsroom that good newspapers traditionally do. *ProPublica*'s funders and directors "never know what we're going to publish before we publish it," Tofel says. "They don't see stories before they're printed. Post-publication, their contact is limited to top editors."

The New York Times reported in December the Justice Department is investigating possible improper conduct by a bank owned until 2006 by *ProPublica*'s major funder and board chairman, San Francisco billionaire Herbert Sandler.[53]

"It could be a good thing," Florida state Sen. Dan Gelber said about the arrangements in his state. "But I do worry. I'm a big believer that there needs to be plenty of competition. A vibrant press corps in our state's capital is crucial."[3]

"If you have fewer people covering things," Ohio University journalism Professor Patrick Washburn says, "you have fewer viewpoints, and fewer viewpoints is not good." A politician can "spin" one reporter to get his views across easier than he can spin several, Washburn adds.

"I think competition makes us better, because it creates more diversity of viewpoints and makes us work harder" says Andrew Alexander, *The Washington Post*'s ombudsman. He worries that quality may decline "when there's no urgency to beat the other guy or to go deeper than someone else."

On the other hand, he adds, "I sympathize with the editors. If you don't have enough staff to cover the local school board meeting, you have to make a choice."

Riley acknowledges that editors and reporters need to be aware of the pitfalls of diminished competition and have to "challenge ourselves to make sure we're doing our job and serving the public good." But, he adds, competition is not necessarily valuable when it leads eight reporters to do the same routine story.

"When that could be done with one and the others could be working on enterprise stories with more importance, you're not being smart," he says. "We could have that group of reporters covering more ground."

Similarly, *Miami Herald* Editor Anders Gyllenhaal said the Florida cooperation "helps us focus on 100 percent more enterprise."[4] In announcing the agreements, *The Herald* promised readers "more deep and probing stories on the important issues across Florida." The arrangements "increase our ability to look beyond the news, to take on investigative projects and to do the kind of explanatory work that is particularly important at the state government level."[5]

Journalism consultant Michele McLellan endorsed the cooperation and predicted more will come.

"Sure, it's important to have more than one watchdog on duty at the statehouse," she said. "But too often the watchdogs became the herd, covering the same hearings, writing up the same turn-of-screw procedural votes, and capturing the same political skirmishes that never quite enlighten real motivations or inform about policy."[6]

[1] "New Tallahassee Bureau Expands Our Coverage," *The Miami Herald*, Dec. 7, 2008, p. L1.

[2] Michael S. Rosenwald, "Washington Post, Baltimore Sun to Share Content," *The Washington Post*, Dec. 23, 2008, p. D3.

[3] "New Tallahassee Bureau Expands Our Coverage," *op. cit.*

[4] Michele McLellan, "Turning Rivalries into Partnerships," Knight Digital Media Center, Jan. 13, 2009, www.knightdigitalmediacenter.org/leadership_blog/comments/turning_rivalries_into_partnerships.

[5] "New Tallahassee Bureau Expands Our Coverage," *op. cit.*

[6] McLellan, *op. cit.*

Some newspaper advocates even have suggested government funding.

Sweden subsidizes newspapers in weak market positions.[54] France is increasing its newspaper subsidies from $362 million to about $620 million annually.[55] The national government is obligated to "make sure an independent, free and pluralistic press exists," French President Nicolas Sarkozy said.[56]

In the United States, owners of *The Inquirer* and *Daily News* in Philadelphia discussed possible state aid with Pennsylvania Gov. Ed Rendell.[57]

On March 24, U.S. Sen. Ben Cardin, D-Md., introduced legislation to exempt newspaper advertising and circulation revenue from taxation, Bloomberg News reported.

irony of saving the watchdog

U.S. newspapers are in such dire straits, Nichols and McChesney argued in *The Nation*, that only government can save them. "Just as there came a moment when policy makers recognized the necessity of investing tax dollars to create a public education system to teach our children, so a moment has arrived at which we must recognize the need to invest tax dollars to create and maintain newsgathering, reporting and writing with the purpose of informing all our citizens," they wrote.[58]

The Knight commission's Shane argues that "we don't have a strong tradition of government-run media, and

research

we have a lot of distrust of government media being an adequate watchdog on government. I'm not sure *The Executive Branch Daily* would be a good substitute for *The Washington Post.*"

For a news organization "to truly do its job as a watchdog," new-media consultant Heilbrunn agrees, "the people who are paying can't be the people being watched."

Nichols and McChesney point out, however, that the government has subsidized news media since the birth of the republic.

"The government implemented extraordinary postal subsidies for the distribution of newspapers," they wrote. "It also instituted massive newspaper subsidies through printing contracts and the paid publication of government notices."[59]

Moreover, they argued, broadcast and cable licenses represent subsidies to newer media.

BACKGROUND

Early Newspapers

Before the first American newspaper was published — in 1690 — a system of private reporting informed 16th-century European businessmen. Scattered about European cities, these journalists prepared handwritten letters that reported on prices, trade, transportation, politics, war and anything else their subscribers might be interested in.

Each letter was sent to just one businessman or company. New York University's Rosen likened them to today's specialty newsletters "that only big firms and rich people can afford." Like today's traditional media, Rosen said, the newsletters needed to be accurate, interpretive and entertaining.[60]

That was not true for the early American newspapers, which were partisan, opinionated and often owned by the political parties they wrote about.[61] Colonial authorities shut down the first American newspaper, *Publick Occurrences Both Forreign and Domestick*, after one issue in 1690 because the publisher had not obtained a government license.

Before American newspapers began to proliferate in the 18th century, historian Fellow says, news was disseminated orally at coffeehouses. "People would come in and say their news and they'd discuss the news." The Internet, on which "everybody can be a journalist," harkens to those days, Fellow observes.

What Harvard historian Jill Lepore termed "the real birth of the American newspaper" occurred in 1721, when James Franklin began publishing the *New-England Courant.*[62]

Without a license, he published political essays, opinion, satire and some news. "I hereby invite all Men, who have Leisure, Inclination and Ability, to speak their Minds with Freedom, Sense and Moderation, and their Pieces shall be welcome to a Place in my Paper," he proclaimed.[63]

Franklin's contrarian publication scandalized Puritan minister Cotton Mather of Boston, angered government officials and got Franklin jailed twice. Ordered to submit his publications to government review or cease printing, he turned the paper over to his younger brother Benjamin, who continued as an irritant to the establishment.

"The Business of Printing has chiefly to do with Men's Opinions," Benjamin Franklin acknowledged. Another early newspaperman declared: "Professions of impartiality I shall make none. They are always useless, and are besides perfect nonsense."[64]

These early papers tended to read like "one long and uninterrupted invective," Lepore said.[65] But their inflammatory protestations helped touch off the American Revolution. And they took important strides toward the press freedom that the Constitution and Supreme Court rulings guarantee today.

Partisan attack and character assassination became so common in the early days of the republic that journalism historian Frank Luther Mott labeled the first third of the 19th century "the dark ages of partisan journalism."[66]

"Right after the revolution, parties paid newspapers to support them, and you had no ethical codes," explains Ohio University journalism Professor Patrick Washburn, editor of the *Journalism History* journal.

According to Fellow, "Journalists were basically stenographers for politicians. Their job was to take what a politician said and improve it."

Early newspapers also experienced something that plagues a growing number of 21st-century publishers — failure. Between 1690 and 1820 more than 2,100 went out of business after two years or less. Nevertheless, the number of newspapers soared from 37 at the end of the Revolution to 1,258 in 1835.

As late as 1850, only 5 percent of American newspapers were considered "neutral and independent." At about that

CHRONOLOGY

1900s-1920s *Newspapers experiment with financing, launch crusades to improve society.*

1906 Referring to newspaper and magazine exposés, President Theodore Roosevelt complains of "muckrakers" who can't lift their eyes above "the filth of the floor."

1908 Church-supported *Christian Science Monitor* begins publishing.

1911 *Chicago Day Book* tries to publish without advertising.

1912 *New York Independent* Editor Hamilton Holt prepares model for an endowment-supported newspaper.

1914 Los Angeles government begins publishing the *Municipal News.*

1930s-1970s *Industry consolidation is followed by "Golden Age" of newspapers.*

1930 Consolidation leaves just one newspaper in eight cities with more than 100,000 residents.

1937-1939 Ninety-eight papers close or disappear in mergers.

1948 Television networks cover the 1948 political conventions, pose tough competition for newspapers.

1950 Newspapers sell more than 35 percent of U.S. advertising, but begin steady decline.

1966 Mid-size dailies earn average profit of 23 percent. . . . Gannett chain sells stock to the public, opening itself to shareholder pressure.

1967 *New York Times* goes public with two classes of stock, leaving Ochs-Sulzberger family in control.

1968 Newspapers sell $5.2 billion in ads versus $3.1 billion for television.

1970 Chains own half of daily newspapers with two-thirds of circulation.

1971 *New York Times* publishes secret "Pentagon Papers" history of Vietnam War; Supreme Court says newspapers can publish without "prior restraint" from government.

1974 *The Washington Post*'s Watergate reporting leads to President Richard M. Nixon's resignation.

1980s-Present *Free content from electronic media threaten newspapers.*

1980 Number of daily newspapers drops below 1,750, beginning steady decline.

1982 Gannett launches *USA Today*; other papers copy its style.

1984 Daily newspaper circulation peaks at 63.3 million.

1991 World Wide Web invented.

1993 *New York Times* goes online.

1998 Cyber-gossip Matt Drudge reveals *Newsweek* investigation of Clinton-Lewinsky affair.

1999 All but two of 100 largest newspapers publish online.

2005 All but two of 20 largest papers lose circulation. Papers cut 2,200 jobs.

2007 Classified advertising plummets; newspapers eliminate nearly 1,500 jobs. . . . *Politico* Web site becomes popular source of political news.

2008 Internet surpasses newspapers as Americans' favorite source of national and international news, but newspapers top Internet as local news source.

2009 Circulation for 1,400 dailies drops to 51 million; newspaper Web sites draw 75 million. . . . *Rocky Mountain News* shuts down (Feb. 27), *Seattle Post-Intelligencer* shifts to Web-only publication (March 17) and *New York Times* borrows $250 million from Mexican billionaire. . . . *Ann Arbor News* announces it will stop publishing and become a Web-based community-news operation (March 23). . . . U.S. Sen. Ben Cardin, D-Md., introduces Newspaper Revitalization Act to exempt newspaper ad and circulation revenue from taxation. . . . Not-for-profit Chicago News Cooperative established (Oct. 22). . . . Nielsen Co. ends publication of nine trade publications, including *Editor & Publisher* (Dec. 10).

2010 *The New York Times* announces plan to start charging readers for online content beginning in January 2011 (Jan. 21). . . . Bloomberg News announces new enterprise – Bloomberg Government – to be based in the Washington, D.C., market (March 3). . . . Apple releases iPad tablet e-reader. News Corp. CEO Rupert Murdoch calls product a potential "game changer" for news media (April 3). . . . Not-for-profit ProPublica wins Pulitzer Prize for investigative journalism (April 13). . . . Not-for-profit Bay Citizen begins operations (May 26). . . . Amazon.com begins shipping third generation of its Kindle e-reader (Aug. 25). . . . *USA Today* announces plan for "digital makeover," resulting in 130 layoffs (Aug. 26). . . . Pew Research Center reports 31 percent of Americans get news from newspapers, while 34 percent get it online (Sept. 12).

Frustrated Newspaper Executives Fight Back

Industry is "a long way from dead."

Randy Siegel is president of Parade Publications, publisher of the colorful, quick-reading tabloid that is delivered with nearly 450 newspapers each Sunday. Although he plays a very different role from Jay Smith, Brian Tierney and Donna Barrett, head of the primarily small-town Community Newspaper Holdings, all share one thing in common: Frustration over continual obituaries for the newspaper industry.

So late last year they launched the Newspaper Project to counter all the doomsayers. Thus far they've produced three pro-newspaper advertisements, which have appeared in more than 400 papers. The first proclaimed that more Americans read newspapers on Super Bowl Sunday than watched the football game. The others carried the themes "Defending Freedom Daily Since 1776" and "America's First Portable Information Device."

Smith, who retired last year as president of Cox Newspapers, says the new organization wants to "bring balance and perspective to the discussion of where newspapers are headed in these times. It's really important that we quit hanging the crepe and talking about newspapers in the past tense, because they're a long way from dead."

Smith and Tierney, the CEO of the company that owns *The Philadelphia Inquirer* and *Daily News*, know from personal experience about the challenges the industry faces. The Philadelphia papers recently sought Chapter 11 bankruptcy protection. A few months after Smith retired, Cox decided to sell most of its newspapers, even though most are profitable. Still, the industry's problems aren't as unsolvable as many people seem to think, Smith and Tierney argue.

Some newspapers are much healthier than others, he points out, and all are suffering from the current recession. Some of the most prominent newspapers — including in Philadelphia — are in trouble because their owners took on too much debt, Tierney says. Without the debt service, he says, the Philadelphia papers would be profitable.

Even in their current state, newspapers provide much more thorough coverage than any other medium, Smith argues.

"The hometown newspaper is the source of the most complete and the most credible information that people in that community have," Smith says. "If you're in the public sector in that community, you don't make a move without thinking, 'What if this ends up on the front page of the paper.'"

No other Philadelphia medium "does what we do," Tierney says, ticking off several recent investigative projects that required "months of reporting and tons of editing, fact-checking and lawyering" — plus several hundred thousand dollars of staff time and expenses, he adds.

Despite circulation and revenue declines, he says, the two newspapers have an unduplicated daily readership of 1.2 million, and another 500,000 to 1 million people visit the publications' Web sites.

While the percentage of 18-to-34-year-olds who read a newspaper has declined from 62 percent in 1978 to 34 percent now, that's still a hefty number, Tierney says. The maker of Red Bull energy drink "wishes one-third of that group bought a can of Red Bull today. If McDonald's had one of three people visiting McDonald's today, they'd be happy."

"What newspapers are facing right now," Smith says, "is the double whammy of dealing with structural change that has been ongoing for more than a decade and continues to accelerate and that is compounded by the historic economic turmoil. Economic cycles have a way of changing, and one of my concerns is that we don't do structural damage while we're in the throes of a bad economic cycle. When that cycle begins to change and begins to improve the economy, I want to make sure we have something left that's worth talking about in the way of newspapers."

time, however, newspapers began to place more emphasis on reporting facts. Partisan papers became increasingly willing to criticize political and government leaders even of their own party.

The decade leading up to the Civil War was a time of great political activism and a great time to be in the newspaper business. Nearly three-quarters of eligible voters participated in the 1852 and 1856 presidential elections.

Newspaper editors and publishers often wielded great political power. Some Northern newspapers became important instruments in the crusade against slavery. Writers commented on newspapers' wide readership and high influence.

Author and political leader Charles Ingersoll termed newspapers "the daily fare of nearly every meal in almost every family." Philosopher Ralph Waldo Emerson described businessmen on a commuter train eagerly purchasing the "magical sheets — twopence a head his bread of knowledge costs — and instantly the entire rectangular assembly, fresh from their breakfast, are bending as one man over their second breakfast."[67]

The *Times* Model

In 1860, *The New York Times* set out an operating plan that eventually would become the underlying principle for most American newspapers: A paper's "proper business is to publish facts, in such a form and temper as to lead men of all parties to rely upon its statements of facts."[68] By 1880, a quarter of American newspapers declared themselves independent, neutral or local, rather than partisan — a proportion that increased to a third by 1890. As newspapers became less partisan, party loyalty among the people declined.

The number of newspapers grew phenomenally during the late 1800s, from 3,000 in 1860 to 4,500 in 1870 to 7,000 in 1880. Many of those were published weekly or less frequently, but the number of dailies also jumped from 574 in 1870 to 2,226 in 1900, when their circulation reached 15 million. Large cities counted their competing papers in double digits.

Investigations and "crusades" grew in importance for newspapers and magazines in the early 20th century. Publications attacked government corruption, political bosses, business monopolies and child labor. They inspired fundraising efforts after disasters and campaigned for better schools, roads and parks. Investigative reporters — derisively dubbed "muckrakers" by Theodore Roosevelt, after the character in John Bunyan's *Pilgrim's Progress* who never lifted his eyes from the muck — exposed wrongdoing by business executives and government officials.

Publishers experimented with various forms of financing their newspapers in the early 20th century.[69] In 1908, the First Church of Christ, Scientist, in Boston began to publish *The Christian Science Monitor*, which printed just one religious article in each issue and became a widely respected publication over the following century. (In 1850, the Mormon church begun publishing the *Deseret News*, which remains one of Salt Lake City's two newspapers.)

New York Independent Editor Hamilton Holt drew up a model for an endowment-supported newspaper, but it wasn't implemented.

The Los Angeles city government published the *Municipal News* for several years after 1914. The mayor, City Council and any political party that won more than 3 percent of the city vote were given newspaper space to use as they wished.

In 1911, the *Chicago Day Book* began publishing without ads, trying to support itself through subscriptions alone. It died during World War I, a victim of readers' preference for having advertising in their newspapers.

The advent of radio in the 1920s increased competition for reader/viewer attention, advertising revenues and political influence. But newspapers continued to thrive, nearly doubling their circulation and more than tripling ad revenue between 1910 and 1930.

Radio networks broadcast the 1924 national political conventions live, and parties and candidates began to cater to the new medium's needs.[70]

'Golden Age'

The 20th century also was marked by newspaper consolidation, which led editors to seek to please a wider range of readers, not just supporters of a particular party or ideology. While earlier years had been marked by fierce competition throughout the country, eight cities with more than 100,000 residents became one-publisher towns by 1930. During the Great Depression, 98 newspapers were closed or disappeared in mergers in the brief period between 1937 and 1939.[71]

Television became newspapers' biggest threat in the 1950s. Networks televised the 1948 political conventions and launched ambitious political reporting efforts thereafter. The parties and candidates began to cater to the new medium, just as they had to radio.[72] On the business side, newspapers' share of advertising revenue began a long, steady decline.[73]

"Radio and television gave you an immediacy that you didn't have before," Ohio University's Washburn points out. "Suddenly you could sit anywhere in the country

[handwritten annotation: difference between code of silence no MLK Jr. & today's journalists]

where you could see television, and you could watch the candidates up close."

The visual immediacy of television reporting also propelled the Civil Rights Movement in the 1950s and '60s and helped turn public opinion against the Vietnam War in the late '60s and early '70s.

Newspaper consolidation continued throughout the second half of the 20th century, creating monopolies or near monopolies in most American cities. "The newspaper became a tollgate between the local retailer and local consumers," Hindman at Arizona State University explains. "If you wanted somebody to go to J.C. Penney or if you wanted to sell your old guitar, you had to take out an ad in the local newspaper."

As a result, publications were able to charge high advertising rates, earn healthy profits, build large news-gathering teams, employ knowledgeable reporters to cover specialized beats and send correspondents around the world. Some publishers wielded their economic and political power selfishly. More often, they emphasized professionalism and civic responsibility. Journalists' educational level rose. Professional organizations and educational institutions emphasized the importance of ethics.

Former *Washington Post* Managing Editor Coll described the period as a Golden Age of journalism, during which metropolitan newspapers were defined by "professional, civil-service-style, relentless, independent-thinking reporting and observation." The newspapers' economic strength enabled "high-quality family owners" to protect journalists from political and commercial pressure — "not perfectly, but largely," Coll said. "Yes, the big papers [sometimes] failed, as in the run-up to the Iraq War, but they succeeded much more often. They practiced a kind of journalism that, on the whole, was better for a democratic constitutional system than any journalism ever practiced before, anywhere."[74]

The era was epitomized by young *Washington Post* reporters Bob Woodward and Carl Bernstein's dogged digging into the Watergate scandal that led to President Richard M. Nixon's resignation in 1974.

Chain Reaction

Journalists' sense of propriety and responsibility before cable television and the Internet stands in stark contrast to the no-holds-barred style of reporting today.

In 1964, FBI Director J. Edgar Hoover invited Washington reporters to his office to listen to tapes that proved conclusively that the Rev. Dr. Martin Luther King Jr. was cheating on his wife. No one wrote a story, and the existence of the tapes was not publicized for nearly 20 years. Journalists generally considered public figures' private lives to be off-limits.

"Imagine Hoover sharing his tapes with professional Internet gossip Matt Drudge," Rosenstiel and Kovach wrote. "How would CNN handle the leaked tapes if the network knew MSNBC was about to be given the same information?

"Harris Wofford, the former Pennsylvania senator who had known King since the early 1950s, believes that in the media culture of the 1990s, one of the most important Americans of the 20th century would have been destroyed, and American history would have been quite different."[75]

In 1982 the Gannett newspaper chain made a profound impact on American newspapers by launching *USA Today* — the first nationwide general-audience paper. Newspapers across the country soon mimicked *USA Today*'s emphasis on colorful graphics and short articles.

In the latter 20th century, newspapers also became consolidated into large chains whose shares traded on public stock markets. Investors with little interest in quality journalism pressured publishers to increase profits. While some founding families maintained control through special classes of stock, they also were pressed to ramp up earnings. A 2001 study by three journalism professors concluded that investors in publicly traded companies were "concerned with . . . continuously improved profitability" and "indifferent to news or, more disturbingly, its quality."[76]

The number of daily newspapers remained above 1,750 until 1980, when a steady decline began, leaving just more than 1,400 publishing now. Total daily circulation peaked at 63.3 million in 1984 and dropped to about 51 million today.[77]

Dean Singleton, CEO of MediaNews Group, which owns more than 55 daily newspapers, said last June the industry was done in by "the proliferation of cable news channels, the inexorable trend toward two-wage earners per household working outside the home, time-pressed lifestyles, the emergence of the Internet, the explosion and fragmentation of all forms of media . . . consolidation in our industry, combined with public ownership and subsequent pressure from institutional and large shareholders."[78]

Consolidation in other industries hurt, too. "The merger of Macy's and the May Co. resulted in substantial consolidation of department store print spending," Singleton continued. "The merger of Sears and K-Mart had the same effect." Craig's List and other online services cut deeply into classified advertising, which comprised 40 percent of newspaper ad revenues in 2000.[79] Classified revenue dropped by more than half between then and 2007.[80]

In retrospect, newspapers have been criticized for letting others seize opportunity on the Internet. They didn't ignore the Web entirely, however. By 1999, 98 of the 100 largest newspapers were publishing online and several — notably *The Washington Post*, *The Wall Street Journal* and *USA Today* — had established staffs dedicated to Internet journalism.

CURRENT SITUATION

Cutting Back

After conducting a nationwide survey of news executives, the Project for Excellence in Journalism described the typical American newspaper of 2008:

"It has fewer pages than three years ago. Its stories are shorter. It publishes less news about foreign and national affairs, science and the arts. It has shrunk the crossword puzzle and may have dropped television listings and stock tables.

"Buyouts of veteran reporters have left the staff smaller and younger, with less institutional memory, less knowledge of the community, less understanding of individual beats and less experience gathering news. The staff also is under greater pressure, and there are fewer editors to catch mistakes."

The survey did find some bright spots: Today's newspaper journalists are "more tech-savvy and more oriented to serving the demands of both print and the Web." Their newspaper has strengthened some local coverage, and "investigative reporting remains highly valued."[81]

Hall at the American Society of Newspaper Editors calls this "the most exciting — and most scary — time imaginable for media." Newspapers are shrinking — and dying — left and right. They are trying desperately to figure out how they can make money with their widely read Internet sites. And they are witnessing an uncountable number of competitors pop up online.

"We need to experiment boldly and guard our values," Hall said. "I think we can do both."[82]

On the one hand, newspapers — especially larger ones — are cutting back to save money. Over the last three years, 85 percent of dailies with more than 100,000 circulation reduced staff, and 52 percent of smaller papers did.[83] All together, U.S. newspapers eliminated nearly 1,500 jobs in 2007 alone and another 5,000 in 2008.[84] *The Chicago Tribune* sliced its news staff by a third over the last year.[85]

Editorial cartoonists, once a staple of nearly every metropolitan newspaper, have not escaped the cuts. Cartoonists have been laid off or not replaced at such major papers as *The Baltimore Sun*, *Chicago Tribune*, *Los Angeles Times*, *Akron Beacon Journal*, *Cincinnati Enquirer* and *St. Paul Pioneer Press*. Papers that use syndicated cartoons will feel the pinch, too, because most syndicated cartoonists earn the bulk of their income from their newspaper employers and wouldn't be able to survive on syndication alone.[86]

"Syndication is really just beer money for most cartoonists," said Stuart Carlson, who accepted a buyout from his cartooning job at the *Milwaukee Journal Sentinel* last year.[87]

Beyond direct staff cuts, *The Detroit News* and *The Detroit Free Press*, once among the largest newspapers in America, cut home delivery to three days a week, telling readers they can buy the papers at newsstands at other times or use the publications' Web sites. The decision will save newsprint and delivery costs.[88] McClatchy Newspapers — publisher of 30 dailies and more weeklies — froze its pension plans, suspended contributions to employees' 401(k) retirement accounts and imposed a companywide pay freeze.[89] For only the second time in its 86-year history, the American Society of Newspaper Editors canceled its annual convention because many members decided they couldn't justify the expense of attending. (The previous cancellation was during World War II.)[90]

MediaNews has shipped some production functions overseas.[91] Journalists in India are writing news stories, such as about corporate earnings reports, for the Thomson Reuters wire service.[92]

New Partnerships

To continue covering public affairs with shrinking staffs, a growing number of publications are entering into partnerships — both with other professional media and with volunteers.

A Growing Lineup of Online Sources

Many Internet sites in recent years have begun offering news and opinion — from the left to the right — including the following:

DailyKos.com — News, commentary and debate for readers and activists on the left-liberal side.

Drudge Report, drudgereport.com — Demonstrated power of Internet by reporting *Newsweek*'s investigation of Clinton-Lewinsky affair before magazine was ready to publish. Consists almost entirely of links to news reports, columnists.

FreeRepublic.com — A popular site for political conservatives, featuring news and discussion.

GlobalPost, www.globalpost.com — Experienced editors coordinate more than 60 freelance correspondents in more than 40 countries.

The Huffington Post, www.huffingtonpost.com — Perhaps the most prominent public-affairs site, now calls itself "The Internet Newspaper." Contains many left-leaning blogs, links to mainstream news reports and creative use of volunteer "citizen journalists."

Kaiser Health News, www.kaiserhealthnews.org — Financed by the Kaiser Family Foundation, two veteran journalists supervise staff and freelancers who cover health.

Knight Citizen News Network, www.kcnn.org/citmedia_sites — Provides links to nearly 800 community news sites of varied quality.

MinnPost, www.minnpost.com — Former editor and publisher of the *Minneapolis Star Tribune* leads professional staff providing news and analysis about Minnesota.

Politico, www.politico.com — A professional staff, led by *Washington Post* veterans, quickly made *Politico* a popular site for news of the 2008 campaign. Now focuses on the federal government. (Also publishes free paper in Washington.)

ProPublica, www.propublica.org — Philanthropy-supported organization, led by veteran journalists, does investigative reporting that can be reproduced by other media.

Screenshot/CQ Researcher Staff

Philanthropy-supported *ProPublica* is among scores of online news and opinion sites launched in the past 15 years in response to the decline in newspaper publishing and the increasing popularity of blogs and other new media.

Seattle Post-Intelligencer, www.seattlepi.com — Internet-only survivor of the daily newspaper that shut down its presses on March 17.

SFGate.com — One of the earliest and most popular major-market newspaper Web sites, launched in 1993 by *San Francisco Chronicle*.

Slashdot.com — Daily aggregation of news reports of interest to techies.

Talking Points Memo, www.talkingpointsmemo.com — One-man blog has grown to a staff of 17 who report, analyze and comment on public affairs.

Technorati.com — Content-rich site offers news, blogs, commentary involving the technology universe.

Voice of San Diego, www.voiceofsandiego.org — Staff of young professionals, supported by philanthropy, covers local public affairs, with emphasis on investigative reporting.

The *News-Press* in Fort Myers, Fla., has created a three-reporter investigative reporting team that will be assisted by 15 volunteers from the community, including retired attorneys, accountants, police officers, educators and even an FBI agent.[93] Use of amateurs reminds Ohio University's Washburn of small-town papers publishing students' reports of high-school activities and news about clubs submitted by club members.

Meanwhile, newly created organizations are attempting to fill the gaps left by newspaper cutbacks, and often they make their work available to the traditional media.

Should newspapers shut down their presses?

YES

James Moore
Media consultant and Co-author,
Bush's Brain

Written for *CQ Researcher*, March 2009

Stop the presses. They're wasting paper. Newspapers have lost their place in our culture. A few are clinging to life, but they are only dinosaurs too blind and dumb to find a tar pit to stumble into and die.

It is argued that papers still make money and that many people still don't have computers. There was once a time when a lot of people didn't have telephones or televisions either. Those devices are now ubiquitous, and computers can also be publicly accessed just as easily.

Businesses don't make money by marketing to customer segments at the margins. People clinging to inky newsprint tend to be older and more attached to tradition. Their demographic, however, is not the source of the money. Advertisers want to reach that gold-encrusted and acquisition-hungry 25-48 demographic. Print ads aren't going to dip into those wallets and purses.

Publishers are also desperately hugging their printed copies because they still make money. The car dealers in local communities love to see their Thursday morning full-page ads. But my guess is most people buying cars today go to Cars.com or one of the other automotive Web sites and price shop. They may even begin by shopping on the Web. Eventually, the buyer links back to the local dealer's Web site. Tell me again how that print ad fits into this? It wastes paper, ink, time and money.

Drop the printed version, and paper pushers have nowhere to go but onto the Web. Traffic on the paper's news site goes up and, consequently, so does ad revenue.

Publishers complain that there isn't enough space on a Web page to sell the most lucrative ads. Web technology, though, now allows specific ads to pop up that target viewers logging on from particular ZIP codes. This is productive and meaningful advertising that small businesses like a family-owned restaurant can afford, and it will drive their foot traffic. Otherwise, they are stuck with the 4-inch x 4-inch ad on a big page and nobody notices.

New eyeballs viewing that Web page might also buy single articles of special interest or enter archives placed behind a pay wall. Big-money operations can purchase the top-dollar banner ads and drop-downs, and the money will flow like a righteous stockholder river.

Newspapers are for wrapping fish. The Internet is for providing information.

NO

John F. Sturm
President and CEO, Newspaper Association
of America

Written for *CQ Researcher*, March 2009

At the heart of the debate over the future business model of newspapers — print versus online — some might see a logical question: Why are we having this conversation? Online is growing audience, while print circulation is on the decline. Print is expensive to produce, while online is fantastically cost-efficient. What's to discuss?

When you take a closer look at print, the answer is, "quite a bit." The future is not print or online. It is both, creating a combined digital and print platform that makes newspapers the most efficient medium — and media buy — in any given market.

Those who point to a recent string of bankruptcies and a few shifts to Web-only publication as the end for print are rushing to some shaky conclusions.

One mistake is to focus on the decline while ignoring the base audience. Every day, 105 million adults read the print product. We must not ignore the steep downtrend in circulation, or that print faces challenges as audiences get younger, but if a new medium had more than 100 million loyal, daily users we would be calling it the face of a new age of communication.

Perspective is also important in understanding the decline in print advertising. Declining classified ads are a problem — in part self-created because newspapers were slow to protect the franchise. But despite 2008's economic turmoil, print does not have an audience problem. It has a recession problem — the same recession that incinerated trillions of dollars in global equity and shut the doors of a growing list of well-known companies.

There is also the matter of relative revenues. Newspaper Web sites continue to attract advertisers, and digital — in all its forms — is clearly a big part of our future. The shift in the balance, however, is going to be gradual. It will take time, experience and confidence before online spending reaches parity with print — and pricing for online reflects its value.

Most important to the communities we serve: Print is the home of the talented reporters and editors who have the skill and responsibility to find the facts and present them fairly and in depth.

Recessions end. By the time the economy heals and ad spending improves, the media landscape may be forever changed. But the newspaper industry — and its print component — will remain a strong source of high-quality, credible reporting for years to come.

Since 2006, journalism students at five universities have been producing in-depth reports on major public issues that they post on the Web and let other media republish. Called News21, the project is funded by the Knight Foundation and the Carnegie Corp. Their reports have been carried by *The Miami Herald*, *The National Journal*, United Press International and other professional news organizations.[94]

And journalism students at Northeastern University in Boston have produced a dozen investigative reporting projects since 2007 that have appeared on the front page of *The Boston Globe*. The students are taught by Walter Robinson, who retired in 2006 as head of *The Globe's* investigative reporting team.

Robinson calls the arrangement "win, win, win. The kids love it — you can't imagine how much fun it is for them to go out to find a story nobody else can find and then see their names on the front page of a major paper. It's great for the newspaper, because the newspaper can use all the extra horsepower it can find at a time when every newspaper has fewer resources. And it's great for the university."

One of the most ambitious uses of amateurs was *The Huffington Post's* "Off the Bus" project during the 2008 presidential campaign.

In 2007, Arianna Huffington's blog invited readers to become volunteer reporters. By the end of 2008, 12,000 had participated.[95] They were coordinated by a handful of professional staff.[96]

Volunteer Mayhill Fowler attracted the most attention with reports that embarrassed Obama and former President Bill Clinton. She recorded Obama at a San Francisco fundraiser when he gave his analysis of why "bitter" small-town residents "cling to guns and religion" — a comment used against him throughout the campaign. She recorded Clinton calling *New York Times* reporter Todd Purdum "sleazy" and a "scumbag" — a rant for which Clinton later apologized.

The reports created controversy not only for the politicians' comments but because Fowler failed in both cases to identify herself as a journalist.[97] That led *The Huffington Post* to instruct correspondents to make their affiliation clear.[98]

Less controversially, "Off the Bus" assigned a large number of volunteers to compile the biographies of super delegates to the Democratic National Convention

and sent 18 to observe Obama canvassers in the fall. The canvassing project produced a report that the Iraq War was not as big an issue as many thought it would be.[99]

The Pulitzer Center on Crisis Reporting supports international coverage, both by freelancers and news organizations. The center focuses on "independent international journalism that U.S. media organizations are increasingly less willing to undertake." Center-supported reports have appeared in *The New York Times*, *Los Angeles Times*, *The Washington Post*, *The Christian Science Monitor* and other publications, as well as on television and radio.[100]

A new organization in San Francisco is trying to drum up reader-financed reporting of local stories. Freelancers pitch story ideas, with budgets, on the *Spot.us* Web site, and readers can contribute. *Spot.us* contributors have funded reports about aging, wastewater, the health of San Francisco Bay beaches, political advertisements and other topics. The stories appear on the *Spot.us* Web site and have been picked up by other media.[101]

Some newly created news organizations have pulled off major scoops. *The Voice of San Diego*, for instance, uncovered conflicts of interest and hidden pay raises in city government, dissemination of misleading crime statistics and other misdeeds. The Web site "is doing really significant work, putting local politicians and businesses on the hot seat," according to Dean Nelson, director of the journalism program at San Diego's Point Loma Nazarene University.[102]

Impact of the Web

In the midst of circulation declines and financial stress, newspapers' readership may be higher than ever because of the popularity of their Web sites and the larger number of other sites that link to newspaper-produced content. Unique visitors to *The New York Times* site grew from 14.6 million in September 2007 to 20 million just a year later.[103]

"Newspapers and their Web sites generally have the largest audience among local news sources," Hall said.[104] But papers still generate 90 percent of their shrinking income from their printed products.[105]

As they struggle to increase their Internet earnings, newspapers are beefing up their Web sites and expanding into other new media.

Thirty-two newspapers can be read on the wireless Kindle reading device for from $5.99 to $14.99 a month. Subscriptions are available to national publications such as *The New York Times* and *The Wall Street Journal*, regional papers such as the *San Francisco Chronicle* and the *Seattle Times*, and foreign papers such as *Shanghai Daily* and *Frankfurter Allgemeine*.[106]

Almost alone among American newspapers, the *Arkansas Democrat-Gazette* restricts its Web site to its paper subscribers or others who pay $4.95 a month for electronic access.[107]

Newspapers and their staffs also are jumping onto Twitter, Facebook, YouTube and other social-networking sites, some of which are popular on cell phones and other wireless devices as well as through computer Internet connections.[108]

Nearly 800 newspapers have entered a consortium with Yahoo! in an effort to increase advertising on their Web sites. An effort to sell print ads through Google failed.[109]

OUTLOOK

Newspapers Doomed?

A consensus is growing among journalists and scholars that newspapers as we've known them are doomed, but journalism always will be in demand.

What they don't know is when the last newspaper will dismantle its presses — or if a few will survive — and what kind of journalism will be preserved. Could anyone have imagined the enormous changes that have occurred in just the last three years? asks former *Boston Globe* investigative reporter Robinson.

"I think there's an information franchise at the local level that is up for grabs," New York University's Rosen says. "I cannot say newspapers will grab it. I don't see them as the one and only watchdog, as the institution that produces an informed public. When you widen the lens, it's not how many reporters but how do government officials get held accountable."

Jay Smith, who retired last year as president of the Cox Newspapers chain, agrees that "far more important than the future of newspapers is the future of journalism." Smith expects printed newspapers to continue to shrink in size and circulation, while their online presence grows.

The City University of New York's Jarvis says successful newspapers will identify their "core" value to readers, which probably includes "investigative journalism, watchdog journalism, throwing sunlight on government, maybe consumer journalism. I believe the market will demand that core, and journalists will respond."

Except for a rare national publication, a newspaper's core also will be local news, he says. To provide national, international and specialized news, a newspaper's Web site can link to other publications' work, he says.

The Web will enable newspapers to serve neighborhoods better than the printed page, which is limited by how much information it can carry, Rosen says. The Internet also allows newspapers to sell advertising to small businesses that couldn't afford printed papers' rates, he says.

Jarvis and Rosen argue that newspapers will have to recruit amateur volunteers to provide comprehensive coverage, particularly at the local level. "Journalists need to become educators" to train volunteers to be effective reporters, Jarvis says.

Others are less comfortable with that model. "So many public-policy stories today require not just going to meetings and listening to what people say but accessing records, acquiring data and analyzing that data," says Shane at the Knight Commission on the Information Needs of Communities. "Amateurs are better than nothing, but they're not better than having trained people with experience and a deep knowledge of the community."

Similarly, Brian Tierney, CEO and publisher of *The Philadelphia Inquirer* and *Daily News*, scoffs: "The idea that citizen journalists are going to replace traditionally trained and paid journalists is like saying citizen surgeons are going to replace people who actually have a degree in medicine."

Niche Web sites with national audiences enjoy the best prospects, many say. So do sites with valuable information that some audiences will pay premium prices for.

"I think we're going to see an increase in very dense but narrow sites of information for which people will pay something online," Smith says. "If it's a business or a special-interest group that wants that information, they may pay handsomely for it."

But that prospect worries former *Atlanta Journal-Constitution* Editor Kovach and others. If general-circulation newspapers decline and important information is available only from expensive vendors, "the people get less information while the people in power get more information." he said. "If we talk about a government as Abraham Lincoln did — 'of the people, by the people, for the people' — then that democracy is in trouble."[110]

Online journalism will be supported by advertising, just as it has been in print, Jarvis says. Others believe online news organizations must charge for their content.

"The excellence of what we have down the pike will be entirely determined by the quality of the demand," the University of Southern California's Overholser says. "If the public demands news and is willing to pay for it, they'll get it." A "micropayments" system — by which readers would pay a few cents for each story they read or for other content they access — could provide the solution, she says.

New York Times business columnist David Carr said journalists should draw hope from Apple CEO Jobs' success with iTunes. "When iTunes began, the music industry was being decimated by file sharing," he wrote. "By coming up with an easy user interface and obtaining the cooperation of a broad swath of music companies, Mr. Jobs helped pull the business off the brink."[111]

Newspaper executives also are looking to the cable TV model and asking if a fee for news could be built into Internet access fees. And they are exploring the possibility of earning commissions by linking their sites to retailers.[112]

For his part, Tierney says the Philadelphia newspapers are exploring how to charge for online content. "We're going to have to find a way to encourage people to pay for quality journalism," he says. "To create great content, we've got to pay people. We just can't give it away."

UPDATE

Even before the economic recession that began in 2007, traditional news media were hard-pressed by falling readership and advertising revenues. The situation has only grown worse over the past three years.

Newspaper advertising revenues, including online advertising, fell 26 percent during 2009 and 41 percent from 2007 through 2009, according to the most recent figures from the Pew Project for Excellence in Journalism.[113]

And the hard times aren't just at newspapers. Local television advertising revenues fell 24 percent in 2009, and magazine ad pages dropped 19 percent, Pew said in its 2010 report on the state of the news media.

Not surprisingly, the news industry has been shrinking drastically over the past three or four years. Indeed, between mid-September 2008 and a year later, the journalism industry lost jobs at nearly three times the average pace of monthly jobs lost in the general economy, according to a study by UNITY: Journalists of Color, a journalism-advocacy group.[114] From January 2008 through Sept. 15, 2009, nearly 46,600 journalism jobs were cut and 201 news outlets closed, including the Rocky Mountain News, Albuquerque Tribune, Tucson Citizen and Seattle Post-Intelligencer (which became an online-only newspaper in March 2009), UNITY said.[115]

As some analysts point out, it's not that the American public is losing interest in news. It's just that it is getting more of its news from the Websites of traditional news outlets, as well as through social media such as Twitter. And the news media haven't yet figured out how to make money in those channels, at least not to the extent required to fund news-gathering efforts at previous levels.

"The notion that people are abandoning traditional media outlets and that audience fragmentation is at the heart of this is not really it," said Tom Rosenstiel, director of the Pew project. "What it is, more simply, is that the audience is migrating online, often to traditional outlets, but advertisers are not following them.[116]

According to Rosenstiel, the shift to so-called new media has also resulted in changes in the way journalistic resources are allotted and the nature of journalistic products. "The media aren't shrinking. The commentary and discussion aspect of our media culture is becoming more robust," Rosenstiel said. But, he continued, "as that discussion element of our media is growing, the reportorial dimension of media is shrinking."

At the same time, the Pew researchers found that the robust—and often very partisan—debates occurring in new media are overwhelmingly based on reporting by traditional news media. "Our ongoing analysis of more than a million blogs and social media sites . . . finds that 80 percent of the links are to U.S. legacy media," the Pew report states.[117]

The question, of course, is that if traditional news gatherers can't find a way to make money, where will future reporting come from? As the Pew report warned, "Unless some system of financing the production of content is developed, it is difficult to see how reportorial journalism will not continue to shrink."[118]

Some major news outlets are testing ways of charging for access to online content. The New York Times, for example, announced in January that beginning in January 2011 it would charge non-subscribers for frequent access to its Website. Non-subscribers would be able to access an as yet unspecified number of articles before being required to pay for access, a strategy the newspaper's executives said was designed to continue encouraging occasional users to visit while generating revenue from regular readers.[119]

Time magazine is following a somewhat different strategy. The news magazine announced in July that it would try delivering abridged articles and summaries on its Website in an attempt to encourage readers to subscribe to the magazine to access the full stories. "I think we'll see what works and doesn't work," Managing Editor Richard Stengel said. "We'll adapt and change. We're in the hunt like everyone else to figure this out."[120]

In August, USA Today, facing sharp declines in ad revenue and circulation, announced that it was undertaking a major reorganization aimed at putting more emphasis on its digital operations, eliminating 9 percent of its workforce—or 130 jobs—along the way. Last year USA Today lost its crown as the newspaper with the biggest weekday circulation to The Wall Street Journal.[121]

One of the most original news-gathering efforts in new media is Patch.com. Purchased by America Online in 2009, Patch is a network of local news sites that employ a relatively small number of full-time journalists and rely upon a large number of freelancers to gather content. In announcing the launch of Patch's 100th site in mid-2010, AOL officials said they expect to be serving 500 communities by the end of the year.

The long-term viability of efforts such as Patch is not clear since company finances are generally not publicly available. According to one report, Patch pays full-time editors $38,000 to $45,000 a year for 70 hours or more of work a week. And it was reported to be paying local freelancers only 10 cents a word, far below standard market rates. "Paying almost 10 times that as an editor here a few years ago, I learned it wasn't easy to find freelancers who could be counted on to deliver smart, well-written stories on deadline," wrote James Rainey of the Los Angeles Times.[122]

At the same time that news organizations are trying to find ways to earn revenues online, they also are receiving help from a growing number of foundation-funded news-gathering projects.

Foundations have actually been supporting nonprofit news gathering for decades. The Washington, D.C.-based Center for Public Integrity was created with foundation support in 1989 to focus on developing investigative news stories of national and international scope. More recently, New York-based ProPublica, dedicated to investigative journalism, began publishing in June 2008, funded primarily by the Sandler Foundation. Both organizations have won numerous awards for their efforts. In 2010 ProPublica won a Pulitzer Prize for investigative reporting, in collaboration with The New York Times Magazine, for an article on decisions made by the medical staff of a New Orleans hospital during Hurricane Katrina.

Such high-profile projects have recently been joined by those at dozens of smaller regional news organizations, including the Chicago News Cooperative and the San Francisco-based Bay Citizen.

The Chicago initiative was started in October 2009 with $500,000 in support from the Chicago-based John D. and Catherine T. MacArthur Foundation. The Bay Citizen began in May 2010 with $5 million in support from local financier F. Warren Hellman. Both projects offer Websites with original reporting on local issues. And both organizations have agreements to deliver content to regional editions of The New York Times.

In addition to regional news cooperatives, foundations also have funded a growing number of smaller topic-focused efforts. For example, the California Center for Health Reporting, supported by the privately financed California HealthCare Foundation, began in 2009. The center does not have a contract with a large traditional news organization, but rather publishes primarily through partnerships with online and print newspapers in California.

The center is filling a gap left by the economic afflictions at the partner newspapers, says Managing Editor Richard Kipling. At every one of the papers, which range in circulation from 20,000 to 400,000, newsrooms have been "denuded," says Kipling. "We walk into newsrooms where better than half the desks are empty." The lack of journalistic resources at the newspapers means it is up to the Center for Health Reporting to provide the expertise and coverage on health-care topics in the state, Kipling says.

Kipling notes that reliance on outside news-gathering organizations represents a major change for news media. "As little as two years ago many newspapers—especially the big ones—looked askance at this," he says. "There's been a sea change now. That wall is down. It's shattered." At the same time, he says, foundation-funded news projects won't supplant traditional media. "It's going to help fill some holes," he says, "but it's not going to save journalism."

Nor do the dollars being provided by foundations come close to making up for the losses experienced by traditional media in recent years.

According to the Pew report, "For all the invention and energy . . . , the scale of these new efforts still amounts to a small fraction of what has been lost." Estimates cited by the Pew study indicate that about $141 million in nonprofit funds have been devoted to new-media efforts over the past four years. "That is less than one-tenth of the losses in newspaper resources alone."[123]

What's more, relying on foundation support for news gathering carries uncertainty: Namely, can nonprofit news organizations count on continued funding? "Foundation funding isn't forever," says Kipling, noting that his project is guaranteed support for only three years. "As far as we know, we could be doing great work for 25 newspapers in the state of California for the next three years and then suddenly go away."

In fact, says Kipling, that's the normal procedure for foundations. "That's what foundations do," he says. "They seed something. If it isn't successful, they drop it. And if it is successful, they drop it because they say if it is successful it ought to be able to stand on its own two feet."

Relying on outside financial sources also poses potential ethical problems for news organizations: Outside money often comes with strings attached.

"New nonprofit journalism centers must protect the integrity of their journalism, no matter how dependent they may be on a limited circle of funders," warned a report from a gathering of news executives at the University of Wisconsin Center for Ethics in April.[124]

The executives recommended "best practices" for news organizations to follow, including full disclosure of the sources of all funding and conditions attached to the funding.[125]

Yet, despite the potential strings on foundation funding, current market conditions also impose limitations on journalism, news executives point out.

Investigative journalism "should be seen as a public good, and not subject to the whims of the marketplace," said Nick Penniman, executive director of the Huffington Post Investigative Fund, an independent project launched in 2009 with seed money from the Huffington Post and the Atlantic Philanthropies. It has since gained additional support from the Schumann Center for Media and Democracy and the Markle and Knight foundations. "Advertisers generally don't like contentious content, especially contentious content that hammers away at big corporations and high-level government officials," Penniman said. "And that's a lot of what we do."[126]

NOTES

1. "Rocky Mountain News Closing after Friday Edition," *Carlsbad* (New Mexico) *Current-Argus*, Feb. 26, 2009.

2. Dan Richman and Andrea James, "Seattle P-I to Publish Last Edition Tuesday," *Seattle Post-Intelligencer*, March 16, 2009, www.seattlepi.com/business/403793_piclosure17.html.

3. David Cook, "Monitor Shifts from Print to Web-Based Strategy," *The Christian Science Monitor*, Oct. 28, 2008, www.csmonitor.com/2008/1029/p25s01-usgn.htm.

4. "Rocky Mountain News Closing," *op. cit.*

5. Michael Hirschorn, "End Times," *The Atlantic*, January/February 2009, www.theatlantic.com/doc/200901/new-york-times (re debt), and Howard Kurtz, "How Low Will Newspapers' Ad Revenues

Go?" *The Washington Post*, Feb. 19, 2009, p. C1 (re reputation).

6. "The State of the News Media 2009," Project for Excellence in Journalism 2009, www.stateofthenews media.com/2009/index.htm.

7. Hirschorn, *op. cit.* For background, see Kenneth Jost, "Future of Newspapers," *CQ Researcher*, Jan. 20, 2006, pp. 49-72, and Kathy Koch, "Journalism Under Fire," *CQ Researcher*, Dec. 25, 1998, pp. 1121-1144.

8. John Nichols and Robert W. McChesney, "The Death and Life of Great American Newspapers," *The Nation*, March 18, 2009, pp. 11-20, www.thenation .com/doc/20090406/nichols_mcchesney. Their book, *Saving Journalism: The Soul of Democracy*, will be published by New Press in the fall.

9. David Swensen and Michael Schmidt, "News You Can Endow," *The New York Times*, Jan. 28, 2009, www.nytimes.com/2009/01/28/opinion/28 swensen.html?_r=2.

10. For background see Marcia Clemmitt, "Internet Accuracy," *CQ Researcher*, Aug. 1, 2008, pp. 625-648, and Kenneth Jost and Melissa Hipolit, "Blog Explosion," *CQ Researcher*, June 9, 2006, pp. 505-528.

11. *Editor and Publisher International Yearbook*, www .naa.org/TrendsandNumbers/Total-Paid-Circulation .aspx.

12. "Newspaper Web Site Audience Rises Twelve Percent in 2008," Newspaper Association of America, www .naa.org/PressCenter/SearchPressReleases/2009/ NEWSPAPER-WEB-SITE-AUDIENCE-RISES .aspx.

13. Hirschorn, *op. cit.*

14. Alan Mutter, "Monitor Move Doesn't Spell End of Print," *Reflections of a Newsosaur*, Oct. 28, 2008, newsosaur.blogspot.com/2008/10/monitor-move-doesnt-spell-end-of-print.html.

15. Adam Lashinsky, "CEO Eric Schmidt Wishes He Could Rescue Newspapers," *Fortune*, Jan. 7, 2009.

16. For background on the economy, see Kenneth Jost, *et al.*, "The Obama Presidency," *CQ Researcher*, Jan. 30, 2009; Peter Katel, "Vanishing Jobs," *CQ Researcher*, March 13, 2009, pp. 225-248, and

17. Jennifer Dorroh, "Endangered Species," *American Journalism Review*, December/January 2009, www .ajr.org/Article.asp?id=4645.

18. Richard Perez-Peña, "Big News in Washington, but Far Fewer Cover It," *The New York Times*, Dec. 18, 2008, p. 1.

19. Perez-Peña, *op. cit.*

20. "The State of the News Media 2009," *op. cit.*

21. Jim Wayne, "Sue Cross on the News Industry's Bleak State, Bright Future," *Online Journalism Review*, www.ojr.org/ojr/stories/080410wayne-associated-press, April 10, 2008.

22. Marc Fisher, "Bloggers Can't Fill the Gap Left by Shrinking Press Corps," *The Washington Post*, March 1, 2009, p. C1.

23. *Ibid.*

24. Bob Norman, "The Fourth Estate Sale," *New Times Broward Palm Beach*, Jan. 15, 2009, www.broward palmbeach.com/2009-01-15/news/the-fourth-estate-sale.

25. Dorroh, *op. cit.*

26. "International News Web Site Globalpost.Com To Go Live January 12," *Global Post*, www.globalpost .com/sites/default/files/globalpost/infopages/gpre leases/FWIS-FinalLaunchPR.pdf.

27. "Business Model," *Global Post*, www.globalpost .com/businessmodel.

28. "Internet Overtakes Newspapers as News Source," Pew Research Center for the People & the Press, Dec. 23, 2008, pewresearch.org/pubs/1066/inter net-overtakes-newspapers-as-news-source.

29. "Stop the Presses?" Pew Research Center for the People & the Press, March 12, 2009, pewresearch .org/pubs/1147/newspapers-struggle-public-not-concerned.

30. Nielsen Online, www.nielsen-online.com/pr/ pr_081105.pdf.

31. "Long Island University Announces Winners of 2007 George Polk Awards," The George Polk

Thomas J. Billitteri, "Financial Bailout," *CQ Researcher*, Oct. 24, 2008, pp. 865-888.

Awards in Journalism, www.brooklyn.liu.edu/polk/press/2007.html.

32. Sydney Jones and Susannah Fox, "Generations Online in 2009," Pew Internet & American Life Project, Jan. 28, 2009, pewresearch.org/pubs/1093/generations-online.

33. Reyhan Harmanci, "CNN Discovers Downside of 'Citizen Journalism,'" *San Francisco Chronicle*, Oct. 5, 2008, p. A7.

34. Justin Baer, "United Shares Plunge on Old News Story," *Financial Times*, Sept. 8, 2008, www.ft.com/cms/s/0/b843a240-7ddd-11dd-bdbd-000077b07658.html?nclick_check=1; "Old Bankruptcy Story Causes United Stock To Plunge," CBS, Sept. 9, 2008, cbs2.com/business/united.airlines.stock.2.813391.html?detectflash=false.

35. Henry Blodget, "Post Hate Mail about Our Link to Steve Jobs Heart Attack Report Here," *Silicon Alley Insider*, Oct. 4, 2008, www.alleyinsider.com/2008/10/why-we-published-that-steve-jobs-heart-attack-report.

36. Bill Kovach and Tom Rosenstiel, *Warp Speed: America in the Age of the Mixed Media Culture* (1999).

37. www.ireport.com/index.jspa.

38. James Callan, "CNN's Citizen Journalism Goes 'Awry' With False Report on Jobs," Bloomberg, Oct. 4, 2008, www.bloomberg.com/apps/news?pid=newsarchive&sid=atekONWyM7As.

39. Michael Miner, "Citizen Journalism: A Field Day for the Flacks?" *Chicago Reader*, Jan. 24, 2008, www.chicagoreader.com/features/stories/hottype/08124/.

40. "Limbaugh Holds onto His Niche — Conservative Men," Pew Research Center for the People & the Press, Feb. 3, 2009, pewresearch.org/pubs/1102/limbaugh-audience-conservative-men.

41. "Continuing Partisan Divide in Cable TV News Audience," Pew Research Center for the People & the Press, people-press.org/report/467/internet-campaign-news.

42. "Limbaugh Holds onto His Niche — Conservative Men," *op. cit.*

43. "State of the News Media 2007, Project for Excellence in Journalism, www.stateofthenewsmedia.org/2007/narrative_overview_publicattitudes.asp?cat=8&media=1.

44. Swensen and Schmidt, *op. cit.*

45. Steve Coll, "Nonprofit Newspapers," *The New Yorker*, Jan. 28, 2009, www.newyorker.com/online/blogs/stevecoll/2009/01/nonprofit-newsp.html.

46. Jack Stripling, "Fortunes Falling," *Inside Higher Ed*, Jan. 27, 2009, www.insidehighered.com/news/2009/01/27/endowments.

47. Coll, *op. cit.*

48. Zachary M. Seward, "Endowing Every U.S. Newspaper: $114 Billion. Innovation: Priceless," Nieman Journalism Lab, www.niemanlab.org/2009/01/endowing-every-american-newspaper-114-billion-innovation-priceles; "May 2007 National Industry-Specific Occupational Employment and Wage Estimates," Bureau of Labor Statistics, May 12, 2008, www.bls.gov/oes/2007/may/naics5_511110.htm.

49. Jonathan Weber, "The Trouble with Non-Profit Journalism," *New West*, Jan. 30, 2009, www.new-west.net/topic/article/the_problem_with_non_profit_journalism/C559/L559.

50. David Westphal, "The State of Independent Local Online News Part 6: Start-ups Look for Foundation Support," *Online Journalism Review*, Nov. 11, 2008, www.ojr.org/ojr/people/davidwestphal/200811/1568.

51. Kevin Sack, "Filling the Gap in Health Journalism," *International Herald Tribune*, Nov. 23, 2008, www.iht.com/articles/2008/11/23/technology/health.php; "Kaiser Family Foundation to Launch Non-Profit Health Policy News Service," Kaiser Family Foundation, Oct., 2008, www.kff.org/newsroom/khn102908nr.cfm.

52. David Westphal, "Newspapers May Seek Philanthropy to Support News-Gathering," *Online Journalism Review*, Jan. 22, 2009, www.ojr.org/ojr/people/davidwestphal/200901/1627.

53. Michael Moss and Geraldine Fabrikant, "Once Trusted Mortgage Pioneers, Now Scrutinized," *The New York Times*, Dec. 24. 2008, www.nytimes.com/2008/12/25/business/25sandler.html.

54. "Global News Professionals Offer Open-minded Alternatives for American Journalism," Missouri School of Journalism, April 4, 2008, journalism.missouri.edu/news/2008/04-08-npc-centennial.html.

55. Eric Pfanner, "France to Aid Newspapers," *International Herald Tribune*, Jan. 23, 2009, www.iht.com/articles/2009/01/23/business/ads.4-414765.php.

56. Laurent Pirot, "Sarkozy Offers New Help for French Print Media," The Associated Press, Jan. 23, 2009, www.sfgate.com/cgi-bin/article.cgi?f=/n/a/2009/01/23/financial/f090344S36.DTL.

57. Howard Kurtz, "How Low Will Newspapers' Ad Revenues Go?" *The Washington Post*, Feb. 19, 2009, p. C1.

58. Nichols and McChesney, *op. cit.*

59. Nichols and McChesney, *op. cit.*

60. Jay Rosen, "Where's the Business Model for News, People?" *Press Think*, April 22, 2008, journalism.nyu.edu/pubzone/weblogs/pressthink/2008/04/22/business_model.html.

61. Unless otherwise noted, this historical section draws from the following sources: Frank Luther Mott, *American Journalism: A History* (1962); Mitchell Stephens, "History of Newspapers," written for *Collier's Encyclopedia*, www.nyu.edu/classes/stephens/Collier%27s%20page.htm; Jost, "Future of Newspapers," *op. cit.*; Roger Stretimatter, *Mightier Then the Sword: How the News Media Have Shaped American History* (1997); Jean Folkerts, Dwight L. Teeter Jr. and Edward Caudill, *Voices of a Nation: A History of Mass Media in the United States* (2009).

62. Jill Lepore, "The Day the Newspaper Died," *The New Yorker*, Jan. 26, 2009, www.newyorker.com/arts/critics/atlarge/2009/01/26/090126crat_atlarge_lepore?currentPage=all.

63. *Ibid.*

64. *Ibid.*

65. *Ibid.*

66. Mott, *op. cit.*, p. 167.

67. Doris Kearns Goodwin, *Team of Rivals: The Political Genius of Abraham Lincoln* (2006), pp. 140-141.

68. William H. Rentschler, "The Most Illustrious Journalist No One Ever Heard of," *USA Today Magazine*, Society for the Advancement of Education, July 1998, findarticles.com/p/articles/mi_m1272/is_n2638_v127/ai_20954323.

69. Nikki Usher, "New Business Models for News Are Not That New," Knight Digital Media Center, Dec. 17, 2008, www.ojr.org/ojr/people/nikkiusher/200812/1604.

70. Tom Price, "Political Conventions: Have They Outlived Their Usefulness?" *CQ Researcher*, Aug. 8, 2008, p. 663.

71. Jay Smith, "Time To Stand up for Newspapers," *The Philadelphia Inquirer*, Feb. 2, 2009, www.philly.com/inquirer/opinion/38791802.html.

72. Price, *op. cit.*, pp. 660-661.

73. "Making the Leap Beyond 'Newspaper Companies,'" American Press Institute, February 2008, www.newspapernext.org/Making_the_Leap.pdf.

74. Steve Coll, "Nonprofit Newspapers," *The New Yorker*, Jan. 28, 2009, www.newyorker.com/online/blogs/stevecoll/2009/01/nonprofit-newsp.html.

75. Kovach and Rosenstiel, *op. cit.*

76. Jost, *op. cit.*, Jan. 20, 2006.

77. National Newspaper Association, www.naa.org/TrendsandNumbers/Total-Paid-Circulation.aspx.

78. "Dean Singleton's Speech in Sweden: 19 of the Top 50 US Newspapers Are Losing Money," *Business Week*, June 9, 2008, www.businessweek.com/innovate/FineOnMedia/archives/2008/06/dean_singletons.html.

79. Philip Meyer, "The Elite Newspaper of the Future," *American Journalism Review*, October/November 2008, www.ajr.org/article_printable.asp?id=4605.

80. Alan Mutter, "$7.5B sales plunge forecast for newspapers," *Reflections of a Newsosaur*, Oct. 12, 2008,

newsosaur.blogspot.com/2008/10/75b-sales-plunge-forecast-for.html.

81. "The Changing Newsroom," Project for Excellence in Journalism, Aug. 7, 2008, journalism.org/print/11961.

82. Westphal, *op. cit.*, Jan. 22, 2009.

83. "The Changing Newsroom," *op. cit.*

84. "The State of the News Media 2009," *op. cit.*

85. Ann Saphir, "Chicago Tribune Trims Newsroom Staff," *Crain's Chicago Business*, Feb. 12, 2009, www.chicagobusiness.com/cgi-bin/news.pl?id=32995, www.chicagobusiness.com/cgi-bin/news.pl?id=32995.

86. Lindsay Kalter, "As Newspapers Dispense with Their Editorial Cartoonists, Vibrant Local Commentary Is Diminished," *American Journalism Review*, December/January 2009, www.ajr.org/Article.asp?id=4648.

87. *Ibid.*

88. Ed White, "Detroit Papers Drop Home Delivery to 3 Days a Week," The Associated Press, Dec. 17, 2008, www.washingtonpost.com/wp-dyn/content/article/2008/12/16/AR2008121602699.html?hpid=sec-business.

89. Melanie Turner, "McClatchy to Freeze Pensions, Suspend 401(k) Match," *Sacramento Business Journal*, Feb. 5, 2009, triangle.bizjournals.com/triad/stories/2009/02/02/daily59.html.

90. "ASNE Cancels 2009 Convention," American Society of Newspaper Editors, Feb. 27, 2009, www.asne.org/index.cfm?id=7268.

91. "Dean Singleton's Speech in Sweden," *op. cit.*

92. Matt Sedensky, "MediaNews CEO: Outsourcing Could Help Save Money," The Associated Press, Oct. 20, 2008.

93. Terry Eberle, "Watchdog Journalism Page Launches Monday, *The News-Press* (Fort Myers, Fla.), Feb. 8, 2009, p. 10-B; "The News-Press presents Team Watchdog," May 27, 2007, www.news-press.com/apps/pbcs.dll/article?AID=/20070527/NEWS01/705270387/1075.

94. "Latest News," News21, newsinitiative.org; John Mecklin, "The New New Media," Miller-McCune Center for Research, Media and Public Policy, Oct. 2, 2008, www.miller-mccune.com/article/the-new-new-media.

95. Arianna Huffington and Jay Rosen, "Thanks to the People Who Worked on OffTheBus; Here's What Comes Next," *The Huffington Post*, Nov. 17, 2008, www.huffingtonpost.com/arianna-huffington-and-jay-rosen/thanks-to-the-people-who-_b_144476.html.

96. Mark Glaser, "Semi-Pro Journalism Teams Give Alternative View of U.S. Elections," Public Broadcasting System, March 13, 2008, www.pbs.org/mediashift/2008/03/semi-pro-journalism-teams-give-alternative-view-of-us-elections073.html.

97. Paul Farhi, "Off the Bus," *American Journalism Review*, December/January 2009, www.ajr.org/Article.asp?id=4644.

98. Katharine Q. Seelye, "Off the Bus, but Growing Thousands Strong," *The New York Times*, July 23, 2008, www.nytimes.com/2008/07/23/us/politics/23web-seelye.html?ei=5124&en=a86c8467fe83154e&ex=1374552000&partner=permalink&exprod=permalink&pagewanted=print.

99. Farhi, *op. cit.*

100. "Our Mission," Pulitzer Center on Crisis Reporting, pulitzercenter.org/openmenu.cfm?id=1.

101. David Cohn, "Creating a New Platform to Support Reporting," *Neiman Reports*, winter 2008, www.nieman.harvard.edu/reports.aspx; spot.us.

102. Richard Pérez-Peña, "Web Sites That Dig for News Rise as Watchdogs," *The New York Times*, Nov. 18, 2008, www.nytimes.com/2008/11/18/business/media/18voice.html?_r=2&hp=&pagewanted=print.

103. Arielle Emmett, "Traditional News Outlets Turn to Social Networking Web Sites in an Effort to Build Their Online Audiences," *American Journalism Review*, December/January 2009, www.ajr.org/Article.asp?id=4646.

104. Westphal, *op. cit.*, Jan. 22, 2009.

105. Mutter, *op. cit.*, Oct. 28, 2008.

106. www.amazon.com/s/qid=1237150180/ref=sr_pg_1?ie=UTF8&rs=165389011&rh=n%3A165389011&page=1.

107. Jonathan Rauch, "How to Save Newspapers — and Why," *National Journal*, Jan. 14, 2008, www .nationaljournal.com/njmagazine/st_20080614_ 5036.php.

108. Emmett, *op. cit.*

109. Alana Semuels, "Google Gives up on Newspaper Advertising Partnership," *Los Angeles Times*, Jan. 21, 2009, www.latimes.com/technology/la-fi-google21-2009jan21,0,6566191.story.

110. Dorroh, *op. cit.*

111. David Carr, "Let's Invent an iTunes for News," *The New York Times*, Jan. 12, 2009, www.nytimes .com/2009/01/12/business/media/12carr.html?_r=2.

112. "The State of the News Media 2009," *op. cit.*

113. "The State of the News Media: An Annual Report on American Journalism," Pew Project for Excellence in Journalism, 2010, www.stateofthe-media.org/2010/overview_key_findings.php.

114. "UNITY Layoff Tracker Report," September 17, 2009, http://www.unityjournalists.org/images/ UNITY_Layoff_Tracker_2009_Report.pdf.

115. Ibid.

116. Pew Research Center, "Transforming Journalism: State of the News Media 2010," transcript, March 29, 2010, http://pewresearch.org/pubs/1551/ transforming-journalism-state-of-the-news-m.

117. Pew Project for Excellence in Journalism, op. cit.

118. Ibid.

119. Richard Perez-Pena, "The Times to Charge for Frequent Access to Its Web Site," The New York Times, Jan. 20, 2010, p. B1.

120. Jeremy W. Peters, "Time Moves to Limit Free Content Online," The New York Times, July 8, 2010, p. B3.

121. Jeremy W. Peters, "USA Today To Remake Itself to Stress Digital Operations," The New York Times, Aug. 27, 2010, p. B1.

122. James Rainey, "Hyper-local in South Bay," The Los Angeles Times, April 24, 2010, p. 1.

123. Ibid.

124. "Report Recommends 'Best Practices' for Nonprofit Investigative Journalism," The Center for

Journalism Ethics, April 26, 2010, www.journalis methics.info.

125. "Roundtable Report: Ethics for the New Investigative Newsroom," The Center for Journalism Ethics, April 2010, www.journalis methics.info/2010_roundtable_report_27april .pdf.

126. Kinley Levack, "Funding Funds: The Huffington Post Investigative Fund Finds Support from Big Name Foundations," EContent, March 2010, p. 8.

BIBLIOGRAPHY

Books

Fellow, Anthony, *American Media History*, Wadsworth Publishing, 2009.
The director of California State University at Fullerton's journalism program traces the development of American media.

Folkerts, Jean, Dwight L. Teeter Jr. and Edward Caudill, *Voices of a Nation: A History of Mass Media in the United States*, Allyn & Bacon, 2009.
Three journalism professors put the history of American media in a cultural context.

Hindman, Matthew, *The Myth of Digital Democracy*, Princeton University Press, 2008.
An assistant political science professor at Arizona State University argues the Internet has not been such a revolutionary force in American politics after all.

Stretimatter, Roger, *Mightier then the Sword: How the News Media Have Shaped American History*, Westview Press, 2007.
An American University journalism professor analyzes the impact of journalists from Tom Paine to Rush Limbaugh.

Articles

Blodget, Henry, "Post Hate Mail about Our Link to Steve Jobs Heart Attack Report Here," *Silicon Alley Insider*, Oct. 4, 2008, www.alleyinsider.com/2008/10/

why-we-published-that-steve-jobs-heart-attack-report.
A well-read blogger argues that it's OK to post unverified news online.

Carr, David, "Let's Invent an iTunes for News," *The New York Times*, **Jan. 12, 2009, www.nytimes .com/2009/01/12/business/media/12carr.html?_r=2.**
The Times' business columnist suggests newspapers learn from the music business, which defeated free Internet file-sharing and now sells billions of tracks online.

Dorroh, Jennifer, "Endangered Species," *American Journalism Review*, **December/January 2009, www .ajr.org/Article.asp?id=4645.**
Dorroh explores the damage done to democracy when newspapers stop covering their communities' interests in Washington.

Emmett, Arielle, "Traditional News Outlets Turn to Social Networking Web Sites in an Effort to Build Their Online Audiences," *American Journalism Review*, **December/January 2009, www.ajr.org/ Article.asp?id=4646.**
Emmett looks at how news organizations are recruiting audiences through Facebook and other social-networking media.

Nichols, John, and Robert W. McChesney, "The Death and Life of Great American Newspapers," *The Nation*, **March 18, 2009, pp. 11-20, www.thenation .com/doc/20090406/nichols_mcchesney.**
Journalist Nichols and communications Professor McChesney passionately argue that government subsidy is the only way to halt the decline of American journalism.

Swensen, David, and Michael Schmidt, "News You Can Endow," *The New York Times*, **Jan. 28, 2009, www.nytimes.com/2009/01/28/opinion/28swensen .html?_r=2.**
Swensen, who manages Yale University's endowment, and Yale analyst Schmidt argue that philanthropists can save newspapers.

Weber, Jonathan, "The Trouble with Non-Profit Journalism," *New West*, **Jan. 30, 2009, www.newwest .net/topic/article/the_problem_with_non_profit_ journalism/C559/L559.**
The founder of a for-profit online-journalism organization explains his opposition to philanthropic support for news media.

Reports and Studies

"News In the Public Interest: A Free and Subsidized Press," Manship School of Mass Communication, Reilly Center for Media & Public Affairs, Louisiana State University, 2004.
Media executives and scholars discuss the pros and cons of alternative ways to finance journalism.

"The State of the News Media," Project for Excellence in Journalism, 2009, www.stateofthenewsmedia .com/2009/ index.htm.
This annual report looks at American journalism from traditional newspapers to the newest online sites.

Adler, Richard P., "Next-Generation Media: The Global Shift: A Report of the Forum on Communications and Society," Aspen Institute Communications and Society Program, 2007, http://staging.aspeninstitute.org/sites/ default/files/content/docs/communications%20 and%20society%20program/NEXTGENERATION .PDF.
Media's impact on society is discussed by leaders of old and new media, other businesses, government, academe and nonprofit organizations.

Miel, Persephone, and Robert Faris, "News and Information as Digital Media Come of Age," Berkman Center for Internet and Society, Harvard University, 2008, http://cyber.law.harvard.edu/sites/ cyber.law.harvard.edu/files/Overview_MR.pdf.
The authors explore the benefits and dangers to society posed by the migration of news reporters and consumers from print to the Internet.

For More Information

John S. and James L. Knight Foundation, 200 South Biscayne Blvd., Miami, FL 33131-2349; (305) 908-2600; www.knightfoundation.org. Supports research organizations and news media, with recent emphasis on the Internet.

Newspaper Association of America, 4401 Wilson Blvd., Suite 900, Arlington, VA 22203-1867; (571) 366-1000; www.naa.org. Advocates for newspaper interests, publishes information about newspaper performance, such as print circulation, Web site visits.

The Newspaper Project, news.newspaperproject.org. Organized by newspaper executives to promote notion that newspapers are important and not yet dead.

Pew Research Center for the People & the Press, 1615 L St., N.W., Suite 700, Washington, DC 20036; (202) 419-4350; people-press.org. Conducts polls about attitudes toward the news media and public policy issues; publishes reports about the media and public affairs.

The Poynter Institute, 801 Third St. South, St. Petersburg, FL 33701; (888) 769-6837; www.poynter.org. Journalism education organization posts wide-ranging information about the news business.

Project for Excellence in Journalism, 1615 L St., N.W., Suite 700, Washington, DC 20036; (202) 419-3650; www .journalism.org. Conducts extensive research on journalism; publishes annual report on "The State of the News Media."

[Handwritten annotations in top margin:]
- originally published 2003 but updated 2010.
- Viacom → CBS, MTV, Simon & Schuster
- demonstrates synergy & vertical integration

2

Media Ownership

David Hatch and Patrick Marshall

Getty Images/David McNew

Protesters in Los Angeles urge the Federal Communications Commission not to ease media-ownership rules. But on June 2, the FCC voted to allow media corporations to own dramatically more news outlets in any one city. Critics say fewer media conglomerates means fewer choices for consumers. But industry executives say consolidation enables them to stay competitive and provide more selections.

From *CQ Researcher*, October 10, 2003. Updated July 5, 2010.

Major TV networks pulled out all the stops competing for the first televised interview with Pfc. Jessica Lynch after her dramatic rescue during the Iraq war. Big-name anchors called her on the phone, and sent her personalized trinkets, autographed books and photos.

But CBS News offered more than souvenirs. Tapping the synergies of its powerful parent company, Viacom — whose sprawling media empire includes publishing giant Simon & Schuster and MTV — CBS dangled book deals and music specials before the waifish soldier from West Virginia.[1]

After originally defending its efforts, the network conceded it overstepped the boundaries of journalistic ethics. Acknowledging the critics who think media companies are too consolidated and powerful, CBS Chairman and CEO Leslie Moonves blamed the aggressive wooing of Lynch on Viacom's sheer size and web of interconnected businesses.

"As these companies become more and more vertically integrated, you know, sometimes you do go over the line," he said.[2] In the end, ABC snared the first TV interview with Lynch, scheduled for Nov. 11 with Diane Sawyer.

Long gone are the days when media companies were one-horse enterprises specializing only in broadcasting or publishing. Today they are multifaceted conglomerates with stakes in everything from television, radio, movies, newspapers and books to the Internet, theme parks, billboards and concert promotion.[3]

Five media powerhouses now control up to 80 percent of America's prime-time TV programming: AOL Time Warner (CNN, WB, HBO); Disney (ABC, ESPN); General Electric (NBC, CNBC,

[Handwritten annotations:]
- CBS
- vertical integration
- AOL-TW (TV), Disney, GE, News Corp, Viacom
- Radio — my graphic shows Clear Channel

own 25% of channels but control 80% of primetime

Inside Big Media

Media conglomerates today own holdings in broadcast, cable, Internet, music, book, video and movie companies. Here is a look at two of the biggest media corporations.*

Time Warner (formerly AOL/Time Warner) Revenue: $41 billion	Viacom Revenue: $24.6 billion
Selected holdings:	**Selected holdings:**
Broadcasting	**Broadcasting**
The WB Television Network	CBS
Cable	39 television stations
Cinemax	Infinity Broadcasting
CNN	(180 radio stations)
Comedy Central	King World Productions
Court TV	Paramount Television
HBO	Spelling Television
Time Warner Cable	UPN
Turner Broadcasting System	Viacom Productions
Internet	**Cable**
America Online	BET
Mapquest	CMT
Moviefone	MTV
Netscape	Nickelodeon
Film	Sundance Channel
Castle Rock Entertainment	Showtime
Hanna-Barbera Cartoons	The Movie Channel
New Line Cinema	VH1
Warner Brothers Pictures	**Film**
Music	Paramount Home Entertainment
Atlantic Recording	United Cinemas International
Elektra Entertainment	**Video**
Warner Brothers Records	Blockbuster
Publishing	**Publishing**
Little, Brown & Co.	Simon & Schuster
Time	
People	
Sports Illustrated	
Fortune	

* Holdings of other media firms are on the Center for Digital Democracy's Web site: www.democraticmedia.org/issues/mediaownership/industryData.php.

Source: "The B&C 25 Media Groups," *Broadcasting & Cable,* May 12, 2003

New York Times op-ed column that the five mega-companies actually own only 25 percent of today's more than 300 broadcast, satellite and cable channels. "But because of their popularity, 80 percent of the viewing audience chooses to watch them," Powell wrote. "Do we really want government to regulate what is popular?"[5]

Meanwhile, one company, Clear Channel Communications Inc., dominates radio, owning more than 1,200 stations — about 970 more than its closest competitor. Clear Channel is also the largest concert promoter in the world.[6]

Critics note that the number of TV-station owners in the United States has declined from 540 to 360 in the past 25 years, while daily-newspaper ownership has plummeted from 860 owners to 300.[7]

"You're running close to a monopoly or oligopoly situation, there's no question about that," says Michael Copps, a Democratic FCC commissioner and staunch opponent of the panel's recent move to loosen media-ownership rules. "It's about the ability of a very small number of companies to control [the content of] our media. To dictate what the entertainment is going to be, to dictate what the civic dialogue is going to be, to dictate that we'll no longer have as much [local news] and diversity as we had before. So it goes to the fundamentals of our democratic life as a country."

While the number of media competitors may be declining, the amount of diversity of content and technologies is not. Today there are six commercial broadcast networks — double the number from a few decades ago — three 24-hour news networks, cable and satellite television, the

MSNBC); News Corp. (Fox, Fox News) and Viacom (CBS, MTV, UPN).[4]

But Federal Communications Commission (FCC) Chairman Michael K. Powell pointed out in a recent

AOL-Time Warner, Disney, GE, NewsCorp, Viacom   *Do they dictate?*

Internet and a growing number of alternative-media choices, such as low-power FM, satellite radio and Internet "blogs," or Web logs written by everyday citizens. (*See sidebar, p. 44.*) Consumers today have "an overwhelming amount of choice," says NBC lobbyist Bob Okun.

Indeed, the three major networks that dominated prime-time TV for decades have ceded huge chunks of the market to cable and satellite competitors. As of June 2002, more than 85 percent of Americans subscribed to cable, satellite and other pay-TV services.[8] "The competition is real from cable," Okun says. "They put on edgier programming."

To fight back, three broadcast TV networks now operate their own studios so they can produce more content themselves, keep tighter control over the creative process and avoid bidding wars over hit shows. Critics say network ownership of studios has forced many independent producers out of business and left those remaining at the mercy of big media. As a result, they say, the broadcast networks are churning out lowbrow, cookie-cutter programming because independent voices have been locked out. Program diversity, creativity and localism — or attention to local needs or tastes — suffer when too few companies control much of what we see, read and hear, the critics say.

But industry executives say consolidation enables them to grow quickly so they can stay competitive. Mergers also create new opportunities for cross-promotion, content repackaging and elimination of redundant offerings, freeing up resources for other areas.

In response to marketplace changes, Republican Chairman Powell in June shepherded through the commission a sweeping relaxation of the FCC's media-ownership rules by a narrow 3-2 vote along party lines, with the two Democratic commissioners opposed.

Among other things, the commission increased the audience reach of network-owned TV stations, permitting them to reach 45 percent of households, up from 35 percent. It also lifted the ban on a single company owning both a broadcast station and a newspaper in the same market — combinations that until recently were only permitted on a limited basis. In sum, the new rules could allow one company — in a single market — to own three TV stations, one newspaper, eight radio outlets and a cable system. And TV-newspaper mergers would be permissible in about 200 markets, affecting 98 percent of the U.S. population.[9]

The new rules triggered an unexpectedly strong backlash from lawmakers, academics and advocacy groups concerned that media control would fall into too few hands. The rhetoric on both sides has been harsh. Critics insist the new regulations could threaten democracy, while supporters warn that without them, free TV could eventually disappear, as more content migrates to pay TV.

Proponents of the FCC's action point out that network broadcasters today are facing more competition than ever before. "In 1979, the vast majority of households had six or fewer local television stations to choose from, three of which were typically affiliated with

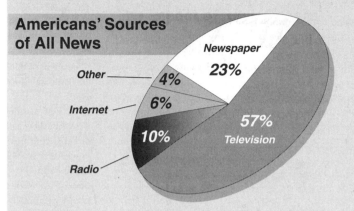

Where Americans Get Their News

More than three-quarters of all Americans consider television and newspapers their most important sources of news, according to a recent study. Watchdog groups use such statistics to rebut claims that Americans get their news from a wide variety of media sources.

Americans' Sources of All News

Newspaper **23%**

Other — **4%**

Internet — **6%**

10%

Radio

57% *Television*

Sources: Federal Communications Commission, "Consumer Survey on Media Usage," prepared by Nielsen Media Research, September 2002, in Consumer Federation of America, "Promoting the Public Interest Through Media Ownership Limits," May 2003

Radio Giant Clear Channel Riles Critics

When a freight train derailed in Minot, N.D, last year, releasing toxic fumes into the air, radio station KCJB-AM didn't answer when police phoned to request public alerts.

Critics of media consolidation say no one responded because the station — one of six outlets in Minot owned by Clear Channel Communications — was running on computers after the company consolidated local operations and slashed personnel.[1] But Andrew Levin, senior vice president for government affairs at Clear Channel, says personnel were on hand and blamed Minot police for not knowing how to operate emergency equipment that automatically prompts on-air alerts.

Tiny Minot, it turns out, was the wrong place for Clear Channel to have such problems because North Dakota Democrat Byron Dorgan sits on the powerful Senate panel that oversees the radio industry. The lawmaker wasn't pleased and is now seeking to clamp down on the looser ownership rules passed by the Federal Communications Commission (FCC) on June 2. He often cites the Minot case as a reason why he opposes further deregulation of television, newspapers and other mass media.

To its critics, Clear Channel provides a sobering lesson on the pitfalls of media mergers. Bolstered by the 1996 Telecommunications Act's deregulation of radio, it grew from 40 stations in 1996 to 1,220 today to become the dominant industry player, with 103 million listeners nationwide and revenue of $3.2 billion annually.[2] It is also the world's largest concert promoter and one of the nation's largest display-advertising companies, with about 770,000 billboards.[3] Coupled with its nearest competitor, Viacom-owned Infinity Broadcasting, the companies control 42 percent of the U.S. radio market and command 45 percent of the revenue.[4]

Detractors say Clear Channel's homogenized playlists make radio sound the same from coast to coast and that its use of "voice-tracking" — programming local radio stations with deejays and announcers in distant cities — undermines localism. "Only about 9 percent of all our programming is voice-tracked," Levin says, adding that the practice enables small communities to enjoy otherwise unaffordable talent. "We think that folks like it."

Noting that Clear Channel owns less than 12 percent of U.S. radio stations, CEO John Hogan said, "I don't see any way possible to conclude that this is a consolidated industry or that Clear Channel has any real dominance inside that industry." Prior to 1996, he noted, up to 60 percent of radio stations were losing money, and many were in danger of going dark. He said Clear Channel should be heralded as an American success story and that the company helped rejuvenate radio.[5]

Clear Channel says it has increased format diversity in many markets, such as Los Angeles, where it owns stations ranging from nostalgia to Spanish hip-hop.[6] But the watchdog Future of Music Coalition (FMC) found hundreds of redundant radio formats nationwide with songs overlapping up to 76 percent of the time. Some stations altered format names without changing playlists.[7]

"Just because it's a [distinct] format doesn't mean that it's diverse," says FMC Executive Director Jenny Toomey. "The public realizes radio has homogenized since the '96 Act passed."

"Radio consolidation has contributed to a 34 percent decline in the number of owners, a 90 percent rise in the cost of advertising, a rise in indecent broadcasts and the replacement of local news and community programming with voice-tracking and syndicated hollering that ill-serves the public interest," railed Sen. Ernest Hollings, D-S.C., at a January hearing.[8]

Eric Boehlert, a *Salon* journalist who writes extensively about radio, told National Public Radio, "You can't have a hit without being on Clear Channel stations. You can't have a career without being on Clear Channel stations. So all of a sudden you have a company that is essentially dictating what gets heard on the radio." That was unheard of before the '96 act, he said.[9]

Don Henley, one of several musicians who accuse Clear Channel of heavy-handed, monopolistic practices, told lawmakers this year: "Artists can no longer stand for the exorbitant radio-promotion costs, nor can we tolerate the overt or covert threats posed by companies owning radio stations, venues and [advertising] agencies."[10]

A just-released report from the watchdog Center for Public Integrity finds that small and medium-sized radio markets have higher levels of radio concentration than large ones. Clear Channel, the report finds, is the main owner in 20 of the top 25 most-concentrated markets.[11]

Fueling the controversy surrounding the San Antonio, Texas-based company are its close ties to Republicans. CEO Lowry Mays is a friend of President Bush and contributes heavily to GOP causes. Tom Hicks, a Clear Channel board member, purchased the Texas Rangers baseball team from Bush and his associates. The company has made a star of conservative radio host Rush Limbaugh, whose show airs on 180 Clear Channel talk-radio channels. Others are concerned that Clear Channel could unduly influence a combined Hispanic Broadcasting Corp. (HBC) and Univision Communications, which recently won FCC approval to merge. Clear Channel is HBC's largest shareholder.[12]

Meanwhile, Rep. Howard Berman, D-Calif., worries that Clear Channel has "punished" Britney Spears and other artists who bypassed its concert-promotion service by burying radio ads for their concerts and denying airplay to their songs.[13] Competitors allege that Clear Channel secretly purchases radio stations — using front groups and shell companies — and "warehouses" them if there is public opposition to the company's expansion in the hope that regulatory limits will later be lifted.[14]

In September, the watchdog Alliance for Better Campaigns accused Clear Channel and Infinity of limiting the sale of radio ads to candidates in California's gubernatorial recall election. The alliance suggested the companies may be withholding ad space for more lucrative commercial clients.[15]

Clear Channel has strongly denied all of these charges, saying it is the target of criticism because it's the market leader.[16]

The National Association of Broadcasters (NAB) emphasizes there are nearly 4,000 separate owners of 13,000 local radio stations in the U.S. today. "The Hollywood movie studios, the record companies, direct-broadcast satellite, cable systems, newspapers — even the Internet — all have more of their revenue share concentrated among the top 10 owners than does radio," NAB President and CEO Eddie Fritts told lawmakers this year. "Spanish-language formats have increased by over 80 percent in the last decade, and other ethnicities are well represented on the dial."[17]

To some, Clear Channel is a harbinger of television's future. "We're already going that way under the old rules," complains Democratic FCC Commissioner Michael Copps, who already sees signs of the "Clear Channelization"

of TV. "I don't think anybody in the Congress really anticipated the extent of consolidation that has ensued from the 1996 act."

But even Copps sees upsides to concentration, such as the "economies and efficiencies" that have allowed some stations to operate more profitably and avoid going under, depriving listeners of service.[18] Nevertheless, he opposes the FCC's new media-ownership policies.

Clear Channel is now in Washington's crosshairs. Although the FCC loosened ownership rules for newspapers and television stations on June 2, it limited the number of radio stations that operators can own in certain markets. The FCC wanted to grandfather in existing non-compliant stations, but Sen. John McCain, R-Ariz., offered legislation to force the divestiture of such properties, including roughly 100 Clear Channel stations.

Meanwhile, the Justice Department is investigating whether Clear Channel requires musicians to sign with its concert-promotion division to get airplay, and whether it wields too much power in Southern California.[19]

---

[1] Marc Fisher, "Sounds Familiar for a Reason," *The Washington Post*, May 18, 2003, p. B1.

[2] From statement by Sen. Ernest Hollings, D-S.C., on radio consolidation before Senate Commerce Committee, Jan. 30, 2003.

[3] Eric Boehlert, "Habla usted Clear Channel?" *Salon.com*, April 24, 2003.

[4] See "Radio Deregulation: Has it Served Citizens and Musicians," Future of Music Coalition, www.futureofmusic.org, Nov. 18, 2002, p. 3.

[5] From NPR's "Fresh Air," July 23, 2003.

[6] NPR, *op. cit.*

[7] Future of Music Coalition, *op. cit.*, pp. 42-52.

[8] Hollings, *op. cit.*

[9] NPR, *op. cit.*

[10] From testimony before Senate Commerce Committee hearing on radio consolidation, Jan. 30, 2003.

[11] See "Big Radio Rules in Small Markets: A few behemoths dominate medium-sized cities throughout the U.S," www.openairwaves.org/telecom, released Oct. 1, 2003.

[12] Boehlert, *op. cit.*

[13] See Rep. Howard Berman, D-Calif., letter to U.S. Attorney General John Ashcroft, found at www.house.gov/berman/, Jan. 22, 2002.

[14] Eric Boehlert, "Washington Tunes In," *Salon.com*, March 27, 2002.

[15] See press release, Sept. 3, 2003.

[16] See "Issue Update," www.clearchannel.com, June 2, 2003.

[17] From testimony before Senate Commerce Committee, Jan. 30, 2003.

[18] Copps was speaking at the University of Southern California Media Consolidation Forum in Los Angeles, April 28, 2003, p. 7.

[19] Bill McConnell, "DoJ Investigates Clear Channel on Two Fronts," *Broadcasting & Cable*, www.broadcastingandcable.com, July 25, 2003.

CNN, Time, Fortune, AOL

a broadcast network," the FCC said in a report accompanying its June decision.[10] Today the average U.S. household receives seven broadcast television networks and an average of 102 channels per home, it said.

But critics say the plethora of media choices can be deceptive. A consumer who watches CNN, subscribes to *Time* and *Fortune* and surfs AOL may think he's consulting several independent sources, but in fact, all are part of media giant AOL *Time* Warner (which recently decided to drop AOL from its name). "You may be hearing many different voices, yes, but they are from the same ventriloquist," said Sen. Byron Dorgan, a North Dakota Democrat.[11]

Because roughly 15 percent of Americans rely on free broadcast TV as their only source of television, a bipartisan coalition of lawmakers is trying to overturn key portions of the new FCC regulations, which a federal court on Sept. 4 barred from taking effect, pending further judicial review.

Meanwhile, the controversy has prompted Congress to re-evaluate whether media deregulation, a trend that has accelerated since Congress enacted the Telecommunications Act of 1996, has met its goal of fostering more competition.[12]

The firestorm has tainted the image of Chairman Powell, who is under attack from influential lawmakers on both sides of the political aisle. The son of Secretary of State Colin L. Powell, he had been a darling of Washington lawmakers for much of his tenure.

Although cable and satellite television sometimes trigger scrutiny into how much market power they exercise, mergers involving broadcasters are of special concern, because they use the public airwaves and are licensed to serve the "public interest."

Commissioner Copps says public-interest requirements have been relaxed over the years and that license renewals are now largely pro forma. In theory, he says, TV and radio stations are supposed to put the public interest ahead of profit, but in reality, that is not always the case. To deflect congressional pressure, Powell launched a new effort in August to promote more localism.

In addition to concerns about content diversity, some critics worry about the ethnic diversity of media owners. Minorities own only 4.2 percent of the nation's TV and radio stations, according to the Minority Media and Telecommunications Council (MMTC), a civil-rights advocacy group. Viewed another way, minorities control 1.3 percent of the value of the nation's broadcast assets, which MMTC Executive Director David Honig calls "a national disgrace."

Meanwhile, a July survey detected a drop in minority employment at local television stations from 20.6 percent to 18.1 percent between 2002 and 2003, and from 8 percent to 6.5 percent at local radio stations.[13]

As Washington politicos debate how the media should be regulated, here are some issues being discussed:

Is the U.S. media industry too consolidated?

In Tampa, Fla., media consolidation is an everyday reality. Thanks to a waiver of the FCC ban on cross-ownership of local newspapers and TV stations, Media General owns both *The Tampa Tribune* and the local NBC affiliate WFLA-TV.* They share a state-of-the-art newsroom, where they sometimes swap story ideas and collaborate on projects. Writers for the paper have appeared on WFLA shows, and some of WFLA's reports make it into the *Tribune*.

Proponents of the Tampa experiment said combining the newsrooms would effectively double the resources available to reporters, producing more in-depth journalism. But Robert Haiman, president emeritus of the Poynter Institute journalism school and former editor of the competing *St. Petersburg Times*, hasn't seen that result. "Where are the huge investigative stories that run simultaneously in the newspaper and on the TV station?" he asked. "I'm not seeing incredible feats of journalism," he said. "I see those promotional connections, but I don't see a great leap."[14]

But others think Tampa's arrangement benefits the marketplace. "It has given power to both sides," says Barbara Cochran, president of the Radio-Television News Directors Association (RTNDA). The newspaper gets exposure to a broader audience with a younger demographic, and the television station has access to the paper's vast reporting staff, she notes, but "they still make very independent decisions."

Does the cross-ownership stifle competition? No, she says, because other voices remain. "You still have competition" in the Tampa television market, she says.

---

* The FCC removed the ban in June, but it remains in effect while lawmakers and the courts decide its fate.

[handwritten: Gauging whether the media [are] too concentrated boils down to perspective.]

[handwritten: cable has 2 revenue streams]

Gauging whether the media is too concentrated boils down to perspective. "Large media companies have become larger, but so has the entire sector," wrote telecom visionary Eli Noam in the *Financial Times*.[15] Industry supporters emphasize that none of the Big Four broadcast networks owns more than 3 percent of the nation's TV stations. Of the 1,340 commercial TV stations in the United States as of March 31, 2003, CBS owned only 2.9 percent, Fox owned 2.8 percent, NBC owned 2.2 percent and ABC owned 0.8 percent.[16]

And while the broadcast networks controlled 90 percent of the audience 25 years ago, today they control less than 50 percent.[17] The networks say the decline is due to the growth of cable, which — because it's a pay service — has fewer content restrictions and thus can offer racier and more violent programming. The major broadcasters insist they're at another disadvantage to cable: It has two revenue streams — advertising and subscriptions — while broadcasters have only advertising.

"You need somehow to create additional forms of revenue," NBC's Okun says, adding that skyrocketing costs for sports, movies, hit TV shows and other marquee programming have forced the networks to consolidate.

But media watchdogs say it's unfair for broadcasters to complain they are losing ground to cable, since broadcasters have migrated most of their channels to cable and satellite for distribution.[18]

Some critics also fear that the news divisions of huge media conglomerates feel pressure to go soft on corporate parents' wrongdoings. "I don't see the problem, frankly. Views are not being suppressed," said Time Inc. CEO Ann Moore, noting that *Fortune* has had tough coverage of its parent company.[19]

Public Broadcasting Service (PBS) President and CEO Pat Mitchell complains that companies often justify consolidation by promising that more resources will be available to invest in news and information-gathering, but they rarely deliver. "The American public seems less informed than ever about almost everything," she says.

That may come as a surprise to FCC Chairman Powell, who cites the emergence of all-news networks and the plethora of local TV newscasts as examples of a robust media environment.

"That's not diversity of news," responds Marvin Kalb, a senior fellow at Harvard University's Joan Shorenstein

Center on the Press, Politics and Public Policy. "That's just multiplicity of news." When TV stations air local newscasts throughout the day they often repeat the same stories, and competing stations usually offer similar coverage, he says. Real diversity would occur if local stations offered a broader range of stories with more depth, he argues.

In fact, a recent study of local TV found that smaller station groups produce better-quality news than network-owned-and-operated stations (O&Os), which have far more resources.[20]

Meanwhile, even though there are many more news outlets today, "There's a lot less news being presented to the American people," says Kalb, a former CBS and NBC News reporter.

Nevertheless, the major broadcast networks remain the first place Americans turn for news, especially during times of tragedy, Kalb says. But the networks, assuming the public is getting its hard news from the 24-hour news stations like CNN, are offering less and less hard news. "They feel that you've already got the news elsewhere, so why bother," Kalb says. "But not everybody watches CNN all day. In fact, probably most of us don't watch it at all."

Did the FCC loosen its media-ownership rules too much?

It's not often that the National Rifle Association (NRA) and the National Organization for Women (NOW) agree on an issue. But their opposition to the FCC's historic June 2 decision easing its media-ownership restrictions put them in the same camp. Such diverse alliances are spelling trouble for the Republican-led FCC. A broad coalition of regulators, lawmakers and advocacy groups argues the commission's action threatens consumers, media diversity and democracy.

Ironically, some of the most outspoken critics have come from Powell's own party. "The FCC made a mistake," said Republican Sen. Trent Lott of Mississippi. "With too much concentration, companies no longer have to be competitive with rates or product," he said. "This is a question of fairness and access for both small media organizations and media consumers."[21]

On the other side of the political aisle, the comments have been all but apocalyptic. "Let me be blunt: I believe the recent changes to the FCC's media-ownership rules

[handwritten left margin: The debate]

[handwritten bottom: diversity ≠ multiplicity]

homogenization of radio

are a disaster for smaller and new entrants [into the media business]," said Democratic FCC Commissioner Jonathan Adelstein.[22]

"The homogenization of radio is a grim predictor of the ravages of deregulation," Sen. Russell D. Feingold, D-Wis., said in a Sept. 16 floor speech.

Former CBS News anchor Walter Cronkite, who lobbied against the rule changes, warned, "The gathering of more and more outlets under one owner clearly can be an impediment to a free and independent press."[23]

But proponents of the deregulation are equally ardent: "It has been said that the rules will allow one company to dominate all media in a community," said GOP Sen. George Allen of Virginia. "It is simply not true . . . If you look at the availability of information and programming, consumers have an unprecedented abundance of choices."[24]

Kenneth Ferree, chief of the FCC's Media Bureau, emphasizing that the agency had to work within parameters set by the courts, says, "I would have gotten rid of the national [network-TV ownership] cap entirely. I'm still doubtful that it can be defended in court, but we tried."

NBC lobbyist Okun says the new rules are "incremental" at best, and that big is not always bad. For instance, he says, increasing the national-audience reach of network-owned TV stations from 35 percent of households to 45 percent would merely "let us own a few more stations in large markets."

The commission lifted the cap after heavy lobbying from the Big Four networks, three of which are at — or above — the 35 percent limit due to waivers while the restriction is in limbo. Raising the cap would let the networks purchase more TV stations and reach more viewers. Fox owned-and-operated TV stations (O&Os, for short) reach 37 percent of U.S. households. CBS-owned stations reach 40 percent. NBC is at 34 percent and ABC, at 24 percent, has more acquisition leeway.[25]

The FCC also lifted its blanket ban on one company owning both a newspaper and broadcast station in a market, permitting the combinations in markets with at least four TV stations. Before, the combinations were allowed only if they were grandfathered in after being banned in the 1970s or with an FCC waiver to help a struggling outlet.

For the first time, the FCC permitted triopolies — single ownership of three TV stations in a market — in large metropolitan areas. But it retained its ban on the Big Four broadcast networks merging with each other.

Democratic Commissioner Copps also complains that the new ownership rules do not factor in the transition of broadcasters to digital. Noting that TV stations will be able to offer multiple digital TV channels in their markets, he asks rhetorically, "Doesn't that change the competitive landscape somehow?"

In fact, the FCC's Republican majority concluded that easing restrictions on common ownership of TV stations in local markets would "spur" the transition to digital because small-market stations face difficulties raising money to convert their facilities.[26]

Copps thinks the FCC should have more carefully considered the effect on advertisers, particularly small businesses that rely on local broadcast ads, and children, who are increasingly exposed to indecent TV images.[27] Some surveys indicate up to 70 percent of Americans think television is inappropriate for children, and 85 percent think it encourages youngsters to engage in sexual activity or commit violence, he says.

"We have no statutory charge to protect advertisers," Ferree says. "That's not what we do. We protect viewers and listeners." He says the agency determined the rules would not cause more indecency.

Copps says the FCC also failed to consider the impact on minorities, in terms of ownership and employment opportunities and diversity of views. Ferree notes the FCC is trying to address minority concerns through a separate advisory committee.

"Any further relaxation in the ownership rules is bad for our industry," says Jim Winston, executive director of the National Association of Black-owned Broadcasters, noting a 20 percent decline in minority-owned TV and radio stations since 1996, when the industry was deregulated. Many African-American broadcasters were forced to sell to bigger players that undercut them on ad rates and had more financial leverage. "Minorities have historically had difficulty raising capital," he says.

But NBC's Okun counters that existing media-ownership restrictions undermine diversity more than consolidation does. His network would like to increase the footprint of Telemundo, its Spanish-language broadcast network, but the network is "severely constrained" from doing so under current ownership rules.

Should Congress reimpose rules limiting television networks' ownership of programming?

Hollywood producer Dick Wolf stood to reap a windfall from NBC — an estimated $1.6 billion over three years — if the network renewed his series "Law & Order" and its spin-offs, "Special Victims Unit" and "Criminal Intent." But all that changed when NBC announced plans to buy Universal Television, a studio that has a partnership with Wolf.

Now, observers say, Universal has essentially switched sides in the negotiations and no longer has an incentive to help Wolf get the best deal from NBC. Victoria Riskin, president of the Writers Guild of America, West, said Wolf will still do well. "I'm more worried about what kind of leverage the Dick Wolfs of the future will have," she said. NBC executives insist the merger with Universal would create more programming opportunities for Wolf.[28]

For more than two decades, the FCC imposed so-called financial interest and syndication rules — commonly known as fin-syn — on TV broadcasters, curbing their ownership stakes in programming. The rules were intended to protect independent producers and promote program diversity. But as the media universe began to expand, the FCC removed some of its fin-syn rules in 1991 and eliminated them entirely in 1995.

The networks opposed fin-syn for financial reasons. Since they were assuming risk by putting up money on the front-end to help cover production costs, they wanted a slice of the lucrative back-end, or revenue from syndication. "It's the ability to generate content in a cost-effective way," says Okun, explaining why the networks have sought to combine with studios.

Critics blame fin-syn's repeal for ushering in an era of "vertical integration," in which the TV networks increasingly produce shows in-house, and for driving most independent producers out of business. The result, they say, is lowbrow, homogenized content that takes few creative chances.

The networks, however, argue that fin-syn is unnecessary. "There's more production going on today in this country than there ever has been, by a factor of 10 or 20," said NBC Chairman Bob Wright. "American consumers have never had video benefits like they have today."[29]

Testifying before the Senate Commerce Committee earlier this year, Rupert Murdoch, chairman of News Corp., which owns the Fox broadcast network, said, "If anyone comes to us with a show that can get us an audience, we'll be the first to buy."[30]

But Jonathan Rintels, president and executive director of the Center for the Creative Community, an advocacy group for independent producers, says it's time to bring fin-syn back. "The market has completely changed. It's gotten re-concentrated," he says. "Of the 40 new series airing on the four major broadcast networks in the 2002 season, 77.5 percent are owned in whole or part by the same four networks — an increase of over 37 percent in just one year — and up from only 12.5 percent in 1990," the group said in FCC comments.[31]

"The harm to the public is that they don't see the best work that can be put on television," Rintels says.

When veteran producer Norman Lear, for example, developed the now-classic sitcom "All in the Family" for ABC, the network balked at the controversial dialogue — mainly from bigoted paterfamilias "Archie Bunker" — so he took it to CBS, where it became a huge hit. Nowadays, networks lock producers into contracts that bar them from taking their ideas to competitors, Rintels says.

Other groups fighting to restore fin-syn include the Coalition for Program Diversity, whose members include Sony Pictures Television, the Screen Actors Guild, the Directors Guild and Carsey-Werner-Mandabach, a big independent-production company; and the Caucus for Television Producers, Writers & Directors.

As part of its June announcement, the FCC rejected the idea of restoring fin-syn. "In light of dramatic changes in the television market, including the significant increase in the number of channels available to most households today, we find no basis in the record to conclude that government regulation is necessary to promote source diversity," the FCC said.[32]

Nevertheless, Commissioner Copps wants the agency to address pending proposals from Hollywood for broadcast networks to devote 25 percent to 35 percent of their prime-time schedules to shows created by independent producers. "There's nothing left for protection against monopoly and . . . oligopoly," he says.

"vast wasteland"
harbinger

Some lawmakers, among them Senate Commerce Chairman John McCain, R-Ariz., and Sen. Ernest Hollings, D-S.C., support independent programmers. McCain and House Energy and Commerce Committee Chairman Billy Tauzin, R-La., are trying to forge a non-legislative resolution between producers and network executives. Lawmakers appear reticent to legislate because an appeals court ruled a decade ago that the FCC hadn't adequately justified its fin-syn rules. "It's clearly been declared unconstitutional by the courts," McCain said.[33]

"People are concerned about the gatekeepers," says PBS' Mitchell, who benefited from fin-syn when she worked earlier in her career as an independent producer. "If it's reached a point now where you've got to own the production as well as the distribution, then what's going to happen to people who are not in that chain? They're going to get left out, and they are getting left out," she says.

"We do need to have some regulatory policy in place," she adds.

BACKGROUND

Regulating the Airwaves

The regulatory structure governing America's media industry was born in the early 1900s, when Congress saw a need to restrict the market power of burgeoning broadcasting companies.

The 1927 Federal Radio Act established the Federal Radio Commission, the precursor to the FCC. Seven years later, Congress passed the watershed 1934 Communications Act, creating the FCC as an independent agency and establishing guidelines for regulating the public airwaves — rules that remain the FCC's guiding principles today.

In the early 1940s, the FCC adopted the National TV Ownership Rule, which prevented networks from owning more than a handful of stations, and restricted their ability to buy radio outlets. In 1943, the FCC and the U.S. Supreme Court ordered NBC to divest one of its networks, which later became its competitor, ABC.

In yet another regulatory step, the FCC in 1946 adopted the Dual Network Rule, barring one radio network from owning another. Later amended to include television, it remains largely intact today, though the FCC amended it in the 1990s to let major networks buy smaller ones.

In the late 1940s, cable television emerged to provide TV service in mountainous and rural areas, but it would take three decades to become a serious competitor to broadcast TV.[34]

During a 1961 speech that was to become a harbinger of the regulatory and political battles ahead, FCC Chairman Newton Minnow, a Democrat, described TV as a "vast wasteland." A decade later, the FCC imposed cross-ownership restrictions designed to limit the influence of major media companies. Under the regulations, an individual media company was barred from owning a TV station and radio property in the same market, or a broadcast outlet and newspaper in the same market.

"It was a good rule for 1975," Dick Wiley, the Republican FCC chairman at the time, said recently of the newspaper-broadcast cross-ownership ban. "We were concerned that newspapers would dominate television, which people forget had only really [become popular] 20 years or so earlier. It's almost 30 years later, and many things are different." Wiley's influential Washington law firm represents clients that oppose the ban.[35]

Also in the '70s, with only three commercial networks and PBS available over-the-air, cable television became more competitive. As it grew in popularity, its fare would become more niche-oriented.[36]

Deregulation Begins

The era of deregulation began in earnest in the 1980s, under the Reagan administration and FCC Chairman Mark Fowler, a Republican who famously likened television to a toaster with pictures — simply another household appliance.

In 1981, the FCC ended its decades-old policy of "ascertainment" for radio stations. The policy required broadcasters to visit community groups and leaders to ascertain what types of programming they wanted and whether broadcasters were serving their needs. The FCC ended ascertainment for TV outlets in 1984. "We determined that it was excessive meddling on our part," says Robert Ratcliffe, deputy chief of the FCC's Media Bureau.

When the idea of requiring ascertainment is broached today with broadcast executives, "Those people jump up and down and say, 'Oh no, that's the heavy hand of regulation coming back. We can't consider something like that,' " Democratic FCC Commissioner Copps says.

CHRONOLOGY

1900-1940s *Government limits the influence of radio and television.*

1901 Italian inventor Guglielmo Marconi sends wireless signals across Atlantic Ocean, paving the way for radio.

1920 The first radio broadcast debuts at KDKA, in Pittsburgh.

1927 Philo T. Farnsworth, the inventor of television, demonstrates the technology for the first time. . . . Federal Radio Commission is established.

1934 Congress passes 1934 Communications Act, setting guidelines for regulating public airwaves.

1938 Orson Welles' realistic "War of the Worlds" radio broadcast about a Martian invasion creates pandemonium across the country.

1941 FCC issues National TV Ownership Rule barring companies from owning more than a few TV stations.

1946 FCC adopts Dual Network Rule, prohibiting companies from owning more than one radio network, later expanded to include TV.

1950s-1960s *Television enters its golden age.*

1950 Cable TV is introduced in rural Pennsylvania and Oregon. . . . FCC institutes the Fairness Doctrine.

1954 Color TV debuts.

1969 Public Broadcasting Service is created.

1970s *FCC seeks to limit media growth.*

1970 FCC prohibits companies from owning radio and TV stations in the same market.

1975 FCC bans cross-ownership of a broadcast and newspaper outlet in the same market.

1980s *New networks revolutionize television.*

1980 Media visionary Ted Turner creates Cable News Network, ushering in an era of 24-hour cable news.

1985 Australian media mogul Rupert Murdoch launches the Fox network, a feisty upstart to the Big 3.

1987 FCC eliminates Fairness Doctrine.

1990s *Media concentration accelerates after Congress deregulates telecommunications and eases media-ownership rules.*

1992 Cable Act requires cable systems to carry local broadcasters.

1995 FCC allows major TV networks to own production studios.

1996 Disney acquires Capitol Cities/ABC, combining a studio with a TV network. . . . Congress passes landmark Telecommunications Act, loosening broadcast-ownership restrictions and deregulating cable.

2000s *Rampant consolidation and FCC action to loosen ownership rules spark national debate.*

2000 Viacom merges with CBS, continuing the trend of "vertical integration."

2001 The largest merger in U.S. history joins AOL and Time Warner.

2002 Comcast and AT&T merge, forming the nation's largest cable company.

June 2, 2003 FCC loosens broadcast-ownership restrictions. Three months later, a federal court orders further review.

Sept. 2, 2003 NBC unveils plan to acquire the film, TV and theme-park assets of Vivendi Universal.

Oct. 6, 2003 Federal court in San Francisco rules that cable providers of high-speed Internet access must include competing Internet services on their systems. The FCC vows to appeal.

2008 Time Warner, the world's largest media and entertainment company, has annual revenue of $50.5 billion, which equals the GDP of Luxembourg. . . . Federal Communications Commission (FCC) approves merger of XM Satellite Radio Inc. and Sirius Satellite Radio Inc.

Continued

Continued

2009 At least 10 newspaper publishers file for Chapter 11 bankruptcy protection. Newspaper ad revenues for print and online versions combined fall 26 percent. . . . The New York Times is forced to borrow $250 million from Mexican investor Carlos Slim Helu, the world's richest man (January). . . . The Rocky Mountain News in Denver shuts down (February). . . . FCC Chairman Michael Copps releases a report on "broadband strategy for rural America." The report is issued as part of the 2008 Farm Bill, which calls on the FCC to work with the U.S. Department of Agriculture to develop a strategy for bringing faster internet service to rural areas (May) . . . . Federal appeals court overturns FCC policy prohibiting cable television companies from exceeding a market share of 30 percent of households

nationally (August). . . . Proposed sale of NBC Universal to Comcast Corp. for $37 billion, subject to FCC and Justice Department approval, leads to concern that the combination would reduce competition and hurt local stations. . . . Congress allots $7.2 billion in the American Recovery and Reinvestment Act of 2009 for broadband loans, grants and loan guarantees (December).

March 2010 — The Third U.S. Circuit Court of Appeals in Philadelphia overturns the FCC rule that prevents media companies from owning a TV station and a newspaper in the same market. . . . The nonprofit media outlet ProPublica wins a Pulitzer Prize for investigative journalism.

In 1985, Fowler oversaw another deregulatory move: The FCC increased from seven to 12 the number of television stations that a single entity was permitted to own.[37]

Fowler also made it his mission to eliminate the Fairness Doctrine. Introduced in 1950, it gave citizens free airtime to reply to criticism leveled against them on TV or radio.[38] Journalists complained that the government should not be dictating editorial content, and the FCC decided that the abundance of media voices made the requirement obsolete. The FCC, which had already concluded that the policy might be unconstitutional, ended it in 1987 after a District of Columbia Circuit Court ruled the agency was no longer required to enforce it.[39]

The prime-time access rule was rescinded along with the Fairness Doctrine. It restricted local TV stations in the top 50 markets to airing only three hours of network programming during prime time, except on Sundays. The FCC had hoped the rule would encourage local public-affairs programming in time slots leading into prime time, but instead broadcasters often ran syndicated game shows, sitcom reruns and the like.[40]

As the broadcast industry was being progressively deregulated, Congress was turning its regulatory sights on

the growing cable industry. In 1992, responding to consumer complaints, Congress passed legislation regulating cable rates and imposing other restrictions on cable monopolies. Meanwhile, direct-broadcast satellite (DBS), which made satellite-TV technology more accessible by offering consumers pizza-sized dishes for reception, was introduced in 1994.[41]

In 1995, when the FCC eliminated the fin-syn rules restricting network ownership of programming, it ushered in an era of vertical integration in which the major networks merged with Hollywood studios. Also in the mid-'90s, after months of congressional hearings, debate and intensive lobbying by affected industry parties, Congress passed the sweeping 1996 Telecommunications Act, giving media companies a green light to consolidate and own more radio and TV properties in various markets.

The act also deregulated cable and expanded the audience reach of network-owned stations from 25 percent of U.S. households to 35 percent. In the ensuing years, broadcast TV networks and major cable companies would merge with other huge companies, transforming themselves into vertically integrated media giants controlling both the production and distribution of content.

In yet another loosening of its rules, the FCC in 1999 permitted more duopolies — the single ownership of two

TV stations in a market — under certain conditions. Eight independent TV stations had to remain in the market after the combination, and none of the combined stations could be among the top four in the market. Before that, duopolies were permitted on a very limited basis, through waivers intended to aid struggling stations.

In June 2003, the FCC tweaked its duopoly rules again: If eight independent TV stations remain after the combination, a top-four TV station can combine with a non-top-four station in the same market.

Although industry executives insist that duopolies result in better-quality news because of the expanded resources available to the combined stations, critics say that's often not the case. "With the joining together of the two newsrooms, there's not a whole lot of original programming," complained Sylvia Teague, a former news executive and producer with the duopoly involving KCBS-TV and KCAL-TV in Los Angeles. She is now director of a project on broadcast political coverage at the University of Southern California's Annenberg School of Journalism.[42]

In October 2001, the two largest DBS companies — DirecTV and EchoStar — decided to merge, claiming the deal would create a formidable competitor to the cable-TV monopolies. But consumer groups said it would be anti-competitive to create a satellite monopoly. In the end, regulators blocked the deal. Now Murdoch's News Corp. is seeking to buy DirecTV, the nation's largest DBS provider.

Some 88 million Americans subscribe to multichannel video services such as cable and satellite, according to the FCC's 2002 report on video competition. The vast majority — 68.8 million — are cable subscribers.[43]

Complaints Increase

In recent years, the public has become increasingly dissatisfied with the media, fueled by concerns about everything from too much explicit sex and violence on TV to the botched predictions made by the networks the night of the 2000 presidential election to the recent journalism-fraud scandal at *The New York Times*.[44]

The public's cynicism was further fueled when big media outlets mostly ignored reporting on the FCC's efforts to relax its media-ownership rules until the agency voted on June 2. Critics smelled a rat because many media properties lobbied in support of some or all of the new rules and stood to gain financially by their implementation.

"I just have to think there's something we should question about the lack of a national debate, the lack of editorials and really engaged reporting on an issue as important as this until the consumers themselves began to respond," says PBS' Mitchell, whose network was not affected by the FCC decision. The PBS program "Now with Bill Moyers" was among the few news shows that devoted significant coverage to the story.

Further exacerbating suspicions about big media companies, some recent studies suggest that media consolidation has taken a toll on news quality and depth of coverage. A five-year study of local television stations finds that despite the fact that network owned-and-operated stations (O&Os) have far more resources, smaller station groups produce better-quality news — by a "significant" margin.[45]

"Affiliates were more likely to air stories that affected everyone in the community, while O&Os were more likely to air national stories with no local connection — those car chases and exciting footage from far away," the report found.

Meanwhile, television stations have eliminated or dramatically reduced their election coverage. During the 2002 midterm elections, "almost six out of 10 top-rated news broadcasts contained no campaign coverage whatsoever," said Martin Kaplan, director of the Norman Lear Center at the Annenberg School, which surveyed election coverage by 10,000 local TV stations.

Of the stations that did cover the election, most focused only on the "horse race" during the final two weeks of the election and ignored the issues being debated. The average campaign story was less than 90 seconds, Kaplan said. "Fewer than three out of 10 campaign stories that aired included candidates speaking, and when they did speak, the average candidate sound bite was 12 seconds long."[46]

New Media Landscape

The raging controversy over the FCC's decision in June to relax its media-ownership rules has triggered plenty of comparisons between today's media marketplace and TV's so-called golden age a few decades ago.

"Even in small towns, the number of media outlets — including cable, satellite, radio, TV stations and newspapers — has increased more than 250 percent during the

Alternative Media on the Rise

By day, Tony Adragna toils for a Washington-area nonprofit and Will Vehrs works in Virginia's state government. But in their free time they're bloggers, filing constantly updated pontifications on their Web log, an online journal called "Shouting 'Cross the Potomac." This summer their log, at www.quasipundit.blogspot.com, garnered them enough attention to be interviewed on C-SPAN.

"Bloggers are a real window on the world, a really great supplement to reporters who may have trouble . . . getting to . . . a story," Vehrs said, noting that blogs (short for Web logs) provided instant coverage of the Sept. 11, 2001, terrorist attacks and the Aug. 14, 2003, blackout in the Northeast.[1]

Blogs and many other big-media alternatives that have surfaced in recent years don't meet the traditional definitions — or standards — of mainstream news outlets, often providing information that's largely unfiltered by professional editors. But that may be less important to citizens today because the major media — from *The New York Times* to the TV networks — have shown they can still get the facts wrong.[2]

While most blogs feature the writings, rantings and musings of everyday people who simply want to post their thoughts, some bloggers are media stars, such as former *New Republic* Editor Andrew Sullivan, whose "Daily Dish" blog can be found at www.andrewsullivan.com, and Glenn Reynolds, the creator of www.InstaPundit.com. Both sites feature continuously updated commentary on the latest news headlines and, in the case of Reynolds, links to other blogs.

The Economist estimates that 750,000 people now blog, and the number is expected to explode. As blogging becomes more popular, the London-based magazine reports, many are taking a closer look at the economic potential of the medium — i.e., charging for access and running ads.[3]

Seizing on the latest wave, the giant Internet service provider AOL now offers its subscribers blogging at no extra charge. And the Internet search engine Google purchased the company that makes Blogger, a free program to create blogs.[4]

Beyond Web logs, Americans also get their Internet news from sites operated by mainstream news organizations, such as CNN or *The Washington Post*, Internet-only magazines such as *Slate* and *Salon* and cybergossip Matt Drudge. Breaking e-mail news alerts are now commonplace, and for many Web users, the headlines on the Internet search engine Yahoo! are the first place they get news.

As competition from new and old news media grows, longtime players are becoming more flexible — and in the eyes of some, softening their standards. Consider Baltimore-based Sinclair Broadcasting, which relies on its Central Casting division to provide news and commentary to half of its 62 stations nationwide. From a studio near Baltimore, its news anchors provide newscasts to Pittsburgh, Raleigh, N.C., Flint, Mich., and other cities. Sinclair says Central Casting enables small, limited-resource stations to offer local news, but critics say the arrangement saves money at the expense of local coverage.[5]

Meanwhile, alternative news sites also have emerged. AlterNet.org, created in 1998 to provide its own brand of "investigative journalism," reaches more than 5 million readers through its Web and print publications.[6]

So far, however, the Internet is hardly a full-fledged alternative to traditional media. According to Nielsen ratings, the 20 most-popular Internet news sites are dominated by major media conglomerates, such as NBC and Microsoft, which co-own MSNBC.com, and CNN.com, operated by Time Warner.[7]

Apart from news, the Worldwide Web also provides alternative, low-cost publishing. Among the newest trends are "online content marketplaces," such as redpaper.com and Lulu.com. The sites provide little editing and let contributors set readership prices as low as pennies a page.

"It's great for grandpa doing his memoirs, and it's great for the family cookbook — people who can't get published

past 40 years," wrote FCC Chairman Powell.[47] But there are fewer media owners. For example, a decade ago there were 12,000 radio stations with 5,100 owners.[48] Today there are more radio stations — 13,000[49] — but only 3,800 owners.[50]

Two or three decades ago, there were more newspapers in large cities, says Kalb of Harvard's Shorenstein Center. Today there are roughly the same number of newspapers nationwide, but that's because there are more small suburban and small-town newspapers, he says. But today's anywhere else," said George Farrier, a 73-year old contributor to Lulu.com from Greenfield, Mo.[8] Lulu, which features lengthier writings, including many books, boasts to visitors that it "allows content to flow directly from creator to consumer. That means creators can keep 80 percent of the royalty from each sale, ownership of their work and the rights to sell it anywhere else."

In addition to alternative news and publishing, new technologies also offer alternative entertainment sources. About 250 low-power FM (LPFM) radio stations have cropped up across the country, mostly in small cities and rural areas. Another 600 or 700 of these 100-watt, non-commercial radio stations are expected to be operational soon.

Low-power radio gives a voice to nonprofits, such as religious groups, educational institutions and local governments, similar to the public access provided by local cable channels. Supporters hope LPFM will gain ground now that a recent study finds they would cause very little interference with commercial stations' signals.[9] Full-power radio broadcasters have opposed licensing LPFM stations in major markets because they feared interference, but supporters say the new report should silence those concerns.

Nevertheless, it could take a while for low-power FM to become a popular alternative to commercial radio. "Right now, a minuscule percentage of the public can tune in," says Michael Bracy, co-founder of the Future of Music Coalition, made up of radio and music interests who support LPFM expansion and oppose consolidation by Clear Channel and other big radio players.

Hedging their bets, some mainstream media companies are switching to newer technologies, or at least making investments in them. Clear Channel Communications, the dominant force in broadcast radio, has invested in XM Satellite Radio, the subscription service that offers 100 stations of music and other programming with few commercials and no cackling deejays. As part of the deal, XM carries some Clear Channel stations.[10]

Broadcast television is also evolving, as it slowly switches from analog to digital technology, which provides crisp, high-definition images and allows each broadcaster to offer multiple signals in each market. The transition, which was supposed to be complete by 2006, is expected to take much

longer because of slow consumer demand, due in part to pricey digital sets and lack of awareness about digital TV. Squabbles with cable systems over signal carriage, industry bickering over copyright-protection standards and stations' difficulties raising capital to convert equipment have contributed to the delays.

In April 2002, the U.S. General Accounting Office (GAO) said many TV stations would not meet the May 2002 deadline for offering a digital signal.[11] Then in November, the GAO said more federal intervention will be needed for the digital transition to occur.[12]

Meanwhile, some Web-based alternative media have made the jump to more mainstream outlets. Thesmokinggun.com, known for obtaining controversial documents and photos, was born during the dot-com boom of the late 1990s and was later purchased by Court TV. This summer, it spawned "Smoking Gun TV," on Court TV, as well as a radio program carried by Infinity-owned stations. There's also a twice-monthly column in *People* magazine.[13]

[1] See transcript of C-SPAN's "Washington Journal," Aug. 15, 2003.

[2] For background, see Brian Hansen, "Combating Plagiarism," *The CQ Researcher*, Sept. 19, 2003, pp. 773-796.

[3] *The Economist*, "Golden Blogs," Aug. 16, 2003.

[4] *Ibid.*

[5] Jim Rutenberg and Micheline Maynard, "TV News That Looks Local, Even If It's Not," *The New York Times*, p. C1, June 2, 2003, p. C1.

[6] For more information, visit www.alternet.org.

[7] See "Top 20 Internet News Sites," Nielsen Media Research (see www.nielsen-netratings.com for more information), November 2002.

[8] Wailin Wong, "Web Sites Offer Unsung Writers Chance to Sing," *The Wall Street Journal*, Sept. 18, 2003, p. B1.

[9] Mitre Corp., "Experimental Measurements of the Third-Adjacent Channel Impacts of Low-Power FM Stations," released on June 30, 2003; http://hraunfoss.fcc.gov/edocs_public/attachmatch/DA-03-2277A1.doc.

[10] Frank Ahrens, "Why Radio Stinks," *The Washington Post Magazine*, Jan. 19, 2003, p. 24.

[11] "Many Broadcasters Will Not Meet May 2002 Digital Television Deadline," General Accounting Office (02-466), April 2002.

[12] "Additional Federal Efforts Could Help Advance Digital Television Transition," General Accounting Office (03-07), November 2002.

[13] Cesar G. Soriano, "The Smoking Gun Joins High-Caliber Media," *USA Today*, Aug. 18, 2003, p. 3D.

small-town papers cover mostly local news and are not substitutes for major dailies, Kalb says.

Some industry observers are nostalgic for the days when there were only three major television networks because they feel the news coverage was more in-depth and less sensational. Robert J. Thompson, professor of television and popular culture at Syracuse University, said the comparative lack of choice when only three networks existed paradoxically served the public interest well.

"All three networks would carry presidential debates, State of the Union speeches and the national political conventions," he wrote.[51] Today, coverage of such events on broadcast TV is far more limited.

CURRENT SITUATION

TV Industry Split

The FCC's decision to raise the broadcast-ownership cap has cast a spotlight on an embarrassing schism within the television industry that threatens to undermine its lobbying muscle on ownership issues.

The networks want the cap upped to 45 percent or removed altogether. But local network affiliates want to preserve the cap at 35 percent, because they worry that if the networks own too many stations, they'll have too much sway over the programs the affiliates air. As the networks grow larger, it's more difficult for local affiliates to resist when the networks want to pre-empt local programming.

"The right to reject or pre-empt network programming must remain at the local level for stations to discharge their duty to reflect what they believe is right for their individual communities," said Jim Goodmon, president and CEO of Capitol Broadcasting Co., which owns five TV stations and radio outlets in the Carolinas. Testifying before a Senate Commerce Committee hearing this year, Goodmon continued, "Whether it is to reject network programming based on community standards or whether it is to pre-empt national network programming in order to air a Billy Graham special, the Muscular Dystrophy Telethon or local sports, I can't imagine that anyone in this room really wants to take away local control over television programming."[52]

The spat has implications for the National Association of Broadcasters (NAB), the TV industry's fierce lobby, which has been abandoned in recent years by the influential Big Four networks over the ownership issue. The networks have indicated they may form a new lobbying organization to push their own deregulatory agenda.[53]

NAB opposed the FCC's decision to raise the cap and says it supports congressional efforts to roll it back to 35 percent. But it's now actively fighting bills that would do just that, because they contain additional language further regulating broadcasters. Some parties are disappointed with NAB's shifting positions.

"The NAB's decision to reverse itself on the issue of the national television-ownership cap is an unfortunate retreat from its proud history of support for localism, diversity and competition in the broadcast marketplace," said Rep. John Dingell, D-Mich.[54]

NAB spokesman Dennis Wharton insists there was no flip-flop or retreat: "If we can get a clean 35 percent rollback bill out of Congress and signed by the president, that is something we would support."

Reaction to Rules

Angered that the FCC relaxed the ownership rules too much, a growing chorus of lawmakers is aggressively moving to rescind at least key portions of it, including Senate Appropriations Committee Chairman Ted Stevens, R-Alaska, Sen. Minority Leader Tom Daschle, D-S.D., Sens. Dorgan and Hollings and Rep. Dingell.

Their top priority: to return the cap on the reach of broadcast network-owned TV stations to 35 percent of the nation's households.

To be sure, the FCC still has allies on the Hill, including House Appropriations Committee Chairman C.W. Bill Young of Florida and House Commerce Committee Chairman Tauzin.

"Only in Washington, D.C., would those who ostensibly want to preserve free speech seek to do so by regulating broadcast rules," Tauzin said.[55]

On Sept. 16, the Senate passed a so-called "resolution of disapproval" — a little-used procedural device that rescinds the rule changes. Spearheaded by Sens. Dorgan, Lott, Feingold and Susan Collins, R-Maine, the vote was 55-40. But House Majority Leader Tom DeLay, R-Texas, warned the bill is dead on arrival in the lower chamber.

Hedging his bets, Dorgan said he'll also try to amend an appropriations bill with a rider to restore the ban on newspaper-television cross-ownership. But his prospects are uncertain because similar efforts have failed in the House.[56]

Putting a positive spin on the vote, Media Bureau Chief Ferree calls it a "huge victory" for the FCC. "This was a freebie for these guys. They know it's not going anywhere in the House." He adds, "I look at today's vote, and I say it's over."

"Were this to become law it would be a disaster," Ferree says. "It would just throw things into chaos. I don't know how we'd stop almost any transaction under old

Are the major TV networks committed to localism?*

YES
Mel Karmazin
President and COO, Viacom Inc.

From testimony before Senate Commerce, Transportation and Science
Committee, May 13, 2003

It is utterly unsupportable and unrealistic that broadcasters should be handcuffed in their attempts to compete for consumers at a time when Americans are bombarded with media choices via technologies never dreamed of even a decade ago, much less 60 years ago when some of these rules were first adopted. . . .

Most television stations in this country are held by multi-station groups owned by large corporations headquartered in cities located far from their stations' communities of license. What does it matter that Viacom's main offices are in New York? The corporate group owners are no more "local" in the cities where they own TV stations than is Viacom. Yet, like Viacom and all good broadcasters, group owners work hard to know what viewers want in each market where it has a media outlet. Localism is just good business.

Networks invest billions of dollars in programming, but most of the return on their investment is realized at the station level. Only two of the so-called "Big Four" networks are profitable in any year [compared] to television stations — run by networks and affiliates alike — which operate on margins anywhere from 20 percent to 50 percent.

If networks are precluded from realizing more of the revenue generated by stations, networks' ability to continue their multi-billion-dollar programming investments will diminish, and more and more programming will migrate from broadcasting to cable and satellite TV, where regulation is less onerous. More Americans then will have to pay for what they now get for free.

[The] argument that affiliates provide more local news than do network-owned-and-operated stations is, again, false. In a study commissioned by Viacom, Fox and NBC, Economists Inc. found that the average TV station owned by a network provides more local news per week — 37 percent more — than the average affiliate, a finding consistent with the FCC's own independently conducted study. . . .

Nor is it true that affiliates stand as the bulwark against allegedly inappropriate network programming. . . . Pre-emptions based on content are rare. But in the handful of cases over the past years when an affiliate has determined that a program's subject may be too sensitive for its market — as was the case last week with our Providence affiliate with respect to the "CSI: Miami" episode dealing with fire hazards at nightclubs — we understand and accommodate. Our own stations would do the same thing for their markets' viewers.

NO
Tom Daschle, D-S.D.
Minority Leader, U.S. Senate

From a statement on the Senate floor, Sept. 16, 2003

Many argue there are an infinite number of media outlets today, especially given the huge growth in cable channels and Internet addresses.

But the vast majority of Americans get their news and information from television news and/or their local newspaper. None of the cable-news channels has anywhere near the viewership of the broadcast media, and most of the major cable and Internet news outlets are affiliated with the print and broadcast media already controlled in large part by just a handful of companies. Diversity of viewpoints is already in jeopardy, and the new rules would only exacerbate the situation. . . .

If many of those so-called diverse viewpoints are actually controlled by a handful of companies, then one can see that localism, too, is in trouble. The loss of localism in radio is well known, sometimes with dangerous consequences like the famous Minot, N.D., case.

In fact, the lack of localism in radio is so undeniable that even the FCC has agreed to address it in the one aspect of the proposed rules that makes sense.

But localism in television is also at risk — local entertainment choices as well as news. James Goodmon of Capitol Broadcasting in North Carolina explained it well in his testimony before the Commerce Committee.

He owns Fox and CBS stations in Raleigh. Out of respect for his local audience's sensibilities, he has refused to carry either network's "reality TV" shows, including "Temptation Island," "Cupid," "Who Wants to Marry a Millionaire" and "Married by America."

His actions have met with intense resistance from the networks, and he has expressed his grave concern that if the networks' ability to own more and more of the broadcast outlets goes unchecked, local stations and communities won't have any ability to choose their own programming. They will be forced to air the network fare, even when it is offensive to local viewers. . . .

Let me be clear: I don't blame the media companies for advocating for their own interests. They have every right to fight for their interests.

I do blame the chairman of the FCC and the other commissioners who voted for these rules for failing to give the rest of the country the consideration they deserved in this debate.

---

*Localism refers to serving a community's needs and tastes.

rules that have been questioned in court and new rules that we couldn't implement."

Ferree continues, "The point is trying to adopt measured, reasonable limits that we can defend in court, which I think we did. And if people on the Hill start to understand that, they'd come around, and we'd get more and more support."

In other action, the House this summer passed an appropriations bill by a vote of 400 to 21 that contained an amendment rolling the ownership cap back to 35 percent.

Stevens has added a similar measure to Senate appropriations legislation expected to be voted on this year. Republican leaders are vowing to strip out the rollback when the House and Senate spending bills go into conference negotiations. If the rollback is removed, it could be pushed by supportive lawmakers next year. The White House has threatened to veto any legislation rolling back the cap.

In addition, the Senate Commerce panel has approved legislation sponsored by Stevens and Hollings that returns the broadcast ownership cap to 35 percent and bars newspaper-broadcast cross-ownership.

Meanwhile, the FCC's new rules face a variety of court challenges. In a surprise 11th-hour move, a federal appeals court in Philadelphia stayed the FCC's June 2 announcement pending further judicial review. The court decision was in response to challenges to the rules filed by advocacy groups.

In addition, the NAB has appealed portions of the FCC decision that reduce the size of many radio markets and ban duopolies between TV stations in small markets. And a group representing local TV affiliates has appealed the raising of the ownership cap to 45 percent. Media General also is appealing because the FCC didn't relax restrictions on its ownership of both newspapers and broadcast outlets in small markets.[57]

Powell Under Fire

The controversy over ownership has focused on more than just regulation. FCC Chairman Powell is now under attack from both parties for shepherding the sweeping rule changes through his agency.

Critics say the FCC, which held only one official hearing on media concentration before it voted, rushed to adopt the changes and refused to compromise with Democratic FCC commissioners.[58] Powell counters that the agency issued 12 studies last fall examining the issues.

Critics insist Powell misjudged the guidance of the courts by developing relaxed ownership rules. In fact, a federal appeals court in Washington has struck down the last five media-ownership rules it has reviewed, tossing them back to the agency. Powell says the court told the FCC to get rid of the rules, but critics say the court instructed the agency to justify them, not discard them.

The FCC received at least 2 million e-mails, letters and postcards expressing opposition to the rule changes, though Powell is quick to point out that three-quarters of the messages were sent by NRA members.[59]

Constant rumors in the press that the chairman might resign have forced him to repeatedly deny he'll leave the FCC before his term expires.

The chairman has been fighting back with a series of op-eds in major newspapers and televised interviews to defend his positions. But he told C-SPAN earlier this year that it is difficult for the FCC, an independent agency, to battle with Capitol Hill on policy issues.

If the FCC is to fight lawmakers over policy issues, he said, "then I think there's a serious argument that we just belong in the administration. There ought to be a secretary of communications, it ought to be the president's policy, it ought to be in a political branch of government, and be treated that way."[60]

To stem the criticism, Powell this summer unveiled plans to promote localism among broadcasters, a key concern of his critics. In the end, the chairman's announcement didn't quiet his detractors, who think his initiative was intended to deflect anger over the agency's broader media policies.

Commissioner Copps says Powell's move should have occurred long before June 2. And he thinks it may not go far enough. "We require stations to keep a public file — we don't look at it when it comes time for license renewal. Can you imagine that?" He says license renewals are now mostly done by postcard. "Unless there is a gross character violation charge against you, you're going to get your license renewed," he says.

In response, Ratcliffe of the FCC's Media Bureau says the agency inspects the files when citizens file petitions against stations. "We constantly review how those things are working," he says.

70% acces
70% of those subscribe

Cable Debate

While broadcast and newspaper outlets have taken the brunt of the criticism lately, cable is not off the hook. If anything, it could be the next regulatory target, industry observers say. In a little-noticed move, the FCC said it wants to know if cable has met the so-called 70-70 test, which would trigger more regulation. The 70-70 threshold is reached if at least 70 percent of U.S. homes have access to cable, and 70 percent of those homes subscribe.[61]

According to a recent report by the consumer group U.S. PIRG, the top 10 cable operators serve about 85 percent of all cable subscribers and the top three — Comcast, Time Warner and Charter — serve about 56 percent, up 8 percent since 1996. Cable operators also dominate the high-speed Internet-access business, yet the cable industry operates largely unregulated.[62]

In 95 percent of all U.S. households, there is access to only one cable service.[63] In most markets, cable offers little in the way of local news, although regional cable-news channels have sprung up in some large metro areas.

Meanwhile, the FCC has to decide the fate of the cable-ownership cap, which a federal appeals court in Washington declared unconstitutional two years ago.[64] The cap limits a single cable company to reaching 30 percent of the national market. According to *USA Today*, the FCC is taking a "measured" approach toward a revised cable cap and would permit case-by-case reviews of cable mergers. In a draft proposal that could change, cable companies would be allowed to serve up to 45 percent of households, but the FCC would have the flexibility to block or approve deals at varying thresholds. AT&T Comcast, the nation's biggest cable provider, is just under the 30 percent cap.[65]

Meanwhile, the average monthly cable fee rose by 8.2 percent — from $37.06 to $40.11 — over the 12-month period ending July 1, 2002, according to the FCC.[66] In response, Commerce Committee Chairman McCain said, "The cable industry has risen to new heights in their apparent willingness and ability to gouge the American consumer."[67]

In a ruling on Oct. 6, a federal appeals court in San Francisco effectively required cable providers of high-speed Internet access to include competing Internet services on their systems. If it stands, the decision would be a blow to cable companies and the FCC, which fears such access

would deter cable companies from investing heavily in super-fast Internet connections, or broadband. The FCC has vowed to appeal and may be able to override the decision through regulatory action.

Over the years, allegations have arisen that some cable companies play hardball with programmers and sometimes refuse to carry competing channels. Cox Communications, for example, which has a 25 percent stake in the parent of the Discovery Channel, doesn't carry the rival National Geographic Channel. "We carry more than 200 channels, and we own 10 of them, and we have 55 movie channels and own three," Cablevision spokesman Charles Schueler said. "To suggest that we favor our own programming is absurd."[68]

Robert Sachs, president and CEO of the National Cable and Telecommunications Association, added, "Since 1992, the percentage of program networks in which cable operators have any financial interest has plummeted from 48 percent to less than 21 percent. At the same time, the number of available channels has skyrocketed from 87 to 308. There are more than six times as many non-cable-owned channels as there were a decade ago."[69]

OUTLOOK

More Mergers?

Before the current ownership brouhaha flared up, many observers were anticipating a new round of deals involving the broadcast television networks, individual TV stations and newspapers. Merrill Lynch and other Wall Street firms predicted TV-station acquisitions by Viacom, Disney, News Corp., Hearst Argyle, Sinclair Broadcasting and LIN TV, among others. "There may be a bantam wave of media mergers, but surely not the tsunami envisioned," Merrill media analyst Jessica Reif Cohen wrote recently.[70]

Several newspaper companies, including Tribune, Media General and Gannett, were widely expected to buy more TV properties. "The only people who can't own a TV or radio station are aliens, convicted felons and newspaper publishers," said Newspaper Association of America CEO John Sturm, before the FCC's announcement.[71]

Fallout from the FCC's decision, coupled with a court-imposed stay, has created considerable uncertainty and dampened the acquisition fervor. Nevertheless, a few transactions have been announced since the FCC's action, the largest being NBC's acquisition of Vivendi Universal's entertainment assets. Some deals were pending before the FCC decision, such as News Corp.'s bid to buy satellite-TV giant DirecTV and the recently approved merger of Univision and Hispanic Broadcasting Corp., which worries Democrats because Univision billionaire CEO Jerry Perenchio, a staunch Republican, would be at the helm.[72]

On Sept. 22, the FCC approved the Spanish-television merger, saying it would not harm diversity of programming for viewers of the networks. But it did require the companies to shed some radio properties to comply with new radio market rules adopted this past summer.[73]

Several Democratic presidential candidates have raised concerns about media consolidation, but it remains to be seen whether the subject will become a full-fledged election issue. Former Vermont Gov. Howard Dean and Sens. John Edwards, D-N.C., and John F. Kerry, D-Mass., have said they oppose the FCC changes. In recent years, Sen. Joseph I. Lieberman, D-Conn., has criticized the networks for airing too much gratuitous sex and violence.

Meanwhile, FCC Chairman Powell has repeatedly argued that free, over-the-air television is in danger of disappearing as programming — particularly sports, movies and children's fare — migrates to pay TV. Letting the broadcast networks own more stations would protect such programming, he said.

"There has been a steady migration of top programming to pay platforms and away from free TV," Powell said. "Free TV is being replaced by pretty low-cost budget programming, like reality TV."[74] If free TV cannot be made competitive with cable and satellite, he said later, "You're going to be wondering what happened [to it]."[75]

A recently released communications-industry forecast by the New York investment bank Veronis Suhler Stevenson indicates he may have a point. Over the next five years, it predicts, consumers seeking to avoid ads will spend more time with cable, DVDs, video games and other media with a pricetag and less time with free, over-the-air TV and radio.[76]

But critics emphasize that media companies reap healthy profits from their TV operations. "They're not a hardship case," FCC Commissioner Copps says. The cable and broadcast networks recently set records for commitments from advertisers for the upcoming television season. Ironically, media concentration helped to encourage the strong buying. "The consolidation of sellers and buyers has made it easy to move a market quickly," said Gene DeWitt, president of the Syndicated Network Television Association.[77]

Copps thinks if the consolidation trend continues, the Internet could be a future regulatory battleground. "I'm worried about the openness of the Internet, and companies having control over the gateways to the information there," he says.

After months of debate, politicking and saber rattling, some observers think there have been fundamental changes. "Something is definitely shifting in the country and in Washington. Where just a few years ago most people did not think about media as an issue . . . now there is a real dialogue going on," said Rep. Bernard Sanders, I-Vt.[78]

UPDATE

The recession that has plagued the global economy since 2008, combined with the growth of Internet media and their inability to find attractive digital-revenue models, has presented severe challenges to media companies.

"Inside news companies, the most immediate concern is how much revenue lost in the recession the industry will regain as the economy improves," write the authors of "The State of the News Media: An Annual Report on American Journalism," from the Pew Project for Excellence in Journalism. "With growing evidence that conventional advertising online will never sustain the industry, what progress is being made to find new revenue for financing the gathering and reporting of news?"[79]

Indeed, in 2009, advertising revenues in nearly all media sectors dropped drastically, with newspapers leading the downward spiral. Newspaper ad revenues — for print and online versions combined — fell 26 percent. Even with rises in subscription prices at many newspapers, overall newspaper revenue fell 22 percent in 2009, and that's on top of a decline in ad revenues of 16 percent in 2008.[80]

Radio stations and magazines have done little better over the period. The former suffered an 18 percent decline in ad revenue, while magazines sold 26 percent fewer ad pages in 2009 compared to 2008.[81]

The one bright spot in traditional media markets through the recession has been cable television. Prime-time viewership rose 7 percent in 2009 to 3.88 million viewers, and profits were up 9 percent over the same period, reaching $1.16 billion.[82] But the numbers mask a potential weakness, says one analyst. "The cost of paying for content to put on all those channels is rising faster than subscription fees," wrote Saul Hansell of *The New York Times*.[83]

While the recent popularity of "reality" TV shows may have helped dropping revenues somewhat, broadcast networks suffered declines in advertising revenue of approximating 20 percent over the past year. And some analysts say there isn't light at the end of the tunnel for networks in their competition with cable television.

"Don't be surprised if at least one of the Big 4 broadcast networks is sold or dismantled in the next 24 months," writes Diane Mermigas, a columnist with *True/Slant*, an online news site. "They are failing business models whose brand value is meaningful mostly to strained local TV station affiliates, many of whom are also fighting to survive."[84]

Largely as a result of the poor revenue performance and outlook, ownership changes in major media outlets over the past two years took place more often in the form of bankruptcies and closures than sales. Among the high-profile departures from the ranks of newspapers were the *Rocky Mountain News* in Denver, which closed its doors in February 2009, and the *Seattle Post-Intelligencer*, which closed its print operations the next month and reverted to an online-only format.

Since 2008 a number of major city newspaper owners filed for Chapter 11 bankruptcy protection, including those owning the *Minneapolis Star-Tribune*, the *Philadelphia Inquirer* and the *Philadelphia Daily News*, the *Orange County* (Calif.) *Register*, and the *Chicago Sun-Times*. According to one report, at least 10 newspaper publishers — many of them owning a dozen or more newspapers — filed for bankruptcy in 2009.[85]

Even icons such as *The New York Times* have struggled in recent years. In January 2009, the newspaper was forced to borrow $250 million from one of its investors, Mexican billionaire Carlos Slim Helu.[86]

Although conversion to nonprofit status was widely discussed as an alternative revenue model to keep newspapers alive, such a strategy has not yet been employed.

According to some analysts, tax laws and the complexity of converting a property from for-profit to nonprofit status have been major obstacles.

At the same time, a handful of nonprofit media outlets — most of which receive foundation funding — have begun to have an impact on journalism. Most notably, ProPublica — an online news publication that began publishing in 2008 and also collaborates with tradition media outlets — won a Pulitzer Prize for investigative journalism in 2010.

Some analysts doubt, however, whether non-profit media can have a significant impact on media markets.

"An obvious issue to address is the cost: Huge endowments would be needed to fund a large national newspaper. ProPublica has annual operating costs of around $10 million, which supports a staff of only 28," wrote Emma Heald, editor-in-chief of *Editors Weblog*, an online service of the non-profit World Editors Forum.[87] According to some estimates, to fund a newspaper such as *The New York Times* would require an endowment on the order of $5 billion.[88]

Far from being a new ownership model, Heald argues that "nonprofit journalism is a way to prop-up existing structures, but will only make newspapers dependent on outsiders rather than encourage them to develop new ways to survive on their own."

In any case, foundations have not yet rushed in to rescue struggling media companies. Instead, write the authors of the Pew report, "an unanticipated class of new owners emerged: private equity firms, banks, investment groups specializing in distressed assets and their advisers." According to the report, these new owners "are in it for the money, running the businesses for a period of time then hoping to exit and sell at a premium to the modest amount they paid."[89]

Magazines have also struggled mightily over the past two years. According to one industry source, while 259 new magazines launched in the first nine months of 2009, 383 magazines folded, including such large-circulation publications as *Country Home*, *Southern Accents* and *Hallmark Magazine*. In addition, Condé Nast killed four of its once high-performing magazines: *Gourmet*, *Cookie*, *Modern Bride* and *Elegant Bride*.[90]

According to the Pew Project for Excellence in Journalism, 41 acquisitions of magazines were made in 2009. Notable were Bloomberg News' purchase of *Business*

Week from McGraw-Hill and the Economist Group's purchase of Congressional Quarterly from the Times Publishing Co. in St. Petersburg, Fla. *TV Guide*, once the largest circulation magazine in the United States, was sold to an investment firm for $1 and the assumption of liabilities estimated at approximately $255 million.[91]

Thanks to rapidly changing economics and technology, some analysts say that the only thing certain about the future of the media is its uncertainty.

"If a new model is to be found it is hardly clear what it will be," states the Pew report. Pew's survey, produced with the Pew Internet and American Life Project, found that only 35 percent of Americans said they had an online news destination they would call a "favorite," and even among those users only 19 percent said they would continue to visit if that site began charging people to view its content. "In the meantime," Pew said, "perhaps one concept identifies most clearly what is going on in journalism: Most news organizations — new or old — are becoming niche operations, more specific in focus, brand and appeal and narrower, necessarily, in ambition."

It is at least clear that traditional media, such as newspapers, are going to have to find a way to earn revenue in new media if they are to survive. "We can't get this halfway right or three-quarters of the way right. We have to get this really, really right," Arthur Sulzberger Jr., the publisher of *The New York Times*, said in announcing that his newspaper would start charging frequent visitors to the newspaper's Website for accessing content beyond a certain minimum.[92] Subscribers to the newspaper will continue to receive unlimited free access to Web content.

Perhaps not surprisingly, the biggest transfer of media ownership in the past two years was in the sector with the best revenue outlook — cable television. Unlike broadcast television, which is dependent almost exclusively on advertising for revenue, cable companies earn revenue from subscription and advertising sales and other activity, such as providing Internet service.

The pending sale of NBC Universal to Comcast Corp., the Pennsylvania-based cable giant, for $37 billion is subject to approval by the Federal Communications Commission (FCC) and the Justice Department, a process that may not be completed until 2011. The proposed deal, announced in December 2009, has generated significant controversy.

Brian Roberts, chairman and chief executive of Comcast, and Jeff Zucker, president and chief executive officer of NBC Universal, both assured lawmakers that the merger would work to the benefit of consumers.[93] Nevertheless, some owners of local stations are concerned that the market power of a Comcast owning NBC would hurt competing stations. "Would they really allow Comcast and NBC to merge? That's controlling all the distribution. That's controlling all the programming," Jim Goodmon, president of the Capitol Broadcasting Co., told *The New York Times*. "There isn't any way that this could be in the public interest."[94]

Comcast was also a key player in an important case decided in August 2009, when a federal appeals court overturned an FCC policy prohibiting a cable television company from exceeding a market share of 30 percent of households nationally. Comcast — with a market share of 24.8 percent — is the only cable provider that is close to the cap.[95]

"Although Congress directed the FCC to establish limits on cable ownership in 1992, the D.C. Circuit Court of Appeals has been disinclined to approve such regulations," said Arnold Schwartzman, president of the Media Access Project, a nonprofit advocacy group. "It is hard to imagine that any rule the FCC could devise would ever withstand review under the standards established in today's decision."[96]

The FCC suffered another rebuff from the courts in March 2010 when the Third U.S. Circuit Court of Appeals in Philadelphia overturned the commission's policy preventing media companies from owning a newspaper and a TV station in the same market.[97] Large media companies don't want any restrictions on their purchases. But many advocacy groups and smaller media companies worry that concentration of ownership in a single market is not in the public interest because it reduces competition and diversity of content.

All of this activity comes as the FCC is just beginning its first quadrennial review of the state of media ownership mandated by Congress, the first under the Obama administration. The Telecommunications Act of 1996 requires the commission to review ownership rules every four years to determine whether changes in the rules are necessary for "the public interest and as the result of competition."[98] Prior to the actual review, the commission undertakes an information-collection effort and solicits and receives comments from industry and the public.

Analysts expect the debate over the rules to split largely along party lines, with Democrats arguing against relaxation of the rules governing media ownership. Democratic FCC Commissioner Michael Copps said that since 1996 there had been a 39 percent decrease in the numbers of commercial radio station owners and a 33 percent decrease in the number of TV station owners. He called the number of minority-owned stations "appalling."[99] According to HearUsNow.org, a non-profit consumer advocacy group, while ethnic minorities make up about one-third of America's population, they own less than 4 percent of America's broadcast licenses.[100]

Commissioner Robert McDowell, a Republican, on the other hand, said that the FCC's media ownership rules don't take into account the impact of the Internet. "This time, I hope, we will get it right," he said. "Burdensome rules that have remained essentially intact for more than a decade should not be allowed to continue impeding, or potentially impeding, the ability of broadcasters and newspapers to survive and thrive in the digital era."[101]

NOTES

1. Jim Rutenberg, "To Interview Former P.O.W., CBS Offers Stardom," *The New York Times*, June 16, 2003, p. A1.

2. Lynn Elber, "CBS May Have Erred in Pursuit of Lynch Interview, Executive Says," Associated Press/TBO.com, July 20, 2003.

3. For background, see Kenneth Jost, "The Future of Television," *The CQ Researcher*, Dec. 23, 1994, pp. 1129-1152.

4. Marc Fisher, "Sounds Familiar for a Reason," *The Washington Post*, May 18, 2003, p. B1.

5. Michael K. Powell, "New Rules, Old Rhetoric," *The New York Times*, July 28, 2003, p. A17.

6. Eric Boehlert, "Habla usted Clear Channel?" Salon .com, April 24, 2003.

7. From testimony before Britain's House of Lords, June 26, 2003.

8. "Annual Assessment of the Status of Competition in the Market for the Delivery of Video Programming, Ninth Annual Report," Federal Communications Commission, www.fcc.gov, Dec. 31, 2002, p. 3.

9. See "Mass Deregulation of Media Threatens to Undermine Democracy," Consumer Federation of America, June 3, 2003.

10. See "Report and Order," www.fcc.gov, July 2, 2003, p. 15.

11. Stephen Labaton, "Senate Debates Repeal of FCC Media Ownership Rules," *The New York Times*, Sept. 12, 2003, p. C3.

12. For background, see David Masci, "The Future of Telecommunications," *The CQ Researcher*, April 23, 1999, pp. 329-352.

13. For background, see "Minorities Lose Ground in Newsrooms" at www.rtnda.org. The survey was by the Radio and TV News Directors Association and Ball State University.

14. Paul Farhi, "Mega-Media: Better or More of the Same?" *The Washington Post*, June 3, 2003, p. C1.

15. Eli Noam, "The media concentration debate," *Financial Times*, July 31 2003, p. A16.

16. "FCC Chairman Powell Defends FCC Media Rules," FCC news release, July 23, 2003.

17. Adam Thierer and Clyde Wayne Crews Jr., "What Media Monopolies?" *The Wall Street Journal*, July 29, 2003, p. B2.

18. See "Free TV Swallowed by Media Giants: The Way It Really Is," Consumer Federation of America, Center for Digital Democracy, Sept. 15, 2003, p. 3.

19. Adam Lashinsky, "Americans Stupid? Media to Blame? Leading thinkers weigh in at Fortune's Brainstorm 2003 conference," *Fortune*, July 31, 2003.

20. See "Does Ownership Matter in Local Television News: A Five-Year Study of Ownership and Quality," Project for Excellence in Journalism, April 29, 2003.

21. See press release/statement, at http://lott.senate.gov/news, June 6, 2003.

22. See "Statement by Commissioner Adelstein before Minority Media & Telecommunications Council," July 22, 2003.

23. Catherine Yang, "FCC's Loner is No Longer So Lonely," *Business Week*, March 24, 2003, p. 78.

24. Labaton, *op. cit.*

25. Frank Ahrens, "FCC Rule Fight Continues in Congress," *The Washington Post*, June 4, 2003, p. E1.

26. See "Report and Order," *op. cit.*

27. For background, see Charles S. Clark, "Sex, Violence and the Media," *The CQ Researcher*, Nov. 17, 1995, pp. 1017-1040.

28. Meg James, "The Vivendi Deal; Creator of 'Law & Order' is Facing Chance of Being Outgunned in Talks," *Los Angeles Times*, Sept. 4, 2003, p. C1.

29. Bill Carter and Jim Rutenberg, "Deregulating the Media: Opponents, Shows' Creators Say Television Will Suffer in New Climate," *The New York Times*, June 3, 2003, p. C1.

30. Bill McConnell, "McCain Weighs in for Fin-Syn," *Broadcasting & Cable*, May 26, 2003, p. 2.

31. See petition for reconsideration filed at FCC by Center for the Creative Community and Association of Independent Video and Filmmakers, available at www.creativecommunity.us, Sept. 4, 2003, pp. 7-8.

32. See "Report and Order," *op. cit.*, p. 15.

33. McConnell, *op. cit.*

34. See "Data Gathering Weakness in FCC's Survey of Information on Factors Underlying Cable Rate Changes," General Accounting Office, May 6, 2003, p. 2.

35. Stephen Labaton, "Behind Media Rule and Its End, One Man," *The New York Times*, June 2, 2003, p. C1.

36. For background, see Adriel Bettelheim, "Public Broadcasting," *The CQ Researcher*, Oct. 29, 1999, pp. 929-952.

37. See "Media Regulations Timeline" at www.pbs.org/now/politics/mediatimeline.html.

38. *Ibid.*

39. *Ibid.*

40. Robert J. Thompson, "500 Channels, But No Clear Picture of What We Want," *The Washington Post*, May 25, 2003, p. B3.

41. See "Issues in Providing Cable and Satellite Television Services," General Accounting Office, Oct. 2002, p. 1.

42. Greg Braxton, "Rewriting the Rules: Synergies Emerge in TV Duopolies," *Los Angeles Times*, May 30, 2003, p. C1.

43. See FCC "Annual Assessment, *op. cit.*

44. For background, see Brian Hansen, "Combating Plagiarism," *The CQ Researcher*, Sept. 19, 2003, pp. 773-796, and Kathy Koch, "Journalism Under Fire," *The CQ Researcher*, Dec. 25, 1998, pp. 1121-1144.

45. Project for Excellence in Journalism, *op. cit.*

46. See testimony of Martin Kaplan of the USC Annenberg School of Communications before Senate Commerce Committee; www.senate.gov/~commerce/hearings, July 23, 2003.

47. Michael K. Powell, "Should Limits on Broadcast Ownership Change?" USAToday.com, Jan. 21, 2003, p. A11.

48. Frank Ahrens, "Why Radio Stinks," *The Washington Post Magazine*, p. 25, Jan. 19, 2003, p. W12.

49. "Broadcast station totals," FCC Audio Division, available at www.fcc.gov, June 30, 2003.

50. Ahrens, *op. cit.*

51. Robert J. Thompson, "500 Channels, But No Clear Picture of What We Want," *The Washington Post*, May 25, 2003, p. B3.

52. From testimony before Senate Commerce Committee, May 13, 2003.

53. Edmund Sanders, "Disney Quits Broadcasters Trade Group," *Los Angeles Times*, June 18, 2003, p. C1.

54. Bill McConnell, "Fritts: No Reversal on 35% Cap Legislation," *Broadcasting & Cable*, July 11, 2003.

55. See "Tauzin Issues Statement In Support of FCC's Media Ownership Process," May 29, 2003.

56. Frank Ahrens, "Senate Votes to Block FCC Media Rules, *The Washington Post*, Sept. 17, 2003, p. A1.

57. Edmund Sanders and Jube Shiver Jr., "ReWriting the Rules: FCC Relaxes Limits on Media Ownership," *Los Angeles Times*, June 18, 2003, p. A1.

58. Christopher Stern, "Bitter Atmosphere Envelops FCC: Under Chairman Powell, Panel Members Maneuver, Criticize," *The Washington Post*, June 3, 2003, p. E1.

59. Interview on C-SPAN's "Washington Journal," Sept. 3, 2003.

60. *Ibid.*

61. Dan Trigoboff, "FCC Eyes 70/70," www.Broad castingandcable.com, Aug. 4, 2003.

62. See "The Failure of Cable Deregulation," at www .uspirg.org, U.S. PIRG, August 2003.

63. "Fighting Media Monopolies 2003," *Consumer Reports*, July 2003, p. 65.

64. For background, see "Judges Lift Cable Ownership Cap," www.broadcastingcable.com, March 4, 2001.

65. Paul Davidson, "FCC Fine-tuning Proposal to Relax Cable Ownership Limits," *USA Today*, July 25, 2003, p. B3.

66. See "Report on Cable Industry Prices," FCC 03-136, July 8, 2003.

67. Press release, July 8, 2003.

68. David Lieberman, "Media Moguls Have Second Thoughts," *USA Today*, June 2, 2003, p. B1.

69. See Robert Sachs, "Television Ownership" letter to the editor, *The New York Times*, Aug. 1, 2003, p. A20.

70. Sallie Hofmeister and Jube Shiver Jr., "Worry Over FCC Rules Not Shared on Wall Street," *Los Angeles Times*, June 4, 2003, p. C1.

71. David Lieberman, "Relaxing Rules Raises Concerns About Diverse Media Voices," *USA Today*, Jan. 15, 2003, p. B1.

72. Juliet Eilperin, "Democrats Fight Hispanic Media Merger, Republican Ownership Could Limit Access to Viewpoints, Groups Tell FCC," *The Washington Post*, May 25, 2003, p. A5.

73. Press release, Sept. 22, 2003.

74. Powell interview, *op. cit.*

75. See transcript of McLaughlin "One-on-One," Sept. 7, 2003.

76. Michael McCarthy, "Forecast: Public to turn to paid media," *USA Today*, Aug. 15, 2003, p. B12.

77. Stuart Elliott, "Trying to sort out the broader trends behind the big surge in spending on TV commercials," *The New York Times*, June 3, 2003, p. C10.

78. Quoted in Robert McChesney and John Nichols, "Media Democracy's Moment," *The Nation*, Feb. 24, 2003.

79. "The State of the News Media: An Annual Report on American Journalism," Pew Project for Excellence in Journalism, 2010, www.stateofthemedia.org/2010/ chapter%20pdfs/2010_execsummary.pdf.

80. *Ibid.*

81. *Ibid.*

82. *Ibid.*

83. Saul Hansell, "The Problem With Cable is Television," *The New York Times*, May 1, 2009.

84. Diane Mermigas, "Why ABC, NBC and Broadcast TV Networks are Toast," *True/Slant*, May 26, 2010, http://trueslant.com/dianemermigas/2010/05/26/ why-abc-nbc-and-broadcast-tv-networks-are-toast/.

85. CBS News, Sept. 1, 2009, www.cbsnews.com/ stories/2009/09/01/business/main5279911.shtml.

86. Eric Dash, "Mexican Billionaire Invests in Times Company," *The New York Times*, Jan. 20, 2009, p. B11.

87. Emma Heald, Could the Non-Profit Model be the Saviour of the Newspaper Industry," ProPublica, in *Editors Weblog*, Feb. 6, 2009, www.editorsweblog. org/analysis/2009/02/propublica_could_the_non-profit_model_be.php.

88. David Swensen and Michael Schmidt, "News You Can Endow," *The New York Times*, Jan. 28, 2009, p. A31.

89. Pew Project, *op. cit.*

90. Marketing Charts, www.marketingcharts.com/ print/top-10-magazine-closures-ytd-2009-10734/.

91. Pew Project, *op. cit.*

92. Richard Perez-Pena, "The Times to Charge for Frequent Access to Its Web Site," *The New York Times*, Jan. 20, 2010, www.nytimes.com/2010/ 01/21/business/media/21times.html.

93. Brian Stelter, "In NBC-Comcast Deal, Quiet Concerns," *The New York Times*, June 20, 2010, www .nytimes.com/2010/06/21/business/media/21 comcast.html?_r=1&scp=2&sq=comcast% 20nbc%20universal&st=cse.

94. Brian Stelter, "Local Level Fears Power of NBC Deal, *The New York Times*, June 21, 2010, p. B1.

95. Bill McConnell, "Appeals Court Rejects Cable Limit," *The Daily Deal*, Aug. 28, 2009.

96. *Ibid.*

97. Joelle Tessler, "Court Lifts Ban on Media Ownership Restrictions," The Associated Press, March 23, 2010.

98. Telecommunications Act of 1996, Section 202(h).

99. Donna Block, *The Deal* (May 26, 2010), www.thedeal.com.

100. HearUsNow, www.hearusnow.org/mediaownership/20/.

101. *Ibid.*

BIBLIOGRAPHY

Books

Klein, Alec, *Stealing Time: Steve Case, Jerry Levin and the Collapse of AOL Time Warner*, Simon & Schuster, 2003.
Reporter Klein describes how the bursting Internet bubble, conflicting management styles, accounting irregularities and other difficulties devalued the largest merger in American history and forced out top executives.

Articles

Fallows, James, "The Age of Murdoch," *The Atlantic*, September 2003.
Journalist Fallows argues that media baron Rupert Murdoch approaches his media empire as just another business — not one charged with serving the public interest.

Fisher, Marc, "Sounds Familiar for a Reason," *The Washington Post*, May 18, 2003, p. B1.
A *Post* columnist and the author of an upcoming book on the radio industry takes a critical look at radio giant Clear Channel Communications.

Kirkpatrick, David D., "Entertainment Industry Faces Problems Mergers Won't Solve," *The New York Times*, Sept. 8, 2003, p. C1.
Kirkpatrick explores whether NBC's proposed deal with Vivendi Universal signals the end of media mergers.

Noam, Eli, "The Media Concentration Debate," *Financial Times*, July 31, 2003, p. A11.
Telecom visionary and Columbia University Professor Eli Noam notes that while media companies are bigger, so is the sector. Local concentration is actually highest among newspapers, not TV stations, and radio-industry growth has slowed in recent years.

Thierer, Adam, and Clyde Wayne Crews Jr., "What Media Monopolies?" *The Wall Street Journal*, July 29, 2003, p. B2.
Analysts at the libertarian Cato Institute argue the broadcast networks are far from monopolies because audience share has decreased dramatically, and many non-network station groups own more TV outlets than networks.

Thompson, Robert J., "500 Channels, But No Clear Picture of What We Want," *The Washington Post*, May 25, 2003, p. B3.
Consumers have far more media choices today, but the quality of news and the quantity of civic-minded programming often pales compared to decades ago.

Reports and Studies

"Big Radio Rules in Small Markets: A few behemoths dominate medium-sized cities throughout the U.S.," Center for Public Integrity, Oct. 1, 2003.
Radio concentration is highest in small and medium-sized markets, where industry giant Clear Channel is a major player. FCC rules limit companies to owning eight radio outlets per market, but companies sidestep the limit by acquiring stations in adjacent markets that can be heard where they've reached the cap. For a copy, visit http://www.openairwaves.org/telecom/report.aspx?aid=63.

"Does Ownership Matter in Local Television News: A Five-Year Study of Ownership and Quality," Project for Excellence in Journalism, April 29, 2003.
This exhaustive study finds that small-station groups tend to produce better newscasts than large ones, and network affiliates tend to have better news than network-owned stations. Moreover, cross-ownership of a TV station and a newspaper in a market usually results in higher-quality news, but local ownership doesn't guarantee quality. Available at www.journalism.org.

"Free TV Swallowed by Media Giants: The Way It Really Is," Consumer Federation of America,

Consumers Union and Center for Digital Democracy, Sept. 15, 2003.

Three watchdog groups challenge the argument that free TV is in jeopardy if the FCC's media-ownership rules are not relaxed, pointing out the broadcast networks are strong financially. Available at www.democraticmedia.org.

Halfon, Jay, and Edmund Mierzwinski, "The Failure of Cable Deregulation," U.S. PIRG, August 2003.

Cable rates have been rising three times faster than inflation, and even higher. Meanwhile, satellite-TV competition is not resulting in lower rates for cable. For a copy, visit www.uspirg.org.

"(Media Ownership) Report and Order and Notice of Proposed Rulemaking," Federal Communications Commission, (FCC 03-127), July 2, 2003.

This 256-page report provides extensive background on the FCC's decision to modify its media-ownership rules. The "Report and order" can be obtained at www.fcc.gov.

"Radio Deregulation: Has it Served Citizens and Musicians?" Future of Music Coalition, November 2002.

The rapid consolidation of the radio industry after deregulation in 1996 is documented in this 147-page report. Available at www.futureofmusic.org.

For More Information

Consumer Federation of America, 1424 16th St., N.W., Suite 604, Washington, DC 20036; (202) 387-6121; www.consumerfed.org. A vocal advocate of regulating the media; frequently issues reports detailing increased consolidation.

Consumers Union, 1666 Connecticut Ave., N.W., Suite 310, Washington, DC 20009-1039; (202) 462-6262; www.consumersunion.org. It has teamed with Consumer Federation to oppose further relaxation of the media-ownership rules.

Future of Music Coalition, 1615 L St., N.W., Suite 520, Washington, DC 20036; (202) 429-8855; www.futureofmusic.org. A nonprofit coalition of radio and music interests that opposes radio consolidation and supports fledgling low-power FM.

National Association of Broadcasters, 1771 N St., N.W., Washington, DC 20036; (202) 429-5300; www.nab.org. The main trade association representing television and radio broadcasters, though the Big Four TV networks are no longer members.

National Cable and Telecommunications Association, 1724 Massachusetts Ave., N.W., Washington, DC 20036; (202) 775-3550; www.ncta.com. The premier trade association for cable TV companies; many also offer high-speed Internet access.

Radio-Television News Directors Association, 1600 K St., N.W., Suite 700, Washington, DC 20006-2838; (202) 659-6510; www.rtnda.org. Opposes curbs on press freedoms and promotes journalistic ethics.

May 2009   Updated August 2010

3

Future of Books

Sarah Glazer and Charles S. Clark

The recent Google Book Search settlement among Google, authors and publishers promises to make millions of out-of-print books available online that were once limited to the New York Public Library and great university collections. But many librarians worry that digital access to the world's great books will be in the hands of a private company.

From *CQ Researcher*,
May 29, 2009.
Updated August 27, 2010.

The university bookstore ran out of the textbook assigned for your course? No problem. The young woman behind the counter can print one out in the time it takes to make an espresso.

Don't like the way the latest episode of the novel you're reading online has turned out? Write in a plot development of your own. (But be forewarned: Another reader may edit you out.)

Forgot to bring a book with you on the subway? You've got President Barack Obama's *Dreams from My Father* on your cell phone, right at the place you stopped reading last night on your Kindle.[1]

The world of reading is changing before our eyes. More books are becoming available than ever before, and in many more formats. It remains to be seen whether readers will flock to these or even more futuristic ways of reading. But already the innovations have caused anxiety in the troubled publishing industry because they suggest radical changes in how books are supplied to readers, much as technological changes are threatening the very existence of the newspaper industry.

"The publishing industry is in a difficult position," says Mike Shatzkin, CEO of the Idea Logical Co., a digital-publishing consulting firm. "We have all these new challenges to invest in, and meanwhile the old model for producing money is in trouble. So publishers are squeezed from both sides."

Amid troubling layoffs in publishing over the past year, cutbacks in new manuscript acceptances and tough times for bookstores, digital books have entered publishing's mainstream for the first time. In this pivotal year for e-books, Amazon.com introduced the

Wholesale E-Book Revenue Tops $50 Million

U.S. electronic book sales have risen steadily since 2002. Last year wholesale revenues exceeded $52 million, or nine times higher than in 2002. Digital books still make up less than 1 percent of books sold in the United States, however.

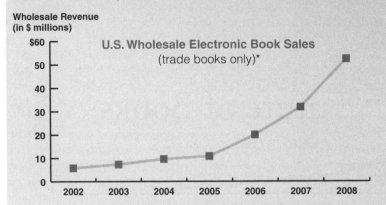

Wholesale Revenue (in $ millions)

U.S. Wholesale Electronic Book Sales
(trade books only)*

*Library, educational and professional electronic sales not included; retail figures may be as much as double the above wholesale figures.

Source: International Digital Publishing Forum

e-books, "this year is about smart-phones," says Bhaskar. His company was one of the first major publishers to make its titles available on the iPhone and the Black-Berry and now plans to bring most new titles out in electronic as well as print format.

The fact that today's new books start out from the writer's desk as digital files has contributed to the growth of another way of producing books — print-on-demand. Theoretically, books can remain digital files until they're ordered by the customer, at which point they are printed on laser printers, order by order. Increasingly publishers are using this method for books about to go out of print and for scholarly or obscure books with low readership. For non-bestsellers, publishers can print out one book at a time, saving the expense of big print runs, storage and bookstore returns, while retailers can avoid holding inventory that doesn't sell.

Yet all these innovations still account for a small percentage of what passes for reading a book. Despite rapid growth, sales revenue generated by electronic books, whether read on a laptop, Kindle or cell phone, still accounts for only about 1 percent of the $11 billion adult trade book market in the United States, estimates Michael Smith, executive director of the International Digital Publishing Forum, a trade association.

Similarly, volumes produced through print-on-demand account for less than 1 percent of the more than 3 billion books printed each year in the United States, according to David Taylor, president of Lightning Source, the leading print-on-demand company.[5]

The Espresso Book Machine, which can deliver a bound paperback in less than five minutes, is currently installed in only a handful of bookstores in North America and England, but its manufacturers envision widespread use in college bookstores, on cruise ships and in remote areas of the world. (*See sidebar, p. 64.*)

Kindle 2.0 and the larger-format Kindle DX — which both permit the wireless download of a book in less than a minute — and Sony Reader acquired 500,000 titles from Google. Both companies' electronic readers employ a technology that does not require backlighting, making its glare-free text easier on the eyes than a computer screen.[2]

For years, e-book enthusiasts have said the product couldn't really take off until the equivalent of an iPod for books was developed.[3] It's not clear whether we're there yet, but the sudden popularity of reading on Apple's iPhone took many by surprise. Over 1.7 million users have downloaded Stanza software, which permits them to read a book on their cell phone from a selection of more than 100,000 titles. The announcements in February that both Amazon and Google were making their titles available on the iPhone only added to the buzz.[4]

"Suddenly there was a sense in 2008 that an e-book program was something a publisher couldn't be without," says Michael Bhaskar, digital editor at publisher Pan MacMillan in Britain. And if 2008 was about

pre I-Pad

Stanza software?

current stats?

online still! (use)

Former Random House editorial director Jason Epstein, co-founder of On Demand Books, which markets the machine, says the publishing model of the last 500 years — in which publishers printed large runs and then had to warehouse and ship physical books at enormous costs — is headed for extinction.

Today, "you can go directly from the digital file to the end user with nothing in between," he points out. "That means you can store in theory every book ever written in whatever language at practically no cost. And deliver that file practically anywhere on Earth at no cost. This has a revolutionary effect on the way books are made and distributed."

Eventually, the traditional publishing industry would have collapsed anyway because of structural obsolescence, he says. "With this recession and the arrival of digitization, the process will be hastened."

Publishers are still trying to figure out how to appeal to young readers — who do most of their reading online — by offering free multimedia content digitally, while still making money for themselves and their authors. *Screen vs. page readers*

"We're moving to a post-literate culture where YouTube is a search engine and video gaming is the main form of entertainment. How does that impact storytelling?" asks Pan MacMillan's Bhaskar.

This spring, Penguin Books won top awards at the hip SXSW (South by Southwest) interactive media festival in Austin, Texas, for its online storytelling experiment. Over a period of six weeks, readers clicking on a Penguin Web site could read a developing mystery being written by a novelist online, search for clues planted on the Internet and contribute plot suggestions to the author as the story was being written. Access to the site, "We Tell Stories," was free even though it drew on the skills of several published authors.[6] *similar to 9/29 NPR online music*

Penguin's experiment "is fascinating, but I'm not sure how it ever makes money," comments Shatzkin of Idea Logical, expressing a widely shared worry in the industry. And he's puzzled by those who see it as the future of fiction: "Participatory content creation makes sense, but why are we calling it books?" he asks.

But those experimenting with online forms of literature suggest our definition of "book" itself needs to be more expansive. "A book is an experience, not a chunk of paper," Chris Meade, director of the London literary think tank if:book, recently told an audience of book club members in Oxford, England. "If you think of the experience of reading a great novel and take the novel away," you can still have a "fantastic" experience, he maintained.

An online book about William Blake recently launched by Meade's organization displays Blake's poems along with gorgeous graphics and videos of an interview with a Blake expert and an actor reading Blake's poem "London." Over the next few months, readers are invited to help it grow by contributing via Twitter and Blogger (a free blog-publishing tool from Google) and the Blake "netbook" itself.[7]

The ease of publishing a book from a digital file means many more actors can get into the act. Small presses can be formed in someone's living room or at a local bookstore. Authors who could never interest a big publisher with their family genealogy or purple-prose novel can be listed on Amazon or simply publish online.

With the cost down to a few hundred dollars to have your book published by one of the author-services companies (the new vanity presses), who needs publishers? On the defensive, publishers say they still play an aesthetic filtering role as the curators of good writing. *demise of gatekeepers*

Yet more and more books and experimental writing are becoming available online for free without publishers' filters. And as publishers put out more digital books, it may be easier for hackers to convert copyrighted works into pirated editions. Some publishers are reporting that piracy has surged in recent months along with rising demand for e-books, raising concerns that piracy partly accounts for declining print book sales. Pirated editions of works by children's writer J.K. Rowling have been posted on Web sites like Scribd, and other copyrighted works are cropping up on file-sharing services like RapidShare.[8]

Still, some authors like *Wired* editor Chris Anderson and novelist Cory Doctorow claim that publishing for free online is actually the way to sell more print books because of the exposure it provides.[9] *author of "The Long Tail"*

Indeed, rather than chasing printed books into oblivion, some experts say digitization is making more books

Digital Era Arrives at London Book Fair

Publishers urged to confront "perfect storm" by maximizing digital content.

At the international London Book Fair this April, a stroll through the massive exhibition hall could have lulled a visitor into thinking the book business is alive and well: Publishers were busy striking deals over foreign rights for printed books, sipping white wine to celebrate.

But despite appearances, anxiety about the industry was palpable, as publishers and booksellers attended seminars on digital publishing with gloomy titles like "Where's the Money?"

At the fair's first-ever "Digital Zone," Janet Hawkins, an independent bookshop owner from Blessington, Ireland, was trying out a hand-held Sony Reader as she considered offering digital e-books downloadable from a computer terminal at her shop. Hawkins is "terrified" her business will be destroyed if Amazon's Kindle, a competitor of the Sony Reader now available only in the United States, is introduced in Britain. Unlike the Reader, which must download books from a separate computer, the wireless, hand-held Kindle downloads from Amazon's proprietary online bookstore and would eliminate any role for shops like hers. (Her window of opportunity may soon evaporate, however; the trade press has been reporting that Sony plans to join Amazon in producing a wireless reader.[1])

Last year's drop in American book sales, following years of little or no growth, led Michael Healy, executive director of the Book Industry Study Group, to ask if book publishing was "doomed to follow its dinosaur cousins, newspapers, to extinction."[2]

What little growth the industry has seen in recent years has been driven almost solely by increases in book prices, not the number of books sold, according to Healy, whose group tracks industry statistics. He bluntly told a roomful of publishers that theirs is "an industry in decline."

Publishing faces a "perfect storm" — more book titles every year but fewer people who want to read them, Healy warned, citing declining spending by households on books and independent bookshops struggling to survive.

The keys to survival, he told the publishers, are the proliferating channels of digital content able to reach the tens of millions of readers who look for information on the Web but don't frequent bookshops. Stop putting the physical book at the center of your thinking, he urged: "Experiment at all costs" by offering digital content — and make it free if necessary.

As further proof that the market is changing, the core audience of American book buyers — middle-aged women — will be dwindling in coming years, according to Bowker, a leading source of publishing industry data. By 2016, those baby boomers will be retiring, going onto fixed incomes, while the Gen X-ers stepping into their shoes will constitute a smaller, more screen-savvy generation of buyers.[3]

Despite all the attention to new mobile readers like the Kindle, desktop personal computers and laptops are still the devices used most frequently for reading e-books, and it may have something to do with all those female romance readers, who are leading purchasers of e-books. You're not likely to be detected reading a "bodice-ripper" at work if you do it on your PC, romance publisher Harlequin discovered from reader surveys.

Yet iPhones hold the greatest potential for growth among readers who don't have gray hair, Bowker Vice President for Publisher Services Kelly Gallagher predicted, even though a company survey found iPhones account for only 10 percent of e-book purchases, trailing behind PCs and Amazon's Kindle. Surprisingly, Kindle's largest ownership group is middle-aged, the survey found, countering its reputation as the reading device of future generations.

Over in the Digital Zone, fairgoers could see some of the reasons why 1.7 million (mainly young) people have available than ever before, even if they're in a different format. A massive digitization project by the Library of Congress allows, for the first time, anyone with a computer at home to look at the first edition of Louisa May Alcott's *Little Women* and other 19th-century books too brittle to be handled.

The recent Google Book Search settlement among Google, authors and publishers — if approved by the

relate my research experiences (glove, foam, soft pencil) at Univ. of Chicago

downloaded the Stanza reading application onto their iPhones. Its latest features include 135 new background colors to pair with 21 crisp fonts as well as background "themes" like "bedroom" (red, satiny sheets) and links to a dictionary while reading.

Worries About Piracy

Piracy discussions at the fair underscored a central anxiety — how to make money on digital publishing without being ripped off. One speaker pointed to a decision by a Swedish court as a sign that piracy is being stifled. On April 17 the court sentenced four founders of The Pirate Bay, a popular file-sharing site, to a year in jail for violating copyright.[4]

But skeptics at the fair predicted new piracy sites would pop up in its place. (As of May 27, Pirate Bay's Web site had not been shut down, and similar sites also were operating.)

The day after the digital seminar, *The Independent*, a British daily, reported substitute approaches already emerging. For example, searches for copyrighted material are being conducted by networks of individuals, avoiding the need for a legally vulnerable centralized Web site.[5]

Paradoxically, piracy has stimulated sales of some titles by giving them more publicity, according to a study cited by industry consultant Mike Shatzkin, CEO of Idea Logical Co.[6] He argued that publishers' encryption of e-books to prevent piracy — known as digital rights management — has been ineffective.

It would be more effective to price e-books cheaply enough so consumers don't feel they have to search for free versions on pirate sites, Shatzkin argued. Strong consumer demand for cheaper books is evident in the recent growth in used book purchases, which explain in part why fewer new books are being bought, he said.

Consumers expect e-books to be priced more cheaply than printed books, and they will be because publishers and booksellers have fewer expenses, Shatzkin predicted. That couldn't have been reassuring to the publishers in the room who wondered aloud why they should be investing in a sector that now commands barely 1 percent of U.S. book sales.

Online books and hand-held digital readers were a big feature of this year's London Book Fair.

Indeed, British publishers at the packed "Where's the Money?" session argued heatedly against lower pricing for e-books. Such a move, Penguin Group Chairman and CEO John Makinson told the standing-room-only crowd, would be "short-changing authors."[7]

[1] Marion Maneker, "How the Next Kindle Could Save the Newspaper Business," *Wired*, May 6, 2009.

[2] The Book Industry Study Group (BISG) tracks publishing statistics. All statistics cited are for the U.S. market. According to the BISG, the number of books sold fell 1.5 percent from 2007 to 2008.

[3] Sixty-five percent of U.S. book buyers are women, according to Bowker, which publishes the authoritative *Books in Print*.

[4] "Court Jails Pirate Bay Founders," BBC News, April 17, 2009, http://news.bbc.co.uk/1/hi/technology/8003799.stm. The decision was expected to be appealed.

[5] Pat Pilcher, "Pirate Bay 'could soon be obsolete,'" *The Independent*, April 20, 2009, www.independent.co.uk.

[6] The study was conducted by Magellan Media Consulting Partners of New York City, www.magellanmediapartners.com/index.php/mmcp/Research/.

[7] See Lynn Andriani, "British Publishers Try to Find the Money in E-Books," *Publishers Weekly*, April 21, 2009, www.publishersweekly.com.

court — promises to make millions of out-of-print books available online that were once limited to great university libraries. But the fact that this vast collection of 20th-century literature will be in the hands of a private company

has many librarians worried as the world's treasure trove of books — past and future — becomes increasingly digital.

Here are some of the questions being debated by publishers, librarians and the ultimate consumers — readers:

Is This the Future of Book Publishing?

"Espresso" machine produces a book in five minutes.

About as big as a large photocopier, the machine is probably the last thing one would expect to see at the flagship store of Blackwell — Britain's leading academic bookseller. But tucked in an alcove at the store on Charing Cross Road in London, it offers a glimpse at a possible future for book publishing. As signs alluringly promise: "Become an author — Print your own book" and "Out of print, Out of stock books — Available Right Here Now."

The Espresso Book Machine, which its makers hope will one day become the ATM of books, can dispense a paperbound book in under five minutes from a digital file, using ink-jet technology for the cover and high-end laser printing for the pages. To the average reader, the color cover and black-and-white pages are indistinguishable from the traditional published version.

"Suddenly, it's increased our stock by a million titles," says store manager Marcus Gipps, citing the number of digital files in the catalog offered by On Demand Books, the manufacturer. That's the equivalent of 23.6 miles of shelving, according to Blackwell. At least 250,000 of those titles are out of print, once inaccessible to most customers.

Previously, when customers asked for a book that wasn't on the shelf, the typical response was, "Can we order it for you?" Often the customer decided to look elsewhere."Now we say, 'Can we print it for you?' " says Gipps.

The Espresso was installed in the store in April as a test. If successful, it will be installed in more Blackwell shops, many located at universities, says Blackwell CEO Andrew Hutchings. He expects it to be particularly popular for self-publishing, publishing theses and printing course packs — selected chapters from textbooks assigned by professors.

As of mid-May, the Espresso had been installed in a dozen sites in North America, England and Australia, according to Dane Neller, CEO of On Demand Books. In the United States, an Espresso machine is in use at the University of Michigan Library, where it prints out-of-copyright and rare books from the library's digitized collections, and at Northshire Books, an independent bookstore in Manchester Center, Vt., among other sites.

Eventually, as On Demand Chairman Jason Epstein envisions it, customers will be able to order any book they want from a computer or cell phone and pick up a freshly printed copy in their neighborhood shop. (To accomplish that, publishers will have to digitize all of their titles, which some are just starting to do.) In addition to bookstores, Epstein sees the Espresso being used in libraries, schools, hospitals, cruise ships and developing countries that lack book distribution networks.

Will the Google Book Search settlement restrict public access to digital books?

Last October, Google announced that it had reached a $125 million settlement with authors and publishers who had sued the company for scanning millions of books from university libraries without compensating them.[10]

The proposed settlement permits Google's Book Search engine to make entire copyrighted books available online for a fee and to show up to 20 percent of a copyrighted text at no charge. Google will keep 37 percent of the revenue from online book sales and advertisements that run next to previews of book pages; the remaining 63 percent will go to authors and publishers.

University and K-12 school libraries will be able to access the entire Google database, currently about 10 million books, by buying a subscription, while public libraries will be provided a terminal with free access to the digital collection. The biggest impact will be on books still under copyright but no longer in print — about 5 million of which have been scanned so far. Under the settlement agreement, 51 percent of these out-of-print books scanned into the database will be priced initially at $5.99 and below.[11]

"For many of these books the only way you can get to them is if you're a student at Harvard," or some other

Blackwell's machine cost about $100,000, according to a company spokesperson, but Gipps expects it to pay for itself in about six months. The machine can produce a book for about $3, with retail prices set by the publisher. The makers expect the Espresso's cost to decline significantly as more are marketed, and eventually hope to lease it out for about the same price as a photocopier.

That could make it attractive to libraries trying to save on purchasing and storing books, says Kari Paulsen, president of EBook Library, which markets e-books to more than 1,000 libraries worldwide. Increasingly, libraries trying to save on storage are telling her that if a book is not in e-book form they don't want it. With an Espresso, a librarian could tell a patron, "You can get it as an e-book or pick it up downstairs printed out in 15 minutes." A library might also make some revenue back by selling Espresso-printed books.

At the University of Alberta Bookstore in Edmonton, Canada, the Espresso has printed some 13,000 books since November 2007. "Edmonton is a long way from pretty much everything, so we have huge shipping bills and long delays," says Todd Anderson, director of the bookstore. The store has saved on shipping costs by acting as a local printer for publishers who would have to send a book thousands of miles; it saves inventory costs by printing only as many copies as students request. It's been able to save students money by printing assigned classics that are out of copyright, like *Frankenstein*, and selling them for less than the standard publisher's sticker price. The bookstore has also printed books of local interest like a 1908

Customers can print their own books on the Espresso machine at the Blackwell bookstore in London.

visitors' guide to Edmonton, local self-published genealogical histories and original small-press books by local authors.

Because of the ease of printing digital files at outposts like Edmonton, the machine could make it possible to distribute "virtually every book ever published, in any language, anywhere on Earth as easily, quickly and cheaply as e-mail," claims On Demand's brochure.

Epstein, a former editorial director of Random House, thinks the effect on publishing could be revolutionary — and could even save precarious independent bookstores. "I think independent bookstores will flourish, and some will become publishers, as they were in the 18th century," he predicts.

major university, says Dan Clancy, engineering director at Google. "One of the things we found exciting was the fact that it broadened access not just to subscription holders but also to users at home, who get a free preview and the book for what looks to be an inexpensive price."

However, some librarians have harshly criticized the settlement because of fears that it puts too many restrictions on public access.

Harvard Library Director Robert Darnton has criticized the agreement for placing what could be the largest digital library in the world in the hands of a private company. In effect, he has written, the settlement hands Google a monopoly over the digitizing of "virtually all books covered by copyright in the United States."[12]

The settlement gives Google permission to continue scanning copyrighted books as long as they were published before Jan. 5, 2009.

"No new entrepreneurs will be able to digitize books within that fenced-off territory . . . because they would have to fight the copyright battles all over again," Darnton wrote in the *New York Review of Books*. "[O]nly Google will be protected from copyright liability."[13]

"What will happen if [Google's] current leaders sell the company or retire?" he asks. What will stop Google from charging exorbitant prices or favoring "profitability over access"?

"The settlement locks in a single player to offering access to the vast majority of the 20th-century's works," concurs Brewster Kahle, founder of the Internet Archive, a nonprofit organization that has scanned some 1.2 million works in the public domain (out of copyright), which it makes available to the public for free via an online platform.

Kahle says he's particularly disturbed that the settlement gives Google legal immunity to scan potentially millions of books whose copyright holders can't be located easily — so-called "orphan" books. His organization would also like to scan those works but would risk being sued for copyright infringement. Kahle favors legislation to protect all scanners from copyright suits.

"Increasingly, people are gathering that Google has been granted a release of liability to exploit that group of works that no one else has," Kahle says. Legislation could have made orphan works accessible to anyone. Google is in effect "legislating through settlement," he says.

Kahle also contends Google will feel no competitive pressure to do a good-quality job that ensures digital copies are as readable as possible. "Once you have a monopoly, the temptation is just to defend your monopoly as opposed to working to make it better," he says. Moreover, the way Google structures its searches is not intended to help serious researchers do large-scale searches quickly but involves "speed bumps" aimed at maximizing the number of times a person views a search page with its accompanying ads, according to Kahle.

Google's Clancy responds that the settlement gives Google a "non-exclusive" arrangement to scan these works, meaning other groups could copy the books as well. And Paul Aiken, executive director of the Authors Guild, one of the parties to the suit, says authors "want real competition in getting these books out to the world." At the same time, he cautions, these books "are out of print for a reason" — they're not commercially in demand. (*See "At Issue," p. 80.*)

Out-of-print books are vital to researchers, however, and Kahle contends the agreement is exclusive in practice: Libraries in the past have been unwilling to let his organization in to scan once Google has knocked on their door. Indeed, it's not clear why a library would let anyone in to scan except Google, since their legal protection for scanning copyrighted works appears to extend to the host library, according to Randall Picker, a professor of law at the University of Chicago.

Many libraries worry that Google is likely to abuse its monopoly by charging them exorbitant subscription prices, according to Jonathan Band, a lawyer representing the American Library Association and the Association of Research Libraries. His associations don't oppose the settlement. But in comments filed with the court responsible for approving the settlement, they are proposing "vigorous" court oversight to prevent artificially high pricing in the absence of competition. The libraries have also asked the judge to protect the privacy of users who read Google's books online.[14]

"I'm concerned that as Google seeks the market for this it could be so expensive for a public library that it will be out of our reach," says Sari Feldman, executive director of the Cuyahoga County Public Library in suburban Cleveland and executive president-elect of the Public Library Association.

Feldman is also concerned that the one terminal per building where Google will provide free access to its database "is not nearly going to satisfy the customer demand we have," especially since the agreement does not permit the database to be accessed remotely from library members' homes.

According to Clancy, the free terminal is intended to help libraries that can't afford the institutional subscription and could be expanded later. "It's a start," he says. University libraries that purchase subscriptions will be allowed to provide remote access to students and faculty. By contrast, K-12 school libraries will not have access to a free terminal; they will have to purchase a subscription. Nor will they be able to provide remote access to students and teachers; readers will have to use the database on school property to access full-length copyrighted works that are out of print. (In comments filed with the court, the American Library Association and Association of Research Libraries cite these differences as inequities between K-12 schools and higher education institutions that could deepen the "digital divide.")[15]

Google has discretion as to which books it copies, and under the agreement it does not have to make public its entire list of scanned books.[16] "A foreign government might put pressure on Google to exclude books about the Armenian genocide or [the 1989 protest at Beijing's] Tiananmen Square," library association attorney Band observes. And if Google has employees in those countries, Google might agree to leave those books out. "You could have a very important research base with holes dictated by foreign governments," he says.

Parties to the settlement — the American Association of Publishers and the Authors Guild — defend the agreement, maintaining that without Google such a vast digital library would never have existed.

"Wouldn't it be much better if the Library of Congress had done this? Yeah, probably it would have," said Patricia Schroeder, outgoing president of the publishers' association and a former Democratic congresswoman from Colorado. "But they didn't have the money to do it, and they didn't do it, and the libraries have copies of everything now. What do we do at this point as rights holders?"[17]

Before Google started scanning library books in 2004, even well-endowed libraries were digitizing less than 10,000 volumes per year — a rate Google ratcheted up to tens of thousands of volumes per week, observes University of Michigan librarian Paul Courant.

In his article, Darnton charged that the special status granted Google under the settlement dashes the Enlightenment philosophers' dream of establishing a Republic of Letters, in which anyone who could read would have access to the entire universe of knowledge. But Courant retorts: "In the absence of the settlement, we would not have the digitized infrastructure to support the 21st century Republic of Letters."[18]

Will traditional print books disappear from the marketplace?

The mother of a 10-year-old boy recently described the way her son reads a printed book: "He'll put the book down and go to the book's Web site. Then, he'll check what other readers are writing in the forums, and maybe leave a message himself, then return to the book. He'll put the book down again and Google a query that's occurred to him."

This description was recently posted on the Web by Bob Stein, founder and co-director of the Institute for the Future of the Book, a think tank based in New York and London. He suggested that "we change our description of reading to include the full range of these activities, not just time spent looking at the printed page."[19]

In Stein's view, as electronic books start to have links to yet more references and multimedia enrichment, the centrality of printed books in our culture will fade. "They'll stop being the principal way people exchange ideas," he predicts. "That role is shifting to things happening on screens on our desks or in our pockets. In all likelihood the future of the book is as an art object — beautiful objects that look like books — not what most of us will use as the way we take ideas from the culture."

Despite such futuristic scenarios, e-books — the main form in which digital books are sold — remain less than 1 percent of the entire U.S. book market, and some in the industry are skeptical that e-books will ever take over.

"When I first came to this job [more than eight years ago], people were predicting that e-books were here and any minute they would be taking over the world," says outgoing AAP president Schroeder. "The other thing people would tell me is, 'I don't know why you're going into books. Young people want whistles and bells and noise.' Then along came *Harry Potter*." As for e-books, "it's been a lot slower conversion than many people thought."

Publishing consultant Shatzkin agrees. "We're having a lot of conversation about something that doesn't have a lot of commercial heft right now," he says. "This is not a profit center for anybody in regular book publishing yet; this is still an experimental investment." As an example, he points to Amazon's policy of pricing most of its bestselling Kindle books at $9.99, significantly below publishers' retail prices, which means the company is taking a loss.

Some in the industry think 2009 will be the year that changes all that, with the introduction of the Kindle 2.0 and DX, the availability of Kindle books on the iPhone and Google Book Search's deal to provide millions of books to the Sony Reader. A new, lightweight, large-format reader, which feels like a plastic sheet of paper, Plastic Logic Reader, is due for commercial release next year.[20]

Yet skeptics note that electronic readers are expensive, and many find them annoying to use. On-demand publishers think digital will take over in another way — by making it possible to print out books on demand from digital files. For Taylor it means glorified printers at central plants; for Epstein it means ATMs for books widely distributed at bookstores, hotels, airports, cruise ships and remote locations in Africa and Asia.

If there's consensus, it's that non-fiction references like encyclopedias, atlases and dictionaries will continue to migrate online, where they can be updated continually, and where community efforts like Wikipedia have benefited from many contributors.

Whether read on screen or on paper, the classical book format has a much better chance of survival than newspapers and magazines, because books don't have advertisers to lose or subscribers they need to hold onto, according to Peter Osnos, founder of the independent publisher PublicAffairs.[21]

By the early 2000s, well over 30 percent of all books were publishers' excess inventory — largely the result of their policy that books shipped to retailers could be returned for full credit, Osnos observes. The costs in wasted paper, manufacturing, packing, shipping and the glut of remaindered books all depress profits.

That will begin to change after the current recession, Osnos predicts, now that digital technology for reading, listening and printing on demand is becoming easier to use. In the future, he predicts, bookstores will become mainly showrooms — places "to engage in the time-honored pleasures of browsing and conversation, with reading and discussion groups, author visits and a renewed commitment to customer service."

An even more radical future is seen in China and India, countries without sophisticated publishing distribution. They may skip the traditional book stage entirely and move directly into electronic readers with purchasing enabled by their extensive cell phone network — much the way Kindle users buy books — to wirelessly download and purchase books; Amazon provides a free, perpetual cell phone subscription to Kindle users for this purpose.

In his 2008 book *Books as History*, David Pearson, director of the University of London Research Libraries, argues that books as owned objects have been important for historical research and may continue to be — at least if book owners still write in the margins. For example, by recording who the owners were and their margin notes on all surviving copies of the first two editions of Copernicus' *De Revolutionibus*, scholar Owen Gingerich was able to show how quickly Copernicus' heliocentric ideas were accepted (or not) by 16th-century astronomers across Europe.[22]

Although many find the prospect of vast digital libraries that can be accessed on screens exciting, others see dire consequences if printed books are abandoned entirely in favor of digital storehouses.

Computers crash, they argue, and obsolescent digital information in the form of, say, old floppy disks sometimes can't be accessed with modern computers.

"Imagine if all the printed books disappeared," says Epstein. "If we blew a fuse, we'd all be savages again. Whoever we are is in these books."

Will literary reading and writing survive online?

The success of Wikipedia, written by thousands around the world, suggests that collaborative or "networked" books could be the wave of the future — at least in non-fiction. But what about fiction?

In a recent post, Stein of the Institute for the Future of the Book suggests that novels will no longer be the dominant form of fiction in the future but will be replaced by something that looks more like the multi-player online game "World of Warcraft." Its 10 million subscribers assemble into teams of 30 or more to accomplish specific goals.

"It's not a big leap to think of the person who developed the game as an author whose art is conceiving, designing and building a virtual world in which players (readers) don't merely watch or read the narrative" but actually contribute to it, Stein writes. In this vision, digital fiction would include video, sound and readers' comments.[23]

Many readers and publishers react in horror to the idea of communal creativity — what happens to the single, narrative voice that creates a world of the imagination into which the reader can plunge?

And what author would want to participate? As writer Cory Doctorow commented on Stein's post, "many authors lack the capacity to interact with their audiences. They are grumpy. To publish these authors successfully, publishers will either have to hire 'ghost-bloggers' or give them charm lessons."[24]

Already there have been several closely watched experiments online. In 2007 Penguin Books sponsored a wiki-novel writing experiment, *A Million Penguins*, written by hundreds of readers collaborating online. Penguin CEO John Makinson called it "not the most read, but possibly the most written novel in history."

Penguin kicked the novel off on a special Web site with the opening line from Charlotte Bronte's classic

The Long Tail Phenomenon

How "low-sellers" revolutionized bookselling.

In 2001 the first so-called digital natives came of age. Children who had started using the Internet in 1995 at age 12 turned 18, graduating into the 18-34-year-old demographic most sought after by advertisers. But they were fundamentally different from previous generations — TV viewership in their age bracket dropped for the first time in half a century.[1]

Instead they were occupying an online space where "niche economics rule," in the words of *Wired* magazine editor-in-chief Chris Anderson, using blogs and Web sites rather than mass-audience TV to explore interests and buy products.

In an October 2004 article in *Wired* (expanded into a 2006 book), Anderson introduced the term "The Long Tail," now widely used in the publishing and digital industries. He pointed out that the traditional marketing strategy of focusing on best-sellers at the top of the demand curve was missing the many low-sellers, which form the endlessly "long tail" of the same demand curve.[2] (*See graph, at right.*)

When aggregated, the low-sellers make up a big portion of the market, Anderson argued — a market that the new online sellers were uniquely positioned to take advantage of. For example, he pointed out that one-quarter of Amazon's book sales came outside their top 100,000 titles.[3]

Anderson credits Jeff Bezos with being the first to test this idea when he launched Amazon in 1995. Amazon uses online retail to aggregate a large inventory of low-sellers. At the time, even superstores carried only about 10 percent of the titles available in English.

Unlike brick-and-mortar retailers, Amazon didn't have to worry about filling up shelf space in valuable real estate. And with no shelf space to pay for, a niche product is just another sale with the same or better margins than a hit, Anderson points out.

The 1988 low-seller *Touching the Void* is an example of how specialist niches help unknown books. By 2004 it was outselling Jon Krakauer's best-seller *Into Thin Air* on the same subject of mountain climbing tragedies, because of word of mouth and Amazon reader reviews.

The long tail phenomenon affected other aspects of the book business, too. In 1997 Alibris was launched as an online retailer for used books. It aggregated the inventories of some 12,000 used-book stores and made the database available to Amazon and Barnes & Noble's bn.com, bringing millions of users to the used-book market. Even though

The Impact of 'Low-Sellers'

Best-sellers sell the most copies and make the most money. While books far down on the sales charts sell fewer copies and make less money individually, they bring in a large portion of total publishing revenue because so many so-called low-sellers (the long tail of the graph) are sold overall.

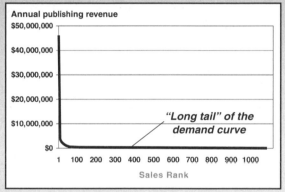

Source: Book Industry Study Group

used books are usually sold one at a time, Alibris was soon growing at double digits.

The long tail phenomenon has tapped into a growing community of people interested not only in consuming but also producing information about a huge range of topics, many of them obscure. In 2001, Jimmy Wales, a wealthy options trader, came up with the idea of getting millions of amateur experts to create an online encyclopedia, using a software application called wiki. Wikipedia was a far cry from the *Encyclopaedia Britannica*, which recruited experts to write its entries. Yet by 2005, Wikipedia had become the largest encyclopedia on the planet, with more than 1 million articles compared to the *Britannica*'s 80,000.[4]

---

[1] Chris Anderson, *The Long Tail* (2006), p. 95.

[2] *Ibid.* Also see Chris Anderson, "The Long Tail," *Wired*, October 2004, www.wired.com/wired/archive/12.10/tail.html.

[3] Anderson, *The Long Tail*, *op. cit.*, p. 23.

[4] *Ibid.*, p. 66.

Jane Eyre: "There was no possibility of taking a walk that day."

"Within about five minutes it had completely changed. We had 1,500 edits the first couple of days," recalls Bruce Mason, a research fellow at the University of Edinburgh specializing in folklore who helped to run the experiment. So many people tried to get onto the site in the first few days the server was overwhelmed, and the project had to be moved to another. At first, vandals tried to delete much of the novel, and along the way some contributors insisted on reshaping the plot continually according to their liking.

When the wiki-novel finally closed on March 7, 2007, at least 75,000 different people had viewed the site. Of those, 1,476 people had registered as users of the wiki. The ultimate, chaotic product, which involved 11,000 edits and 1,500 pages, wasn't really literature, most observers agreed, but it demonstrated the way that passionate, online literary communities can form.[25]

"The final product itself . . . is more akin to something produced by the wild, untrammeled creativity of the folk imagination," researchers Mason and Sue Thomas, professor of new media at Britain's De Montfort University, Leicester, wrote, describing it as "rude, chaotic, grotesque, sporadically brilliant, anti-authoritarian and, in places, devastatingly funny. As a cultural text it is unique, and it demonstrates the tremendous potential of this form to provide a stimulating social setting for writing, editing and publishing."[26]

Yet the narrative didn't really hold together as a single story line, and the writing varied from "exciting and talented to really bad clichés," according to Mason.

"I don't really think the wiki novel makes sense," says Thomas, who co-authored the research report and helped run the experiment. "A novel has to be quite controlled. We didn't produce a novel; we produced something fascinating."

In another Penguin-sponsored exercise, an award-winning novelist was asked to write a detective-story version of *Alice's Adventures in Wonderland*, to which readers were invited to contribute. Readers searched for clues hidden on Craigslist and other Internet sites, interacting in real time with the novelist/narrator to give her solutions to the mystery.

The result: a charming story, written with a sly slant. Unlike *A Million Penguins*, it succeeded as a coherent story — probably because the novelist had ultimate control over how the story was composed and which contributions to incorporate. (*See sidebar, p. 78.*)

Publishers are experimenting with these new formats because they think the younger generation reads in a fundamentally different way from older generations, requiring more multimedia content and more participation, says Pan MacMillan digital publisher Bhaskar.

Networked books (like *A Million Penguins*) are "quite a nebulous concept in that nobody really knows exactly what one might look like. Almost by definition it's an experiment," says Bhaskar. And with the current recession, "I think right now the climate is less forgiving for these eye-catching, high-profile experiments that have no revenue stream attached."

And so far, even in networked book communities, barely 1 percent of those who sign on tend to be interested in actively contributing; the rest just read what's going on.[27]

University of Chicago sociologist Wendy Griswold thinks there will continue to be readers of print books, but they will be an elite reading class that is highly educated, older and predominantly female — much like today's core group of book buyers.

Surprisingly, though, a similar demographic group has been drawn to the Kindle. The largest group of Kindle owners is middle-aged (56-64 years old) and includes slightly more women than men, according to a survey of 120,000 book purchasers presented by Bowker at the London Book Fair on April 19.[28] (Men are more frequent adaptors of the iPhone, the survey found.)

And other traditional literature is migrating onto the new screens.

Narrative — an online literary magazine that publishes stories by celebrated veterans like Joyce Carol Oates as well as new talents — has become the first literary magazine available on Kindle.

If readers are going to be viewing literature on a screen no bigger than a beer coaster, the writing needs "to be sharper, smarter and more economically and elegantly expressed than ever," writes Philip Gwyn Jones, publisher of Granta and Portobello books. In his view, most of the debate so far is about "transport methods" rather than the cargo being shipped. "Everyone wants to be captivated by a great story or a great argument."[29]

Mary Harrington, an associate at the Institute for the Future of the Book in London, is more skeptical that long-form fiction will migrate from print to digital. "The Internet is very good for conversation, but once the conversation's been had, it makes sense to finalize it in print," she says. She points to the new science fiction novel *Playing for Keeps*, by Mur Lafferty.[30] It started out as free digital content (in this case podcasts), built up an online community and then became a print book.

The physical nature of a book gives it qualities that are completely inverted when it comes to the Internet, Harrington points out. As a fixed entity between covers, a book must limit and choose its words carefully. Its authorial voice has made the book authoritative ever since the creation of sacred works like the Bible, and its message can be universal.

By contrast, Harrington says, the Internet is "boundless, never authoritative — there's always someone who has something to add," on a blog or a Web site. "And it's never universal," since writers online are writing for fragmented audiences. "Because the Internet is boundless, intangible and not edited, you can never publish the definitive anything online."

BACKGROUND

In the Beginning

The Greek philosopher Socrates (469-399 B.C.) lamented the loss of knowledge because the media of transmission were changing. Before the invention of the Greek alphabet 2,500 years ago, knowledge and stories were recited aloud, much like Homer's epic poem *The Odyssey.*

The new technology of writing meant stories no longer needed to be memorized, a development Socrates feared would weaken the Greeks' mental capacities for memorizing and retelling. (Paradoxically, we only know about Socrates' concerns because they were written down by his student Plato in his famous *Dialogues.*)[31]

The shape of contemporary books can be traced to the invention of the "codex" — parchment pages bound together between covers, initially made of wood or leather and later of cloth. The form proved usable and durable, and sometimes labor-intensive. The great texts of Greek learning, Christian theology and medieval literature were preserved through laborious hand copying by library scribes and monks.

The next revolution for books came with the 15th-century invention of printing with changeable type. The invention is attributed to German metalsmith Johannes Gutenberg, who cast type in molds using a melted metal alloy and constructed a wooden-screw printing press to transfer the image onto paper.

Gutenberg's first and only large-scale printing effort was the now iconic Gutenberg Bible in the 1450s — a Latin translation from the Hebrew Oldament and the Greek Newament, copies of which can be viewed on the British Library Web site. Gutenberg's invention made mass production of texts possible for the first time. Although the Gutenberg Bible itself was stratospherically expensive, printed books began to spread widely over European trade routes during the next 50 years, and by the 1500s printed books had become more widely accessible and less costly.[32]

By the 17th century, books were being printed by the thousands, instead of hundreds. By this time, too, America had its first printers — in Boston, Cambridge and Philadelphia.

By the 19th century, publishing was an established industry in both Europe and the United States, and publishing houses emerged that dealt in a general book list, which they sold to a growing mass market of readers.

Golden Age

From its origins more than two centuries ago, the American publishing industry has followed a historic pattern that has varied little: Copy is delivered to a printer who ships inventory to a publisher's warehouse from which it is sent to bookstores.[33]

Technological developments have made the process more efficient: Steam presses were invented in 1810, and stereotype plates developed in 1846 made it possible to produce longer runs at less cost per copy. The type produced printed sheets that were then folded, sewn together and bound, much as in Gutenberg's times.

Much as today's traditionalists fear the disappearance of print books, there were those who decried what they saw as the mediocrity of machine-made books. The private hand-press movement began in the 19th century as a reaction to the loss of this craft, led by Arts and Crafts

19th Century *Publishing becomes an established industry in Europe and the United States; modern presses speed printing and reduce the cost of books.*

1810 Steam press invented.

1817 Harper Brothers, one of the nation's earliest publishers, begins as a New York printer.

1850 By mid-century, New York is shipping millions of books to the rest of the country.

1891 International Copyright Act passed by Congress extending protection to foreign copyright holders.

1920s-1930s *Readership expands during golden age of publishing.*

1926 Book of the Month Club founded.

1928 Random House founded.

1939 Pocket Books launched, introducing paperbacks.

1960s-1980s *Mergers and takeovers by conglomerates combined with migration of Americans from cities to suburbs kill downtown bookstores and large inventories.*

1965 RCA acquires Random House.

1975 Gulf & Western Industries acquires Simon & Schuster.

1980 German publisher Bertelsmann acquires Bantam, later Dell, Doubleday and Random House.

1989 Rupert Murdoch's News Corp. acquires HarperCollins.

1990s *Publishing industry becomes more concentrated; World Wide Web introduces digital reading, online bookstores.*

1994 Viacom acquires Simon & Schuster.

1995 Amazon founded as online bookstore. . . . Germany's Holtzbrinck Group acquires St. Martin's Press.

1997 Alibris, an online retailer for used books, launched.

1998 Bertelsmann acquires Random House, making half of top 20 U.S. publishers foreign-owned.

2000s *New electronic readers like Kindle and iPhone boost e-book sales.*

2000 Best-selling American author Stephen King publishes novella *Riding the Bullet* solely in electronic form.

2001 Wikipedia, an online encyclopedia written by readers, is launched; first "digital natives," who used computers at age 12, turn 18.

2004 *Wired* magazine editor Chris Anderson publishes seminal article about "The Long Tail" in publishing.

2007 Penguin sponsors online wiki-novel, *A Million Penguins.* Hundreds contribute, 75,000 view it.

2008 Google reaches landmark settlement over book scanning. . . . Troubled publishing industry hit with layoffs and pay freezes on "Black Wednesday" (Dec. 3). . . . Amazon's Kindle sells out in United States by Christmas.

2009 American Association of Publishers announces 2008 book revenue dropped 2.8 percent from 2007. . . . Book Industry Study Group reports 1.5 percent fewer books were sold in the U.S. in 2008 than in 2007, for a total of 3.1 billion books sold, including e-books and traditional trade, educational and professional books. . . . Amazon launches Kindle 2.0 (February) and large-screen Kindle DX. . . . Google announces deal to provide 500,000 e-books to Sony Reader. . . . University of Michigan announces its scholarly publications will be digital only. . . . More than 1.7 million people have downloaded Stanza reading applications onto an iPhone. . . . Scribd.com launches online vanity press (May 18). . . . On Oct. 7, 2009, the U.S. District Court for the Southern District of New York will hold a hearing to accept or reject the Google Book Search settlement with authors and publishers. . . . After one year on the market, Apple-based e-book reader Stanza tops 4 million downloads (July 13).

Feb. 18, 2010 — District Court in New York conducts hearing on proposed amended Google Book Settlement with authors and publishers on book copyright ownership.

July 19, 2010 — Amazon reports e-book sales surpass those of hardcovers.

August-September 2010 — Court decision expected in Google Book Settlement.

Print-on-Demand Flips Traditional Publishing Model

'Sell first, then print' is publisher's new motto.

When Sarah Palin was picked last August as Sen. John McCain's presidential running mate, the publisher of the only existing biography of the once-obscure Alaskan governor found itself in a quandary. Printing more copies on a traditional offset press would have taken weeks — and missed the sales window for the book.

Instead, Epicenter Press turned to a leading print-on-demand company. Within a few hours of receiving a digital file, Lightning Source was producing copies of *Sarah* on its giant, high-quality laser printers, and within days — not weeks — it had 30,000 copies.[1]

A sudden spike in demand is only one of the ways that traditional publishers are starting to use print-on-demand (POD). More than a decade ago, Ingram Book Group, the word's leading book wholesaler, was trying to cut down on the unsold books crowding its warehouse. Out of this need it created a company that would print books from digital files only when Ingram needed them.

Today that company, Lightning Source, makes a profit printing an average order of only 1.8 books — capitalizing on the "long tail" phenomenon, in which individual orders for unpopular books add up to a lot of sales.

Print-on-demand technology is best known for fueling the recent explosion in self-publishing. Authors who can't break into mainstream publishing get their book listed on Amazon or another database, usually expecting to sell only a few copies to their friends and families, each one printed in response to an order.

But increasingly, large publishing houses and retailers like Amazon are also using print-on-demand to fill orders when books are out of stock or out of print.

As David Taylor, president of Lightning Source, puts it, print-on-demand reverses the traditional sequence of printing, warehousing and then selling. Instead, his motto is "sell first, then print."

Now the world's leading POD printer, Lightning Source more than doubled its monthly printing volume from 600,000 books in 2005 to more than 1.4 million last year.

The company's plant in Milton Keynes, a sprawling "new town" 60 miles northwest of London, produces a stunningly eclectic variety of books. A single copy of an accounting dictionary in Spanish was pumped out right after eight copies of *E-business in Healthcare* and *Multivariate Density Estimation*.

"I've been amazed at the most obscure books that someone wants to read," says Taylor. Many of those titles would be dead without print-on-demand, he says, because "you would never print them speculatively" hoping for a sale.

Only about 40 percent of Lightning Source's production is for mainstream publishers; the remainder is for non-traditional publishers like self-publishers, micro-publishers with as few as one or two titles and content aggregators like bibliolife.com, which offers out-of-print books that are printed only in response to an order.

Despite the significant cost savings to be gained from avoiding storing, shipping and pulping unsold books, mainstream publishers have been slow to adopt print-on-demand, mainly because the printing cost per book is higher — especially for best-sellers. Many publishers also have sunk costs in warehousing or haven't realized that there are potential cost savings, according to industry analysts.

However, some publishers aiming for a small, professional readership in areas like medicine and accounting, as well as some academic presses, are going straight to print-on-demand, because it is economical for small printings.

POD has also stimulated some innovative new uses: Readers can assemble their favorite articles from Wikipedia or Wikitravel, for example, and have them bound in a customized book by the German company PediaPress.[2]

Digital printing now accounts for only about 1-3 percent of all the books printed in North America, but the business is projected to grow 15-20 percent over the next three years, according to Gilles Biscos, president of Interquest, a market research company in Charlottesville, Va.

Increasingly, Lightning Source's business is shifting toward traditional publishers as they rethink the way they do business, according to Taylor. He thinks this trend will continue, particularly in an economic climate where publishers are looking to cut costs wherever possible.

---

[1] "Gov. Sarah Palin Biography brought to market by Epicenter Press and Ingram Content Companies," Lightning Source press release, Sept. 2, 2008.

[2] http://pediapress.com.

CQ Press/Sarah Glazer

The Lightning Source print-on-demand company prints some 1.4 million volumes a month. About 40 percent of the printing is for mainstream publishers, but President David Taylor, above, at the plant in Milton Keynes, outside London, expects the percentage to increase as publishers revamp the way they do business. Digital printing now accounts for only about 1-3 percent of all the books printed in North America, but the business is projected to grow 15-20 percent over the next three years.

artists like William Morris, and such works continue to be valued by collectors.[34]

Harper Brothers, one of the earliest American publishers, began as a New York printer in 1817. The firm was soon competing with other printers to ship books via the Erie Canal, which gave New York printers an advantage over competitors in Boston and Philadelphia, and helped turn New York into publishing's center.

American publishers made a brisk business of publishing pirated works by British authors like Charles Dickens, William Thackeray and the Bronte sisters throughout most of the 19th century, ignoring international copyright. By the 1840s, the American market had become big enough for Dickens to cross the ocean to protest the theft of his property, but his plea for copyright protection was ignored.[35]

Soon after, however, American authors asked for protection for their own works in foreign editions. By the end of the century Congress had passed the International Copyright Act, which allowed publishers to contract for exclusive rights to the works of British and other foreign writers and earn a profit from them.

By the 1850s, New York publishers were shipping millions of books to the rest of the country.

The 1920s have been called "the golden age" of American publishing. The firms that were launched in the '20s were still run by some of these distinctive personalities in the 1950s. Bennett Cerf founded Random House. Richard Simon, Max Schuster and Alfred A. Knopf all founded houses that bear their names. They introduced to American readers many of the great modernist writers of the time, from James Joyce to Gertrude Stein. Thousands of bookstores in towns and cities were the main distribution channel for these writers.

Publishers also saw a growing readership for their books as U.S. illiteracy declined from 7.7 percent in 1910 to 2.9 percent in 1940. School enrollments and libraries grew, and the increasingly urbanized nation created receptive homes for bookstores. Book readership also expanded through the Book of the Month Club, founded in 1926, and paperback books, launched by Pocket Books in 1939.

The explosion in recreational reading was an historical exception to a tradition in which reading had been limited to elites — and it didn't last, argues University of Chicago sociologist Griswold. "The period from the mid-19th to mid-20th century was unusual because you had high, universal literacy and a middle class, but you didn't have a lot of alternatives" for entertainment, she says. By the 1950s TV began to erode the primacy of reading as entertainment. "We're returning to a period where lots of reading is a minority pastime," she says, even though many people read for work and online.

Decline of the Backlist

By the mid 1970s, as American book customers migrated from the city to the suburbs, the great downtown bookstores with their large "backlists" — inventories of books other than new releases and current bestsellers — began to disappear.

Bookstores cropping up in shopping centers now had the same limited space and high rent as the clothing store next door and needed the same quick turnover — forcing them to focus on best-selling authors and books by celebrities. By the 1980s, backlists were in steep decline. Thousands of titles disappeared into the "orphan" category — no longer in print but still in copyright.

In the 1950s, no publisher survived without its backlist, and best-sellers were viewed as lucky accidents, according to former Random House editorial director Epstein, who first worked for Doubleday in the 1950s. "Publishers depended on the existence of thousands of independent bookstores that knew how to sell backlist," he recalls. In Epstein's view, the steep decline in backlists turned the industry upside down, forcing publishers to shave their profits by vying for best-selling authors with unrealistically high advances and guarantees.

Such difficulties forced increasing consolidation of the industry. But the big entertainment conglomerates — CBS, ABC, RCA and MCA-Universal — that acquired publishing houses in the 1970s and '80s found them a burden on the balance sheets and sold them off.[36]

Between 1986 and 1996, 63 of the 100 best-selling titles were written by only six writers — Tom Clancy, John Grisham, Stephen King, Dean Koontz, Michael Crichton and Danielle Steel. Publishers often sacrificed much of their normal profit and incurred losses to keep these highly successful authors.[37]

"Publishing was never a profitable business," says Epstein. "You didn't do it to make money; you did it as a vocation."

By the beginning of the 21st century, U.S. publishing was dominated by five financial empires: the German conglomerates Bertelsmann, which had acquired the Random House group, and Holtzbrinck, which now owns St. Martin's and Farrar, Straus and Giroux; London-based Longmans, Pearson (owner of Viking, Penguin, Putnam and Dutton); Rupert Murdoch's News Corp., which owns HarperCollins and William Morrow, and Viacom, which had taken over Simon & Schuster and Pocket Books.[38]

Dawn of the Digital Revolution

In the 1990s as the World Wide Web's popularity grew, entrepreneurs began jockeying to use Web sites to reach millions of customers at little cost — driving the first dot.com bubble from the mid-1990s to its collapse in 2000. By the end of the '90s, the publishing world was filled with speculation about electronic books and Internet publishing.

At the time, industry analysts optimistically predicted the nascent e-book market would reach $2.5 billion by 2002. But the market remained remarkably sluggish until recent years. Even by 2006, it had increased to a total of only about $20 million, from $7 million in 2003.[39]

Publishers also hoped to make money selling CD-ROMs (acronym for "compact disc: read-only memory"). Although the CD encyclopedia *Encarta* proved popular

at first, CD-ROMs failed to become significant sellers. After the CD-ROM bubble burst, "a widespread cynicism arose about digital publishing, which has continued among publishers into the networked era and has only begun to adjust," write Harrington and Meade in a recent report on digital possibilities for literature.[40]

CURRENT SITUATION

Publishing Woes

Some observers think the tough times for publishing signal the end of traditional ways of doing business, not just a temporary reaction to the recession.

Last November, Houghton Mifflin Harcourt — whose authors include literary giants such as Philip Roth, Gunter Grass and J.R.R. Tolkien — was awash in so much debt that it announced an unprecedented buying freeze on new manuscripts.[41] At the time, other houses had also frozen acquisitions unofficially.[42]

Then on Dec. 3 — dubbed Black Wednesday — Penguin and HarperCollins announced pay freezes. The same day Random House announced it was dissolving Doubleday and Bantam Dell and distributing their remainders among the conglomerate's other three publishing groups, ultimately causing more layoffs.[43]

"To be a journalist or author these days in America is to be a lumberjack in Wisconsin in the 1930s or a steelworker in Pennsylvania in the 1980s or an auto worker in Michigan, well, right now. It is to be watching your industry, and indeed your way of life, collapsing around you," Samuel Freedman, an author and professor at the Columbia School of Journalism, recently wrote.[44]

In recent years the U.S. book market as a whole has remained relatively static at 3 billion books sold annually. At the end of last year, book revenues tracked by the American Association of Publishers were down 2.8 percent from 2007.[45]

The continuing trend towards conglomerates got some of the blame. In 2006 an Irish firm, Riverkeep, bought Houghton Mifflin and by July 2007 had taken over one of Mifflin's largest rivals, Harcourt, in a $4 billion acquisition that left the parent company billions of dollars in debt.

"There were hedge fund guys with no background in publishing buying up publishing houses," New Press

Reading Devices, Here and Now

More than 1.7 million users of the Apple iPhone (top) have downloaded Stanza software, which permits them to read a book on their cell phone from a selection of more than 100,000 titles. In March Google announced plans to offer its more than half a million digitized public-domain books on the Sony Reader (bottom).

Founder Andre Schiffrin told *Salon.* In his view, corporate owners expected unheard-of 15-20 percent profit margins in an industry with traditional margins of 3 to 4 percent.[46]

The practice at Barnes & Noble and Borders of requiring publishers to pay "co-op" fees to get their books placed prominently in a store also pinches publishers' profits. American publishers' practice of accepting returned books from stores for full credit has become another major expense; returns now represent nearly 40 percent of all hardbacks shipped.[47]

While the big book chains have been blamed for driving out small bookshops and squeezing publishers, they're now having their own problems. Borders hovers near bankruptcy, after investing heavily in music sections just as CDs were going out of style. By February, Barnes & Noble's stock price had fallen by more than half in the previous 18 months, triggering job cutbacks.[48]

Meanwhile the Internet has been invading newspapers' book reviewing territory, with a flourishing dialogue on literary blogs. Two years ago, bloggers were already reporting that they were being courted by publishers sending them pre-publication galleys in hopes of a mention. As of mid-May, only two newspapers still had separate book-review sections: *The New York Times* and *The San Francisco Chronicle.*[49]

Reference books also have been badly hit by Wikipedia and other free works on the Web. Estimates of online retailers' current share of the U.S. market are as high as 30 percent. Their heavy discounting further squeezes publishers' profit margins and spells more difficulty for brick-and-mortar bookshops.

Revolutionary Changes

This past year, almost every month seemed to herald a revolutionary development in the still small but growing e-books market.

In February, Amazon launched a sleeker version of its $359 Kindle, with wireless access to more than 230,000 electronic books. The following month Google announced plans to offer its more than half a million digitized public-domain books on the Sony Reader device. Industry analysts described the two deals as jockeying by industry giants to make their device the iPod of books.[50]

But some were betting on another horse. At year's end, *Forbes* magazine declared Apple's iPhone the most popular e-reader, given that 395,000 users had downloaded the Stanza reading application, which enables the downloading of 100,000 book titles — half of them for free.[51]

Now more than 1.7 million unique users have downloaded Stanza — along with more than 7 million e-books — according to Lexcycle, Stanza's maker. On April 27, Amazon purchased Lexcycle, leading some industry observers to suggest that Amazon really seeks to dominate the entire electronic books market, not just Kindle devices.[52]

Is iPhone the most popular e-reader? It's hard to say because rival companies like Amazon won't say how many Kindles they've sold. But industry analysts say up to 500,000 Kindles were sold last year, and up to a million of both versions have been sold so far.[53] As of mid-March, Sony had sold 400,000 of its $350 Readers.[54]

Stanza is only one of several reading applications accessible to iPhone users (owners can also download Kindle and Google books, among others), which suggests even more iPhone users are reading on their phones. But most e-book reading still occurs on laptops or desktops, according to the recent Bowker survey, which found 48 percent of all e-book purchases are for PCs. The survey found the Kindle came in second at 22 percent, followed by the iPhone at 10 percent.

But how many people want to read a book on a tiny screen? When Lexcycle CEO Neelan Choksi is confronted with that question, he retorts, "Aren't you the same person who read 50 e-mails on your BlackBerry yesterday?" And some users say they find the crisp iPhone screen with its ability to choose 125 background colors easier to read than the gray and black Kindle.

Most people will go back home to get it if they've forgotten their cell phone, not so likely with a Kindle, Choksi points out. "If you're 30 or under, you're used to reading blogs and Facebook on your cell phone already."

The ultimate reader, Choksi thinks, will have to be "something with the convenience of the iPhone." (Unique uses reported in Stanza's customer survey included in the bathroom at work and on a submarine.) "It has to have color and be multifunctional; it will have to have video." All the content you get on your PC, not just books, will have to be available through it, Choksi believes.

Mary Klement, a San Diego engineer who travels frequently, has 150 books loaded onto her iPod Touch, which she also uses to watch her favorite HBO series while flying and to check e-mail. She likes the convenience of always having a "book" with her that's easy to hold in her palm while waiting at the airport baggage claim. She can download books anywhere in the world where there's a wireless Internet connection — an advantage over the Kindle, which only works over Sprint's U.S. cell phone network.

With so much activity, e-books are "getting closer to a tipping point" for market success, says Smith at the International Digital Publishing Forum.

E-book retail sales last year increased 68 percent over 2007 to an estimated total of $107 million, according to the organization. (*See graph, p. 60.*) But that doesn't include some of the largest publishers that have been reporting triple-digit growth, according to Smith. Nor does it include library or higher-education sales, sectors that both boast twice the electronic sales of trade publishers. Meanwhile, Overdrive, a leading seller of e-books to libraries, logged 10 million downloads in 2008.

In addition, e-books' fourth-quarter sales doubled last year over the same period in 2007, Smith pointed out, and this January sales jumped 174 percent over the first month of last year. Penguin announced its e-book sales jumped 500 percent in 2008 over the previous year, although e-book sales are still less than 1 percent of total revenue.[55] Random House and Simon & Schuster also expected e-book revenue to at least double.[56]

"I don't think the traditional print book will be replaced, but I do expect reading habits of the younger generation will change," says Smith. "My 9-year-old gets in the car and wants the Sony Reader all the time; she reads her *Nancy Drew* titles on it."

Appealing to Youths

Publishers are enticing young readers using combinations of Web content and books. For instance, Scholastic's *The 39 Clues* — aimed at 9-12-year-olds — combines online game playing and card collecting with a series of traditional books; its first one, *Maze of Bones*, became a bestseller.[57]

Penguin's children's division ran a month-long giveaway of Johan Flanagan's *The Ruins of Gorlan*, which included posting downloadable e-books on Scribd.com (a YouTube for books); in the first two weeks, 20,000 people downloaded the book.[58]

Just this winter, HarperCollins started releasing e-book versions along with its new print titles for children in six e-book formats including Kindle and Sony Reader.[59] The top three novels downloaded from libraries last year were from Stephenie Meyer's popular teen vampire *Twilight* series, according to library distributor Overdrive.[60]

Aiming for the millions of Nintendo DS machines in British children's hands, HarperCollins launched its *100 Classic Book Collection* in December, making 100 classics from *Romeo and Juliet* to *Treasure Island* readable on the portable devices. The publisher has sold 200,000 copies

Writing a Tale With Help From Your Readers

Readers collaborate with novelist to create a modern take on Alice in Wonderland.

"I looked at the black mirror, and suddenly it was like I was falling into a dream." Alice Klein is a character in a novel who suffers from writer's block — until she finds a strange, black mirror in the second-hand bookshop where she's working. When she looks into the mirror, it sends her into a trance and seems to get her writing again. But the mirror also turns out to have evil powers.

That's the plot real British novelist Naomi Alderman cooked up when Penguin Books asked her to write an online tale based on Lewis Carroll's classic, *Alice's Adventures in Wonderland.* [1]

But she didn't write the story by herself.

Over six weeks, Alderman posted (almost) daily blogs written in the voice of her protagonist, Alice Klein. Readers were sent to six different locations on the Web to search for secret messages providing clues to the mystery of the mirror that Alice was trying to untangle. These ranged from answering an ad on Craigslist to showing up at a live event in London where readers could meet a character who had valuable information. Then they e-mailed helpful suggestions to the author.

At one point in the story, Alice decides to break into the offices of an evil doctor to steal the mirror. While Alice was attempting to break in, she asked readers — blogging live with her — to offer clues. "What buttons do you think I should press?" she asked when she reached a locked door with a mysterious design. Readers sent solutions. "You're all geniuses! It worked!" Alice responded.

Alderman calls this kind of writing a literary form that is in its infancy. But it has historical antecedents. The earliest English novels, Samuel Richardson's *Pamela* (1740) and *Clarissa* (1748), are told through characters writing letters in "real time." Dear reader, my pursuer is knocking at my door at this very moment!

"It was very exciting to be involved in something so new where you're making the rules as you're writing," Alderman says. "It's a different kind of writing; it's much more collaborative." Readers' suggestions about the direction of the plot ranged from great to "lousy," according to Alderman, who likened the activity to a chef choosing ingredients.

As the lead writer on the Alternate Reality Game "Perplex City," which has sent hundreds of players running around London searching for clues to a murder mystery, Alderman says the rewards in this kind of collaboration are different from writing novels. But she insists she enjoys both. Alderman won the distinguished Orange Prize for New Writers for her first novel, *Disobedience*, published in 2006, about growing up in an orthodox Jewish family in England.

"If I just sit in my house and write novels all day, eventually I go crazy because being alone with the imaginary people you've made up in your head does send you crazy," Alderman says. "But if I'm constantly working with other people, I begin to feel like I don't have any ownership over my own work, and that also sends me crazy."

of the collection, which can also play appropriate background music for about $23 extra.[61]

In February, Sourcebooks became the first major print publisher to release a digitally enhanced picture book. Readers of Laura Duksta's *I Love You More* can hear the voice of the mother and the son as they read along.[62]

The market position of e-books could be improved by the adoption last year of a uniform standard for e-books known as .epub, developed by Smith's organization. Usable on a variety of platforms, it saves publishers the cost of producing digital files in several different formats.

Some publishers see a big digital future. HarperCollins CEO Victoria Barnsley has estimated that "within 10 years more than half our sales will come from digital downloads."[63]

Last October, *Newsweek* announced it would publish four books about the presidential and vice presidential candidates, available only electronically on the Kindle.[64]

In March, the University of Michigan Press announced that it will shift its scholarly publishing from a primarily print operation to digital-only editions, although readers will be able to produce printed versions with print-on-demand systems.

What about the widely held view that art has to be the product of a single imagination?" I think we're a little too hung up on the idea of the artist as this magnificent individual with his or her magnificent genius that comes only from them and has nothing to do with the wider world," Alderman responds. "Actually, we're all products of the stories that we hear, of conversations and writers we've been exposed to."

She likens readers' real-time responses to the experience of a playwright, where the live audience responds to the words as they are spoken. Her "Alice in Storyland" had about 1,000 unique hits, with about 150 people actually contributing ideas, according to Alderman. In that sense, she says, it's similar to a magic show where only a few audience members will volunteer, "but it's quite fun to watch" everyone else.

"Alice in Storyland" is filled with sly references to the classic, starting with the character's names: Alice Klein (Klein means "little" in German/Yiddish) is a stand-in for Alice Liddell, the "little" girl for whom Carroll wrote the classic and who inspired the Alice of his *Wonderland* tales. Another character, Mr. Marsh Ayre, is reminiscent of the March hare.

In the last episode, Alice is awakened by a phone call from her agent congratulating her on writing her second novel — something she has no memory of writing — much the way the original Alice wakes from her Wonderland dream.

"Apparently I've written my second novel," she writes in her final blog post. "At least according to Penguin I have."

The link takes readers to a real Penguin Web site that seems to be selling a book entitled *A Trickle of Ink*, described as a "rip-roaring" instant classic by Alice Klein, complete with a price and reader review. [2] Except that no matter how

Getty Images/Chris Jackson

With help from online readers, British novelist Naomi Alderman wrote a tale based on Lewis Carroll's classic, *Alice's Adventures in Wonderland*.

hard you click, you can't buy the novel. Like Alice Klein, it doesn't really exist.

---

[1] http://wetellstories.co.uk. For "Alice in Storyland," see http://treacleandink.wordpress.com/category/uncategorized/.

[2] www.penguin.co.uk/nf/Book/BookDisplay/0,,9780141885025,00.html.

"Why try to remain in a territory you know is doomed? Scholarly presses will be primarily digital in a decade," said press director Phil Pochoda. Other university presses, including Penn State, are moving to digital-only for some books. [65]

Settlement Fallout

As a result of the Google Book Search settlement, up to 10 million out-of-print books where copyright holders can't be located could now be the exclusive province of Google to scan and commercially exploit, according to Internet Archive founder Kahle's estimate.

A variety of groups are planning to file comments in court raising concerns over the settlement, including the Internet Archive, the Institute of Information Law and Policy at New York Law School (which has financing from Microsoft), the American Library Association and the Association of Research Libraries. [66]

At the end of April, *The New York Times* reported that the Justice Department was launching an inquiry into the antitrust implications of Google's settlement and was talking with groups opposed to the settlement, including the Internet Archive and Consumer Watchdog. That same

Will the Google book settlement expand access to digital books?

YES
Dan Clancy
Google Engineering Director

Written for *CQ Researcher*, May 26, 2009

Six years ago, Google embarked on a massive project to digitize millions of books to make them as searchable as Web pages. Today, as a result, anyone in the U.S. can search across the entire texts of more than 10 million books for free, simply by visiting Google Book Search. People can read and download 1.5 million public-domain books in their entirety, from the works of William Shakespeare to Benjamin Franklin.

Until now, though, we've only been able to show our users a few snippets of text for millions of in-copyright books we've scanned. Since most of these books are out of print, to actually read them you have to hunt them down at a library or a used bookstore. And if the only known copy is on the other side of the country — you're out of luck.

If approved by the court, our groundbreaking agreement with a broad class of authors and publishers stands to open access to millions of such books in the U.S. By unlocking access to these books, anyone, any place in the country will be able to benefit from the wealth of knowledge contained in our nation's most renowned libraries.

Users will be able to preview millions of works online from anywhere in the U.S. If they want to read the whole thing, they'll be able to go down to the public library to use a computer station with access to the whole book for free. And if they want a copy for themselves, they'll be able to purchase access to an electronic copy of the book. Meanwhile, schools around the country can obtain an institutional subscription to give their students access to most books that we've scanned.

Our non-exclusive agreement requires that these new services be priced for "broad access," which means they must be affordable enough to allow universities and libraries across the country to take advantage of them. Partners like the University of Michigan will be able to review the prices of all institutional subscriptions and challenge them through arbitration if they believe they're too high.

What's more, the settlement creates an independent, not-for-profit Book Rights Registry run by authors and publishers that can work with others (including Google's competitors) to build alternative or even competing digitization services.

Just because the University of Michigan — one of Google's many partners — isn't down the road or around the corner doesn't mean people around the country should be denied access to its library. As the discussion continues, it's important to understand what readers stand to gain.

NO
Brewster Kahle
Founder and digital librarian, Internet Archive

Written for *CQ Researcher*, May 26, 2009

In the short term, the settlement negotiated between Google, the Authors Guild and the Association of American Publishers will certainly expand access to digital books. Google's 7 million books (and counting) is an important addition to the recent flood of digitized books. In the medium and long terms, however, the settlement will stall and stifle the exciting future of digital books by granting a single entity too much power and control.

If the settlement is approved, the outcome will be not one but two court-sanctioned monopolies. First, Google will be the only organization with an explicit license to scan and sell access to in-copyright but out-of-print books, which make up the majority of books published in the 20th century. The settlement also creates a new entity, called the Book Rights Registry (essentially, a monopoly), which, in conjunction with Google, will set prices for all commercial terms associated with those digital books.

We need to learn from our experiences with other companies that have come to dominate different types of digital content: Lexis-Nexis and Westlaw in law publishing and Elsevier with academic journals. Each aggressively pursued acquisitions and digitization to gain a strong position, while enjoying enthusiastic support from libraries and universities. It was difficult for them to see the future effects of allowing companies to gain dominance in a market: Elsevier grabbed control of academic journal publishing by aggregating journals and selling them in bundles to libraries — progressively raising subscription prices. Similarly, Lexis-Nexis and Westlaw left no real alternatives for accessing law materials.

The publishing and distribution of digital books could face the same danger.

But there are alternatives to Google. Hundreds of libraries, publishers and technology firms are already digitizing millions of books, with the goal of creating an open, freely accessible system.

If Google is allowed to create a monopoly on access to a large segment of digitized books, the entire publishing environment will weaken. Publishers will see their opportunities for selling limited. Authors will suffer as one company's Web site increasingly dictates who an author's readers will be. And readers, who for generations have seen their lives enriched by a diverse world of book publishing and libraries, will also suffer.

As controlling entities turn from innovation and competition to defending their dominant positions, access to digital books will suffer. Google might get richer, but society will become much poorer.

month, Judge Denny Chin of U.S. District Court in New York, who is overseeing the settlement, postponed until Sept. 4 the deadline for parties to file briefs opposing the settlement and for authors to opt out of it. The court's hearing to decide whether to accept the settlement and to consider objections was also postponed, to Oct. 7, 2009.[67]

Under the settlement, revenue generated from subscriptions and advertising on Google search pages will be split — with 37 percent going to Google and 63 percent going to authors and publishers. Some of the settlement money will go to establish a Book Rights Registry to administer the system and ensure that authors and publishers get paid.

"The court needs to supervise the registry in its interactions with Google very carefully to make sure that the monopoly the settlement creates does not abuse its power," says attorney Band, who represents the library associations.

Legislation passed by the U.S. Senate last year (but not by the House) would have limited the copyright infringement liability for libraries or companies wishing to scan or otherwise use "orphan" books.[68] At press time, no new orphan-works bill had been introduced in this congressional session.

Google's Clancy notes that his company supports even stronger orphan-works legislation than the Senate measure and that Google's efforts to identify rights holders under the settlement could actually help clarify which books still have identifiable copyright holders. But most observers agree the settlement takes the wind out of the sails of new legislative efforts — at least for books covered by the settlement.

Bypassing Publishers

On May 18, Scribd, the popular Web site that bills itself the YouTube of writing, launched an online vanity press and bookstore that allows anyone to upload and sell their own work. Although other companies offer digital self-publishing, the announcement received a lot of media attention because Scribd claims 60 million users a month, and its audience has been doubling every six months.[69]

Several authors (none famous) announced they would be publishing their new books for the first time in digital form and selling them on the site for only $2 but would still make more money than going the conventional publishing route. Scribd allows authors or

Scribd, the popular Web site that bills itself the YouTube of writing, launched an online vanity press and bookstore on May 18 that allows anyone to upload and sell their own work. The announcement received heavy media attention because Scribd claims 60 million users a month, and its audience has been doubling every six months.

publishers to set the price and keep 80 percent of the revenue. (Mainstream publishers pay authors royalties of 15 percent or less.)

"As more and more authors become bloggers, individuals now can market their own books in a way they never could before," says Choksi of Lexcycle, which added a self-publishing company, Smashwords, to its Stanza iPhone application earlier this year. Admittedly, he notes, many of these books are amateurish affairs like family genealogies, which might only attract a few buyers who know the author personally.

However, one sure-fire big seller went the self-publishing route to get a bigger cut of the revenues. Amy Fisher's 2004 memoir about shooting her lover's wife when she was 17, *If I Knew Then . . .*, was published as a print-on-demand book by self-publisher iUniverse and appeared briefly on *The New York Times* bestseller list.[70]

Some publishers fear that kind of authorial entrepreneurship could cut into their business. But so far, successful writers have, for the most part, continued to seek out name-brand publishers.

In addition to its vanity press, Scribd is trying to position itself as a potential rival to Amazon by offering books for sale that can be read on any device, unlike Amazon's Kindle, and hopes to carry the full digital catalog of books from publishing partners like Random House.[71]

Scribd claims to offer publishers an advantage over Kindle, which sets the price and keeps the majority of revenue on some titles. Some publishers are worried that Amazon is gaining too much market power and may start squeezing publishers' revenue even more — especially if it continues to price bestsellers as low as $9.99.[72]

In a move reminiscent of iTunes, which sold one song at a time for $1, Scribd will now sell a chapter or two of a travel guide for as little as $3, under arrangements with publishers like Lonely Planet.[73]

Meanwhile, the National Endowment for the Arts (NEA) reported in January that for the first time since 1982, the number of adults who said they had read a novel, short story, poem or play in the past 12 months had risen — from 47 percent of the population in 2002 to more than 50 percent in 2008.[74]

While one expert called the rise "just a blip," others cited a 24-percent rise among young men ages 18-24.[75] The survey questions did not distinguish between online and print reading.

Former NEA chairman Dana Gioia called the rise at least partly a reaction to earlier reports of a reading crisis. "Reading has become a higher priority," he said.[76] Still, 22 percent of Americans did not read a book last year because they couldn't — one of the worst illiteracy rates among wealthy countries.

OUTLOOK

The iPod of Books?

Books may be changing, but in a direction that appeals to many different audiences — from the computer-linked to the print loyalists.

For years, publishers have said, "We're looking for the iPod for books" — the universal device that makes it easy to load and read books whenever and wherever you want.

Have we found it with the iPhone, Kindle or Sony Reader? Probably not yet. Some think the next generation will be a lightweight electronic reader — offering the advantages of a large-format screen, which can display the front page of a newspaper or a complicated nautical chart, with the convenience of a gadget that can be folded up.

The Plastic Logic Reader, which almost fits that description (it's bendable and is thinner than a pad of paper but can't be folded up and put in your pocket), is to be introduced in pilots later this year and will be widely available by early next year.

Amazon's new, large-format Kindle DX appears to be targeting the same market — business travelers — since it also permits wireless exchange of documents. It's not clear Amazon's other target audience, student textbook readers, will be enticed by a device costing close to $500. Major textbook publisher Pearson Education reports about 25 percent of its sales are digital — with most of them read on laptops.[77]

Amazon's April release of the DX seemed timed to beat not only Plastic Logic but also other devices whose announcement is expected imminently from Apple, Palm and possibly Murdoch's News Corp. Sony's expected release of a wireless version of its Reader will likely intensify competition.[78]

Some are skeptical of all the devices and think print is still the perfect technology. "I don't think there will ever be an iPod moment" with the book, says Lightning Source's Taylor. Instead, he sees print-on-demand exploding in the next few years as publishers try to cut costs in a tough economic climate. Marketing researcher Interquest projects annual growth of 15-20 percent over the next three years for the digital-printing market because of new ink-jet technology that will make somewhat longer press runs more economical.

Smaller on-site computer printers, like the Espresso, could make it possible to print out books almost anywhere — whether in bookstores, rural African outposts or on ships at sea.

It's still unclear how big an e-book audience will emerge. Ironically, if electronic devices come down in price, some think they could have a bigger market in the underdeveloped world, which has little publishing infrastructure but is quickly installing cell phone networks, the method for purchasing and downloading books on the Kindle.

Publishers must also decide whether to continue to exercise so-called digital rights management (DRM) over e-books, aimed at preventing piracy and free sharing of files. (*See sidebar, p. 63.*)

Some see protective encoding as an impediment to further adoption of digital books because it locks in each e-book to a proprietary format and limits the variety of devices on which it can be read. "It's as if you had a DVD you can't play on your laptop or on a friend's DVD player," says Lexcyle's Choksi. "I think e-books as an industry would do so much better if DRM were used only for encryption and for managing the rights the publishers want managed."

Most authors and publishers can be expected to stand by DRM as the only bulwark protecting their copyright and income.

Eventually, piracy could become irrelevant if publishers turn to storing e-books "in the cloud" — i.e. in cyberspace like Google Mail, with a user password to gain access. "In the long run we won't need DRM," predicts Idea Logical CEO Shatzkin, because, "We'll stop having hard drives; everything will be on the Internet."

Research libraries are running to catch up with all the online activity. Already, some scholarly journals have been migrating to electronic-only versions, and many libraries are canceling their print-version subscriptions in favor of electronic versions. Some think books will follow suit.

Much like Wikipedia, the sciences are being revolutionized by the ability to share scholarly papers online without waiting for peer-reviewed publication. "We know scholars are depositing and sharing their work way outside the traditional scholarly framework" of publication, says Columbia University chief librarian James Neal. "Our challenge is how do we get in there, capture and preserve that stuff?"

Paradoxically, digitization is preserving many printed books that are now too brittle to be handled. The Library of Congress has digitized some 29,000 books, going back to the early 19th century, which can be viewed on the Internet Archive Web site. Some are so fragile they will be sent to a climate-controlled vault at Fort Meade, in Maryland.

"So for all intents and purposes they will never be handled again," says Mike Handy, who supervises the digitization effort at the library.

Amidst all this activity, the U.S. print-book market will probably continue to hover at about 3 billion sales per year.

"It's a flat market because there's a lot of competition from electronic media," says Gilles Biscos, president of Interquest, a market research company in Charlottesville, Va. "People have other things to do than read books, and they spend a great deal of time on the Internet reading screens."

That's where both the opportunity and the challenge lie for the future of books.

UPDATE

The publishing world marked a milestone in July 2010 when word shot round the exploding array of digital news-reading gadgets that e-books — for the first time ever — had outsold hardcover books on amazon.com. And though the 600,000 books now available electronically represent only a fraction of the online giant's total book offerings, the news led Amazon founder Jeff Bezos to predict that e-books sold for reading on the company's Kindle would overtake paperback sales within 12 months.[79] *Did they?*

In fact, the sales figures released in July looked good for the entire publishing industry. Book purchases were up an encouraging 11.6 percent over the previous year, while trade e-book sales shot up from less than 3 percent of the total market a year earlier to 8.48 percent.[80]

Despite the impressive rise in e-books' market share, some observers doubt that traditional book publishing veterans are adapting quickly enough to the consumer demand sparked by the e-revolution. "Right now, the industry is flush with cash because people are buying digital versions of books from Amazon or Apple," says Dan Visel, a researcher at the Brooklyn-based Institute for the Future of the Book. But "this is likely to prove with time to be similar to the music industry's introduction of the 8-track or the cassette tape, providing, essentially, a new way for consumers to buy the same content. It will provide money in the short term, but I don't think it's sustainable." *naysayers*

A chief concern, Visel says, is the likely rise in publishing piracy once a larger portion of the books being published become available as easily copiable electronic books. "The public is also going to start to wonder why Apple or Amazon has arbitrarily decided that they should pay $10 [per book] for something that isn't really costing Apple or Amazon very much money," he adds, "The consumer isn't getting anything besides digital bits."

The industry deserves credit for catching up and "conquering the first frontier," which is getting printed books converted to the computer screen, says Mike Shatzkin, CEO of Idea Logical, a digital publishing

tough challenge

The millions of Americans now buying Apple's iPhone and iPad (shown above) are in many cases also buying Stanza, the book-reader software developed by Seattle-based Lexcycle, which was acquired by Amazon.com in April 2009.

CQ Press/Screenshot

consulting firm in New York. But to expand e-books from "Ohio and Indiana through the Rocky Mountains to the Pacific," he says, the industry will have to get past two major obstacles that most book lovers know little about.

The first involves "finding a commonly sensible answer to the relationship between costs and consumer demand," Shatzkin says. There is a "wide range" of concepts about what an e-book could be, other than just a book on a screen enhanced by some new "apps" and "perhaps some video." He cites as an example *The Girl With the Dragon Tattoo* and other murder mystery blockbusters by the late Swedish journalist Stieg Larsson. "I wish I could click on some of his Swedish proper names and learn what some of those references mean," Shatzkin says.

`The second challenge involves the setting at which book shoppers go to browse. "We're still working on the analog of the physical store: Barnes and Noble, Borders, and Amazon are all trying to be superstores, where you go to the section on, say, history," Shatzkin says. "But the presentation of choices is clunkier in a digital environment."

He predicts that future book buyers will likely go on Web-sites organized by communities in a given field rather than to bookstores offering all e-books in the same place. "It will take a combination of curation and presentation to rebuild the new subject infrastructure that is connected to a community," he says.

Nonetheless, e-books, which retail for less than half the cost of hardcover books, are making their presence felt. Barnes and Noble, the nation's biggest bookseller, was recently put up for sale, and its board linked the rise of the e-book to the company's slumping sales and customer traffic. Though the chain has marketed its own electronic reader, called the Nook, it is considering expanding into more sales of toys and games.[81]

Meanwhile, the digital revolution continues to smash the longstanding barriers to aspiring authors seeking audiences for their work without benefit of agents, editors or professional marketers.

Efforts at standardizing e-books to maximize interoperability between different readers and software programs were advanced in August, when the International Digital Publishing Forum, a Toronto-based trade group, announced the launch of a program to implement standard specifications for e-publishing (EPUB). "As EPUB is rapidly gaining momentum, it's great to see such wide industry interest in performing the technical work to keep [up] the . . . standards that make EPUB error-free and modern," said Garth Conboy, vice chair of the EPUB Standards Maintenance Working Group.[82]

Also in August, Bowker, the longtime industry compiler of bibliographic information that administers the ISBN catalog numbers used in books, announced that it had created a new Internet-based manuscript-submission service. Bowker says it will bring "authors, publishers and agents together in an efficient online system, where authors present their book proposals to the leading publishers in the industry from one central location, and acquisition editors apply e-tools that allow them to sort through them and zero in on the ideas they find most interesting."[83]

In May, Bowker announced it had teamed up with Google to establish a system to facilitate consistent ISBN numbers to identify, catalog and publicize the e-books to be published as Google Editions, many of which are classics or out-of-print books for which the search-engine powerhouse has been scanning and acquiring rights.

Is it working?

"Publishers, digital intermediaries and their trading partners continue to deal with an increasing array of e-book formats with specific features, attributes or restrictions," said Brian Green, executive director of the International ISBN Agency. "It makes the assignment of separate ISBNs to each format even more important for ensuring that the e-book ordered is the correct one for the user's device or software platform."[84]

Not that putting ink on paper is disappearing. Indeed, digital technology has made publishing on old-fashioned paper more economical. For one thing, near-instant printing of small quantities of books based on advance orders avoids the expense of warehousing. Interquest Ltd., a Charlottesville, Va.-based research and consulting firm, predicts that digital book manufacturing over the next five years will grow 15-20 percent in volume.[85]

Whether the exponential growth of equal-access publishing has harmed the quality and reliability of published literature is another evolving question. Wikipedia, which in its early years was regarded skeptically by journalists, scholars, and makers of traditional encyclopedias, is now armed with fact-checking editors. The free site now offers an astonishing 3.4 million different entries in English, according to its Website, many of them on topics that simply aren't covered by Britannica or Compton's.

But are discerning readers well-served by an over-abundance of books? "There's certainly more bad writing that can be bought now than at any time in the past, but that's a function of volume rather than necessarily a lack of good writing," says Visel. "The volume, however, does increase the chances that good writing will not receive the attention it deserves. Assuming a constant number of readers, which may well be incorrect," he adds, "the amount of attention given on average to each book has gone down; concurrent with this has been the decline of the print book-reviewing establishment. Given this, it's entirely possible that any number of masterpieces have been published and aren't receiving any attention, and the average reader is increasingly adrift in trying to figure out what to read."

Perhaps the most disgruntled players in the transformed world of publishing are the mid-list authors wary of domination of the process by amazon.com, Google and Apple. The millions of Americans now buying Apple's iPhone and iPad are in many cases also buying Stanza, the book-reader software developed by Seattle-based Lexcycle, which was acquired by Amazon.com in April 2009. It's a sign to some that yesterday's economic model for New York-based elite publishing has collapsed, presenting both threats and opportunities as the definition of a publisher broadens.

Another sign of the times came in February 2010, when the U.S. District Court for the Southern District of New York held a hearing on the pending court verdict on what is known as the Google Book Settlement. Supporters of the proposed deal included University of Michigan library science Professor Paul Courant, who argued that Google's plan to scan books is one solution to an age-old problem: To read and study many important but rare books, researchers and scholars must travel to read them. "Broad social progress depends on being able to find, use and re-use the scholarly record," Courant told the court.

Opponents of the settlement, who outnumbered supporters, warned of a Google monopoly. William Cavanaugh, an assistant U.S. attorney general, said the publishers and the Authors Guild lacked the right to enable a third party such as Google to use authors' works without their permission. The settlement "has the effect of rewriting contracts," he said.[86]

Meanwhile, in July Amazon cut a short-lived deal with the Wylie Agency's new publishing arm to publish e-book versions of numerous 20th-century American classics whose print copyright (but not electronic rights) are owned by other publishers. Before the deal fell apart in late August, it drew a mixed reaction from the Authors Guild, which is also a party in the suit against Google. It applauded the move to permit established authors and their families to craft new deals for electronic rights, given that such technology didn't exist when the original contracts were signed.[87]

But the guild also warned that "when an agency acts as publisher, serious potential conflicts of interest immediately come to mind. . . . And Amazon's power in the book publishing industry grows daily."[88]

However, Wylie announced on Aug. 24 that it was largely abandoning the agreement with Amazon in favor of Bertelsmann's Random House, which had challenged Amazon's right to sell some 13 titles in digital form.[89]

NOTES

1. Whispersync permits Kindle owners to access their library of previously purchased books at no additional cost and to pick up where they left off through automatic bookmarks.

2. The screen displays ink particles electronically to create a reading experience much closer to printed paper than most computer displays.

3. For background, see Kenneth Jost, "Future of Books," *CQ Researcher*, June 23, 2000, pp. 545-568.

4. Miguel Helft, "Google and Amazon to Put More Books on Cellphones," *The New York Times*, Feb. 6, 2009, www.nytimes.com.

5. If digital printing used by publishers for short runs of up to 1,200 books are counted, digitally printed books accounted for 3 percent of all books published in North America, according to Interquest, a market research firm.

6. www.wetellstories.co.uk.

7. www.songsofimaginationanddigitisation.net.

8. Motoko Rich, "Print Book are Target of Pirates on the Web," *The New York Times*, May 12, 2009, www.nytimes.com.

9. *Ibid.*

10. Miguel Helft and Motoko Rich, "Google Settles Suit over Book-Scanning," *The New York Times*, Oct. 29, 2008.

11. The formula only applies to books for which the rights holder has not set a price. The purchaser gets perpetual online access to the book.

12. Robert Darnton, "Google & the Future of Books," *The New York Review of Books*, Feb. 12, 2009, www.nybooks.com.

13. *Ibid.*

14. Miguel Helft, "Libraries Ask Google to Monitor Google Books Settlement," *The New York Times*, May 4, 2009, www.googlebook settlement.com.

15. K-12 users will still be able to view up to 20 percent of a book's content, as part of the free search function, as will all other users in the United States. For background, see Kathy Koch, "The Digital Divide," *CQ Researcher*, Jan. 28, 2000, pp. 41-64.

16. Google is obligated to reveal only 85 percent of the books it has scanned into the database, under the agreement.

17. The association announced on Feb. 27 that Schroeder would step down as president on May 1, www.publishers.org.

18. Paul Courant, "Google, Robert Darnton, and the Digital Republic of Letters," *Au Courant*, (Paul Courant's blog), http://paulcourant.net.

19. See www.futureofthebook.org/blog/archives/2008/09/a_unified_field_theory_of_publ_1.html.

20. Brad Stone and Motoko Rich, "Amazon Unveils a Large-Screen Kindle Aimed at Textbooks and Newspapers," May 7, 2009, *The New York Times*, www.nytimes.com. The three newspapers are *The New York Times*, *The Boston Globe* and *The Washington Post*.

21. Peter Osnos, "Rise of the Reader," *Columbia Journalism Review*, March/April 2009, pp. 38-39.

22. David Pearson, *Books as History* (2008), p. 25.

23. Bob Stein, "A unified field theory of publishing in the networked era," if:book, www.futureofthebook.org/blog/archives/2008/09/a_unified_field_theory_of_publ_1.html.

24. *Ibid.*

25. Bruce Mason and Sue Thomas, "A Million Penguins Research Report," April 24, 2008, De Montfort University, Leicester, U.K., www.ioct.dmu.ac.uk/projects/amillionpenguins report.pdf.

26. *Ibid.*

27. *Ibid.*

28. Presentation by Bowker Vice President for Publisher Services Kelly Gallagher, "Understanding tomorrow's digital consumer by knowing what they are up to today," London Book Fair, April 19, 2009, www.bowker.com.

29. "Publishing's High Flyers," *newbooks*, March/April 2009, p. 30, www.newbooksmag.com.

30. www.playingforkeepsnovel.com.

31. Marcia Clemmitt, "Learning Online Literacy," in "Reading Crisis?" *CQ Researcher*, Feb. 22, 2008, pp. 169-192.

32. British Library, "Treasures in Full: Gutenberg Bible," www.bl.uk/treasures/gutenberg/ background.html.

33. Jason Epstein, "An Autopsy of the Book Business," *Daily Beast*, Jan. 8, 2009, www.daily beast.com.

34. Pearson, *op. cit.*, p. 65.

35. Jason Epstein, *Book Business* (2001), pp. 97-98.

36. *Ibid.*, p. 33.

37. *Ibid.*, p. 33.

38. *Ibid.*, p. 11.

39. "Interquest Report: High Growth Segments of Digital Book Printing — Market Analysis and Forecast 2007," Interquest, 2007.

40. Mary Harrington and Chris Meade, "read:write Digital Possibilities for Literature," A Report for Arts Council England, July 2008, www.futureofthebook.org.uk.

41. Motoko Rich, "Book Publisher Suspends New Acquisitions," *The New York Times*, Nov. 25, 2008, www.nytimes.com.

42. Colin Robinson, "Diary," *London Review of Books*, Feb. 26, 2009.

43. Jason Boog, "Read it and Weep," *Salon.com*, Dec. 23, 2008.

44. Samuel Freedman, "In the Diaspora: The ever-dying people of the ever-dying book," *Jerusalem Post*, March 5, 2009, www.jpost.com.

45. American Association of Publishers, press release, "AAP Reports Book Sales Estimated at $24.3 Billion in 2008," March 31, 2009.

46. Boog, *op. cit.*

47. Robinson, *op. cit.*

48. *Ibid.*

49. Freedman, *op. cit.*

50. Geoffrey A. Fowler and Jessica E. Vascellaro, "Sony and Google Team Up to Battle Amazon," *The Wall Street Journal*, March 19, 2009.

51. Dave Caolo, "iPhone the most popular ebook reader," The Unofficial Apple Weblog, Oct. 3, 2008, www.tuaw.com.

52. See Kassia Krozser, "Amazon Buys Lexcycle," April 28, 2009, booksquare.com and Andrew Ross Sorkin, "Dealbook: Amazon Buys Lexcycle," http://dealbook.blogs.nytimes.com.

53. Peter Osnos, "Platform: The Kindle Surge and Beyond," *teleread.org*, May 19, 2009, www.teleread.org.

54. Geoffrey A. Fowler and Jessica E. Vascellaro, "Sony and Google Team Up to Battle Amazon," *The Wall Street Journal*, March 19, 2009.

55. Jim Milliot, "Penguin Posts Solid Gains Worldwide," *Publishers Weekly*, March 2, 2009.

56. Dominic Rushe, "Market Warms to Electronic books," *Timesonline*, Aug. 31, 2008, http://business.timeonline.co.uk.

57. www.the39clues.com.

58. Judith Rosen, "Taking Steps into the Digital Future," *Publisher's Weekly*, Feb. 16, 2009, www.publishersweekly.com.

59. *Ibid.*

60. "OverDrive Announces 2008 Library Download Statistics and Milestones," Jan. 6, 2009, www.overdrive.com.

61. Vicky Frost, "Waiting for the iPod Moment," *The Guardian*, April 20, 2009.

62. Rosen, *op. cit.*

63. Robinson, *op. cit.*

64. Richard Perez-Pena, "Campaign Articles from Newsweek Become E-Books for Amazon Kindle," *The New York Times*, Oct. 13, 2008, www.nytimes.com.

65. Scott Jaschik, "Farewell to the Printed Monograph," *Inside Higher Ed*, March 23, 2009, www.insidehighered.com.

66. Miguel Helft, "Google's Plan for Out-of-Print Books is Challenged," *The New York Times*, April 4, 2009, www.nytimes.com.

67. Miguel Helft, "Justice Dept. Opens Antitrust Inquiry into Google Books Deal," *The New York Times*, April 29, 2009, www.nytimes.com. Also see official Google Book Settlement Web site, www.googlebooksettlement.com.

68. www.thomas.gov/.

69. Kenneth Li, "Scribd launches online book market," *Financial Times*, May 18, 2009, www.ft.com.

70. See Sarah Glazer, "The Book Business: How to Be Your Own Publisher," *The New York Times*, April 24, 2005, www.nytimes.com.

71. Li, *op. cit.*

72. Brad Stone, "Site Lets Writers Sell Digital Copies," *The New York Times*, May 17, 2009, www.nytimes.com.

73. See www.scribd.com.

74. "Reading on the rise," National Endowment for the Arts, www.arts.gov/research/ReadingonRise.pdf.

75. *Ibid.*

76. "Adult literacy: the readers," *The Economist*, Jan. 17, 2009. pp. 411-412.

77. Brad Stone and Mokoto Rich, "Amazon Introduces Big-Screen Kindle," *The New York Times*, May 6, 2009, www.nytimes.com.

78. Marion Maneker, "How the Next Kindle Could Save the Newspaper Business," *Wired*, May 6, 2009, www.wired.com.

79. Claire Cain Miller, "E-Books Top Hardcovers at Amazon," *The New York Times*, July 19, 2010. See also Edward C. Baig, "Volume of Kindle book sales stuns Amazon's Jeff Bezos," *USA Today*, July 29, 2010.

80. Association of American Publishers, press release, July 14, 2010.

81. Julie Bosman, "Quick Change in Strategy for a Bookseller," *The New York Times*, Aug. 12, 2010.

82. International Digital Publishing Forum, press release, Aug. 16, 2010.

83. Bowker, press release, Aug. 11, 2010.

84. Bowker, press release, May 5, 2010.

85. Cassandra Carnes, "Book Publishing Evolves," *DPS Magazine*, March 2010.

86. Greg Sandoval, "Google book settlement draws fire in court," CNET News, Feb. 18, 2010, http://news.cnet.com/8301-31001_3-10456382-261.html.

87. "Wylie Agency Circumvents Publishers on e-Books With Odyssey Editions," POD (Print on Demand), July 22, 2010, http://mickrooney.blogspot.com/2010/07/wylie-agency-circumvent-publishers-on-e.html.

88. Authors Guild, statement, July 26, 2010.

89. Jeffrey A. Trachtenberg, "Amazon Loses E-Book Deal," *The Wall Street Journal*, Aug. 25, 2010, p. B1.

BIBLIOGRAPHY

Books

Anderson, Chris, *Free: The Future of a Radical Price*, Hyperion, July 7, 2009.
"Every industry that becomes digital eventually becomes free," including books, *Wired* editor-in-chief Anderson argues. He has even promised there will be a way to get this book free.

Anderson, Chris, *The Long Tail*, Random House Business Books, 2006.
The editor-in-chief of *Wired* magazine introduced the term "long tail" into the business lexicon to argue that aggregating many low-selling items creates a lot of sales — in books (think Amazon and print-on-demand), music and other areas.

Epstein, Jason, *Book Business: Publishing Past Present and Future*, W.W. Norton, 2001.
The former editorial director of Random House sprinkles personal reminiscence about his 50 years in publishing throughout this discussion of publishing's history and where it's headed.

Pearson, David, *Books as History*, The British Library and Oak Knoll Press, 2008.
In this beautifully produced book, the director of University of London Research Library Services discusses the importance of physical books as artifacts in understanding history.

Articles

"Sony, Google Challenge Amazon," *The Wall Street Journal*, March 19, 2009, http://onlinwsj.com.
The Wall Street Journal describes Google's deal to provide 500,000 books to the Sony Reader as a challenge to Amazon's Kindle.

Courant, Paul, "Google, Robert Darnton and the Digital Republic of Letters," *Au Courant: Paul Courant's blog*, Feb. 4, 2009, ttp://paulcourant.net/2009/02/04/google-robert-darnton-and-the-digital-republic-of-letters.
The University of Michigan's dean of libraries counters Darnton's critique (below), arguing that such a vast digital library could never have been assembled without Google.

Darnton, Robert, "Google and the Future of Books," *New York Review of Books*, Feb. 12, 2009.
Harvard Library's director expresses concern that Google will abuse its "virtual monopoly" over what could be the biggest digital library in the world as a result of its recent out-of-court settlement with authors and publishers.

Osnos, Peter, "Rise of the Reader: How Books Got Wings," *Columbia Journalism Review,* **March/April 2009, pp. 38-39.**
The vice chairman of the *Columbia Journalism Review* and founder of PublicAffairs books imagines the future world of the book, digital and otherwise, in 2014.

Pullinger, Kate, "My Digital Evolution in Fiction," *Internet Evolution,* **March 18, 2009, www.internet evolution.com.**
A published novelist suggests that works of literature by a single author may be a "relic of a cultural moment" as literature becomes increasingly collaborative and multimedia — online and on our phones.

Reports and Studies

"Book Industry Trends 2008," Book Industry Study Group, www.bisg.org.
An industry trade association issues a comprehensive report each year on trends in publishing revenues and output. The 2009 report was to be released May 29.

Band, Jonathan, "A Guide for the Perplexed: Libraries and the Google Library Project Settlement," Nov. 23, 2008, www.arl.org/pp/ppcopyright/google.
An attorney for the Association of Research Libraries provides a detailed description of the Google Book Search settlement from the perspective of libraries.

Harrington, Mary, and Chris Meade, "Read: Write: Digital Possibilities for Literature," Arts Council of England, www.futureofthebook.org.uk, July 2008.
Two members of a London literary think tank, The Institute for the Future of the Book, report on online experiments with literature.

Mason, Bruce, and Sue Thomas, "A Million Penguins Research Report," De Montfort University, Leicester, U.K., April 24, 2008, www.ioct.dmu.ac.uk/projects/millionpenguinsanalysis.html.
Two British academics analyze a wiki novel-writing experiment sponsored by Penguin that attracted hundreds of contributors to a developing plot online.

On the Web

***Songs of Imagination and Digitisation,* if: book, www.songsofimaginationanddigitisation.net.**
Click onto this book by and about the British poet William Blake to get an idea of the future multimedia "netbook," containing poems and essays along with videos, inventive computer graphics and an invitation to contribute online. Published by the London literary think tank if: book with support from the Arts Council of England.

For More Information

American Library Association, 50 E. Huron, Chicago, IL 60611; (800) 545-2433; www.ala.org. Represents librarians in the United States.

Association of American Publishers, 50 F St., NW, 4th Floor, Washington, DC 20001; (202) 347-3375; www.publishers.org. Principal trade association for the publishing industry.

The Authors Guild, 31 East 32nd St., 7th Floor, New York, NY 10016; (212) 563-5904; www.authorsguild.org. Represented authors in the Google Book Search settlement.

http://books.google.com. Google's Web site for searching books explains how the search engine would change under the out-of-court settlement with authors and publishers.

www.googlebooksettlement.com. Official Web site run by the administrator of the Google Book Search settlement.

Institute for the Future of the Book, 74 N. 7th St., #3, Brooklyn, NY 11211; www.futureofthebook.org. Think tank experimenting with future forms of the book in New York and London.

International Digital Publishing Forum; P.O. Box 215, Toronto, Ontario M3C 2S2 Canada; (905) 235-IDPF (4373); www.openebook.org. Trade association for the e-book industry.

Kernochan Center for Law, Media and the Arts, Columbia University School of Law, 435 W. 116th St., Box A-17, New York, NY 10027; (212) 854-7424; http://kernochancenter.org. Streaming video of the center's March 13, 2009, conference on the Google Book Search settlement.

Scribd; www.scribd.com. A Web site where users share and sell original writing, and mainstream publishers are starting to post free excerpts.

We Tell Stories; http://wetellstories.co.uk. This Penguin experiment with online storytelling won the "Best in Show" prize at the SXSW interactive festival in Austin, Texas.

4

Blog Explosion

Kenneth Jost, Melissa J. Hipolit and Charles S. Clark

Former conservative socialite Arianna Huffington created HuffingtonPost.com, a year-old liberal political blog that has risen to the top rank of blogs, with an estimated 1.3 million visitors in April 2006. Huffington says blogging has "leveled the playing field" between the traditional media and the new, independent media who have only a laptop and an Internet connection.

From CQ Researcher,
June 9, 2006.
Updated August 27, 2010.

Getty Images/Andrew H. Walker

Time magazine's special issue promised to reveal "the lives and ideas of the world's most influential people," and many of the faces on the May 8 cover were instantly recognizable: President Bush, Al Gore and Hillary Rodham Clinton from the world of politics. Computer billionaire Bill Gates. Entertainment queen Oprah Winfrey. Rock star turned global activist Bono.

Down toward the bottom, however, *Time* anointed two media stars less familiar to most Americans but well known to the increasing number of news junkies who turn to cyberspace for information and opinion about the day's events.

Matt Drudge appeared in his trademark fedora, looking much the same as the taboo-defying conservative did in 1998 when his online Drudge Report broke the story of President Bill Clinton's liaison with White House intern Monica Lewinski.

Off to Drudge's left, Arianna Huffington presented an image of pensive glamour evoking her dual life as celebrity socialite and proprietress of HuffingtonPost.com, a new but widely read liberal compendium of political news and opinion.

Time's selection of Drudge and Huffington from among many better-known media heavyweights represented the kind of event the weekly news magazine might have noted on its "Milestones" page:

"**ARRIVED**. *The Age of the Blog, the interactive, globally connected medium of communication with revolutionary potential to make politics more democratic, business more productive and knowledge and culture more diffuse.*"[1]

The word "blog" — short for "Web log" — may nevertheless still seem like somewhat obscure jargon to many Americans. A countercultural computer geek coined the word less than 10 years

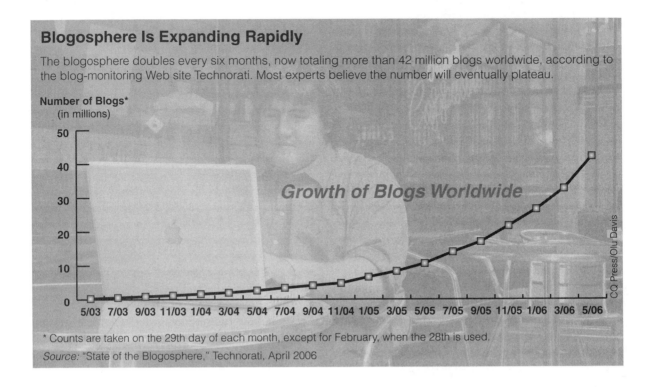

Blogosphere Is Expanding Rapidly

The blogosphere doubles every six months, now totaling more than 42 million blogs worldwide, according to the blog-monitoring Web site Technorati. Most experts believe the number will eventually plateau.

Number of Blogs*
(in millions)

Growth of Blogs Worldwide

CQ Press/Olu Davis

* Counts are taken on the 29th day of each month, except for February, when the 28th is used.

Source: "State of the Blogosphere," Technorati, April 2006

ago to describe the process of logging on a personal site items he found interesting while surfing the World Wide Web. Nearly three-fourths of the country's Internet users had never read a blog as of November 2004, according to a survey by the Pew Internet and American Life Project.[2]

Today, however, the so-called blogosphere has exploded, with more than 42 million sites and counting, according to the blog-finding service Technorati. Admittedly, many of them are little more than personal diaries, such as the growing number of intimacy-revealing blogs published by high-school and college students. (*See sidebar, p. 102.*) But businesses, politicians and even government agencies are now starting blogs to provide information to — and invite feedback from — customers and constituents. (*See sidebar, p. 100.*)

In addition, a growing number of political blogs provide breaking news not found in mainstream media along with corrections or complaints about news coverage and sharp, often vituperative commentary about national and world events. "Blogs have become the new information ecosystem, part of the conversation about policy," says Rebecca MacKinnon, a research fellow at

the Berkman Center for Internet and Society at Harvard Law School in Cambridge, Mass. (*See chart, p. 96.*)

Blogging has also become a global phenomenon and a valuable tool for human-rights and pro-democracy activists in challenging repressive regimes. Bloggers and other Web activists face risks, however. The Egyptian government jailed at least six bloggers among other dissidents in May 2006. China has jailed several Web activists and — with the assistance of U.S.-based Internet service providers — blocked some anti-government sites. And Iran jailed some 20 online journalists and bloggers in January 2005. Some were released after international criticism, but human-rights groups say the government continues to persecute bloggers critical of the regime.[3]

Blogs offer two comparative advantages over other media. Bloggers face few barriers to entry: Anyone with a computer and the nominal costs of easy-to-use software and a Web hosting service can start a blog. The ease of start-up is beguiling, however. The vast majority of blogs go idle after a short period of time. For readers, blogs offer the opportunity to provide instantaneous feedback and to engage in freewheeling dialogue with other blog readers unlimited by space or time.

"Blogs give people the ability to talk to each other, and they're finding that they have more trust in people like themselves, at least in some key areas, than they have in traditional sources of information," says David Kline, a business journalist, consultant and co-author of the book *blog! how the newest media revolution is changing politics, business and culture.*

Drudge himself reportedly dislikes the word "blog," and the Drudge Report invites e-mail and tips but, unlike true blogs, no interactive feedback. Huffington sees her recognition from *Time*, however, as "a tribute to the influence of the blogosphere," which she says "has leveled the playing field between the media haves and the media have-only-a-laptop-and-an-Internet-connection crowd."

In fact, both Drudge and Huffington have clearly arrived in terms of their visibility in political and media circles. Drudge's site drew around 2.7 million "unique" visitors in April 2006, according to the media-tracking service Nielsen/Net.* "Anybody who's dealing with the political world or the political media world, they're checking Drudge's site every day," says Robert Cox, managing editor of TheNationalDebate.com and president of the newly founded Media Bloggers Association.

Huffington's site, which debuted on May 9, 2005, rose within a year to the top rank of blogs. Nielsen/Net estimated 1.3 million visitors in April 2006. "It creates a place for liberals to gather and takes some of the oxygen from conservative sites like the Drudge Report," says the liberal political satirist Al Franken.[4] In the *Time* issue, he claims tongue-in-cheek credit for converting the

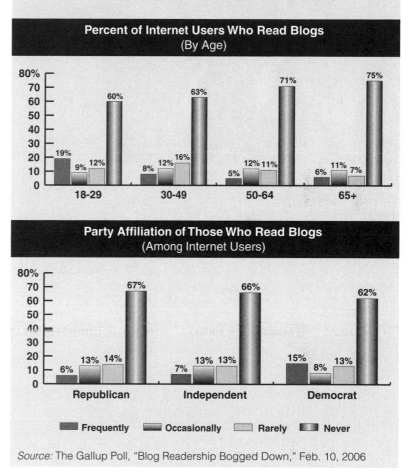

Most Blog Readers Are Young and Democrats

Internet users between ages 18-29 read blogs more than other age groups, and 28 percent of them read blogs frequently or occasionally. Democrats read blogs more often than Republicans or Independents.

Percent of Internet Users Who Read Blogs
(By Age)

18-29: 19%, 9%, 12%, 60%
30-49: 8%, 12%, 16%, 63%
50-64: 5%, 12%, 11%, 71%
65+: 6%, 11%, 7%, 75%

Party Affiliation of Those Who Read Blogs
(Among Internet Users)

Republican: 6%, 13%, 14%, 67%
Independent: 7%, 13%, 13%, 66%
Democrat: 15%, 8%, 13%, 62%

■ Frequently ■ Occasionally □ Rarely ■ Never

Source: The Gallup Poll, "Blog Readership Bogged Down," Feb. 10, 2006

onetime Newt Gingrich acolyte to her self-described views today as "a compassionate and progressive populist."

The mainstream print and broadcast media continue to draw far more readers and viewers than blogs, however — even in head-to-head competition online. NewYorkTimes.com, for example, was reporting 29 million unique visitors per month in March 2006.[5] "We haven't gotten to the point that blogs swamp in readership the aggregate of all newspapers and magazines," says Eugene Volokh, a UCLA law professor and author of a widely read legal-affairs blog, The Volokh Conspiracy.

---

*A "unique visitor" is anyone who goes to a site at least once during the time period.

At Sen. Strom Thurmond's 100th birthday bash on Dec. 5, 2002, Sen. Trent Lott, R-Miss., center, fondly recalled Thurmond's 1948 campaign on a segregationist platform. The gaffe went largely unreported until it erupted in the blogosphere, and the mainstream media then took up the story. An abashed Lott eventually had to give up his post as Senate majority leader — an incident many attribute to bloggers' newfound political muscle. Among others, President Bush, left, attended the party, along with Thurmond's daughter Julie, right.

In contrast to traditional media, bloggers have no established career path, no prescribed course of dues-paying jobs before reaching prime time or the front page. Drudge used a job in the gift shop at CBS Studios in Los Angeles in the early 1990s to gather Hollywood-type gossip for a report that started as an e-mail newsletter and then broadened into political gossip as it moved onto the World Wide Web in 1996. Before starting her blog, Huffington was a columnist and critic in London in the 1970s and an author and socialite after moving to the United States in the 1980s.

Easy access makes the blogosphere "extremely competitive," according to media historian Paul Starr, a professor of sociology and public affairs at Princeton University in New Jersey. But it is unclear "how deeply entrenched the early leaders will be, how long they will be able to maintain the edge that they now enjoy," says Starr, author of the Pulitzer Prize-winning *The Creation of the Media*.

The biggest blogs, however, not only appear to have staying power but also — thanks to advertising — are making their creators rich. Drudge's site has been estimated to be worth as much as $120 million; Huffington has made lucrative deals with Internet giants AOL and Yahoo. *Time* itself hosts one of the older blogs: Andrew Sullivan's Daily Dish, while Mickey Kaus's Kausfiles is featured on the online magazine *Slate.com*.

Still, media watchers emphasize that blogs depend on mainstream media for much of their raw material. "They don't go out and do investigative reporting," says Kline. "But as a complement to traditional media, blogs have been very helpful, adding a real slice of life to reporting, uncovering a lot of mistakes in the mainstream media and allowing more diverse voices to be heard."

As the number of blogs and blog readers continues to grow, here are some of the questions being debated:

Should policymakers be influenced by political blogs?

One month away from becoming Senate majority leader, Sen. Trent Lott, R-Miss., put his foot in his mouth at Sen. Strom Thurmond's 100th birthday bash on Dec. 5, 2002, by fondly recalling the presidential campaign the South Carolinian waged in 1948 on a segregationist platform. Noting that his home state of Mississippi had voted for Thurmond, Lott remarked, "If the rest of the country had followed our lead, we wouldn't have had all these problems over all these years."

Initially, Lott's gaffe went unreported except for a brief mention on ABCNews.com. But the story erupted in the blogosphere, pushed initially by the liberal Joshua Micah Marshall (talkingpointsmemo.com) and the conservative Glenn Reynolds (Instapundit.com). Eventually, the mainstream media took up the missed story, and an abashed Lott had to give up the GOP leadership.

Even as bloggers were demonstrating their impact, however, a noted journalism professor was dismissing their abilities and their role. "Bloggers are navel gazers," Elizabeth Osder, a visiting professor at the University of Southern California's Annenberg School of Journalism, told *Wired News* in 2002. "This is opinion without expertise, without resources, without reporting."[6]

Osder reflected a common view of blogging among journalists and media-watchers in the early years of the phenomenon. But now, blogging is getting respect. "It's

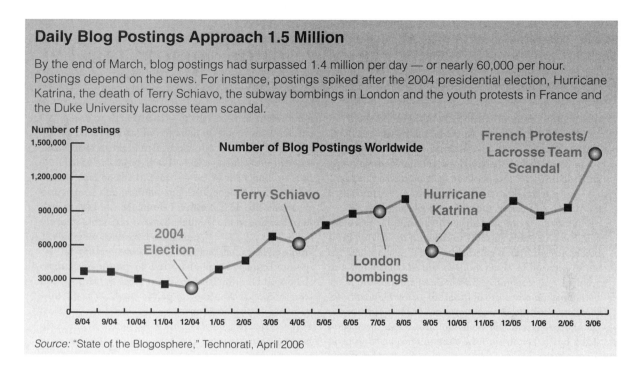

Daily Blog Postings Approach 1.5 Million

By the end of March, blog postings had surpassed 1.4 million per day — or nearly 60,000 per hour. Postings depend on the news. For instance, postings spiked after the 2004 presidential election, Hurricane Katrina, the death of Terry Schiavo, the subway bombings in London and the youth protests in France and the Duke University lacrosse team scandal.

Number of Postings

Number of Blog Postings Worldwide

French Protests/
Lacrosse Team
Scandal

Terry Schiavo

2004
Election

Hurricane
Katrina

London
bombings

Source: "State of the Blogosphere," Technorati, April 2006

moving out of the toddler stage and into the early elementary school age," says Lee Rainie, director of the Pew Internet and American Life Project. Bloggers influence mainstream news coverage by checking facts, adding material and prolonging stories, he says. "In some respects bloggers can keep a story alive a lot longer than it would've been alive in the pre-Internet era."

With literally millions of bloggers, generalizations are necessarily treacherous. But among the highest-profile political bloggers, several of them started — like Huffington and Drudge — without the kind of background or experience ordinarily associated with admission into the top echelons of the commentariat. Marshall, for example, had been in journalism for only two years when he started Talking Points Memo in 2000 at the age of 31. Reynolds was a 41-year-old professor at the University of Tennessee Law School when he started Instapundit in 2001.

But legal-affairs blogger Volokh bristles at the insinuation that bloggers have not paid their dues. "Some bloggers have many more qualifications than the average journalist writing on a particular field," he says. Others may have no special expertise but "end up producing good stuff because they're smart people."

Author Kline acknowledges the uneven quality of some blog content. "A great deal of it is uninformed — maybe 95 percent," he says. "But much of what I read in the newspapers is garbage. And most academic writing is terrible."

As with the Lott story, however, Huffington says bloggers have played an important role by running ahead on controversies that mainstream media were either missing or downplaying, such as the re-examination of the "60 Minutes II" story on President Bush's Air National Guard service and the reassessment of the prewar coverage of Iraq's supposed weapons of mass destruction. "These stories would not have gotten the traction they did without the blogosphere," she says.

But Tom Rosensteil, director of the Washington-based Project on Excellence in Journalism, says bloggers depend on mainstream media to have an impact on events. "If you track the cases where blogs have been influential, it's because they've influenced other political leaders or the media," the former *Los Angeles Times* media critic says.

Whether direct or indirect, bloggers' influence appears to have become a recognized fact of political life. "They have a considerable readership," says Princeton's Starr,

Liberal Political Blogs Are Most Popular

Although conservative blogs dominated immediately after the 9/11 terrorist attacks, most of the top 12 political blogs today are liberal. A blog's popularity is measured by how many other sites link to it, considered a vote of confidence for that blog. The rankings refer to how the Web site ranks among the 100 most popular blogs of all types.

Top 12 Political Blogs

Overall Rank Among All Blogs	Blog/Blogger	Site	No. of Web Sites Linking to This Blog
6	**Daily Kos** Liberal political analysis written by conservative-turned-liberal author Markos Moulitsas Zuniga.	www.dailykos.com	11,798
10	**Huffington Post** Liberal commentary by conservative-turned-liberal Arianna Huffington.	www.huffingtonpost.com	8,960
16	**Michelle Malkin** Written by conservative journalist and author Michelle Malkin; focuses on immigration issues.	www.michellemalkin.com	7,165
17	**Instapundit** Libertarian/conservative; written by University of Tennessee law Professor Glenn Reynolds.	www.instapundit.com	6,460
19	**Crooks & Liars** Liberal virtual magazine by former Duran Duran musician John Amato; features audio and video clips.	www.crooksandliars.com	6,406
5	**Think Progress** Liberal; edited by Judd Legum, research director at the Center for American Progress and former Clinton-era assistant to White House Chief of Staff John Podesta.	www.thinkprogress.org	5,586
35	**Wonkette** Gossipy, satirical blog on Washington, D.C., politics created by journalist Ana Marie Cox.	www.wonkette.com	4,177
39	**Talking Points Memo** Liberal political commentary, reporting from Joshua Micah Marshall, a columnist for the Capitol Hill newspaper, *The Hill*.	www.talkingpointsmemo.com	3,879
55	**AMERICAblog** Liberal blog with focus on the Bush administration, the radical right and gay civil rights; edited by writer and political consultant John Aravosis.	www.americablog.blogspot.com	3,402
56	**Little Green Footballs** Neoconservative war blog by software engineer and guitarist Charles Johnson.	www.littlegreenfootballs.com	3,401
59	**Power Line** Conservative blog dealing with policy issues such as income inequality and campaign finance reform written by lawyers John H. Hinderaker and Scott W. Johnson.	www.powerlineblog.com	3,346
71	**Eschaton** News and politics from liberal points of view; edited by Duncan Black, a senior fellow at Media Matters for America.	www.atrios.blogspot.com	3,147

Source: Technorati.com, as of June 1, 2006

who is co-editor of the liberal monthly *The American Prospect.* "I don't see how anybody can ignore them."

Geneva Overholser, a longtime journalist and now a professor at the University of Missouri School of Journalism in Columbia, agrees, but says readers need better information to evaluate individual blogs. She also worries about a seeming lack of diversity in the blogosphere. "We're not seeing the diversity of voices across the old lines of sex, race, socio-economic level," she says. "Could we really say it's just as easy to find a poor Latina writing a blog that will be heard as it is to find some 35-year-old white guy writing for us?"

Meanwhile, Osder sounds different on the subject today from four years ago. Blogging is "absolutely a wonderful new way to hear the voices of people you might not have heard before," she says. "I think of it more as a way for people in public office to have a new and legitimate ear on their community."

Should blogs tone down their political rhetoric?

Barely an hour after the American Bar Association (ABA) announced it had rated as "unqualified" President Bush's judicial nominee Michael Wallace, one of the bloggers on the pro-Bush site ConfirmThem.org vented his reaction.

"This is complete and utter b.s.," wrote Stephen Dillard ("feddie") in his May 10 posting. "Mike Wallace is clearly qualified to serve as a federal appellate judge, and the hacks that issued this rating ought to be ashamed of themselves. Lord, how I loathe the ABA."

A few days later, the liberal blogger Jerry Tenuto ("Lone Star Iconoclast") weighed in from the opposite perspective on another Bush nominee, Brett Kavanaugh.

"Brett Kavanaugh is just another shiftless Republican sycophant, ready to do the bidding of the King . . . er, Herr Oberst Karl Rove, that is," Tenuto wrote in the posting on OpEdNews.com. "They've really got this Fuhrer prinzip concept working overtime."

Although such caustic blogosphere rhetoric cheers partisans, some fear it risks aggravating political divisions and coarsening political dialogue. Media historian Starr, however, says blogs cannot be blamed for the political divisions in the country.

"You have, in general, a more polarized and more partisan politics, and at the same time you have the development of the blogs," says Starr. "The two feed off each other."

Bloggers themselves defend the sharp language as part of an American tradition and an essential element of their appeal. "There is a long, proud tradition of incendiary, controversial political rhetoric in America that goes back to the days before the Declaration of Independence," says Cox, of the Media Bloggers Association.

At the same time, blog expert Kline is one of many media watchers who expect the tone to change over time. "I don't think the degree of snarkiness is going to last," Kline says. "This phenomenon is going to evolve. The political conversations now, people just talk at each other. Over time, they'll become more reasoned."

Starr notes that blog technology invites intemperate postings. "There is less of a filter with the blogs because somebody's keystrokes go up immediately," says Starr. "Even if that writer has second thoughts, it's too late."

But Rosensteil of the Project on Excellence in Journalism says some bloggers do claim to filter out inflammatory rhetoric. "They try to be more provocative, but the most obstructionist and divisive stuff is kept out," he says.

For some bloggers, sharp rhetoric is part of their appeal. "I'm preaching to the choir for a reason," says Markos Moulitsas Zuniga, whose liberal blog DailyKos reportedly draws 500,000 visitors monthly. "It's because we're trying to organize, we're trying to fundraise, we're trying to win elections."[7]

Huffington, however, says she aims at a wider audience. "I don't think we just preach to the choir," she says. Huffington says her blog is bookmarked by many people

Bloggers post on their Web logs in a special section reserved for them during the Democratic National Convention in July 26, 2004, in Boston, Mass. Bloggers marked an important milestone when both the Republican and Democratic parties credentialed some bloggers to cover their 2004 national conventions.

in the media and in government. "Obviously, these are not all people of the same political persuasion," she says.

UCLA's Volokh cautions against overgeneralizing about blogs. "Some are highly partisan, some are less partisan and some are not partisan at all," he says. In fact, legal affairs blogs include several widely read primarily informational sites, such as SCOTUSBlog about the Supreme Court and How Appealing, which covers appellate litigation.

For his part, Cox of TheNationalDebate.com says the marketplace will operate over time as a check on the kind of rhetoric seen in the blogosphere now. "Bloggers, like anyone else advocating a political point of view, must compete in the marketplace of ideas," he says. "This marketplace is self-correcting. Those that employ language in a way that offends the sensibilities of their readers will find themselves with a dwindling audience and decreased influence."

Journalism Professor Overholser agrees. "There are all kinds of blogs," says Overholser. "Some will seek to be balanced, though most are indeed opinionated. Among the opinionated, some will be shrill, others more thoughtful and fair-minded. We consumers will choose among them, and the ones we choose will flourish."

Should bloggers have the same rights and privileges as reporters?

Sen. Richard J. Lugar, R-Ind., cheered journalism groups in May when he and a group of four bipartisan cosponsors introduced a bill to establish a federal shield law giving reporters a qualified privilege to protect confidential sources of information. "This is important legislation that all Americans should support," David Carlson, president of the Society of Professional Journalists, said in a May 18 press release.[8]

Bloggers had less reason to cheer, however. Lugar's bill would limit the protection to established print, broadcast and cable media — and exclude bloggers. "This bill is more like an 'affirmative action' program for corporate media," says Cox. "It grants special privileges to entities or persons based solely on their relationship to a corporate media organization."

Lugar says the issue is still open for discussion. "As to who is a reporter, this will be a subject of debate as this bill goes farther along," Lugar said in an online reply to a question after introducing the bill.[9] And journalists and media watchers are themselves uncertain about how far into the blogosphere to extend special privileges established for journalists.

"There's so much variety," says Steve Outing, a columnist for *Editor and Publisher Online* who covers interactive media. "Anything from a high-school student who has a personal blog all the way up to a *New York Times* reporter who might be blogging for *The New York Times* or maybe they have a personal blog."

As free-speech expert Volokh notes, the First Amendment itself guarantees certain rights to anyone — whether or not in the news media. The government cannot censor blogs, for example. But journalist shield laws passed by some states are the only protection for guarding confidential sources after the Supreme Court in 1974 refused to recognize a journalists' privilege under the First Amendment.

In addition, governmental and private organizations routinely must decide who qualifies as a member of the media in order to grant them special seating or access to news events. Bloggers marked an important milestone in 2004 when both the Republican and Democratic parties credentialed online journalists — including some bloggers — to cover their national conventions.[10]

For his part, Cox says the rule for bloggers is simple: "When bloggers are acting in a journalistic capacity, they should have the full protections afforded to anybody else who's operating as a journalist. If a blogger is reporting on a story — interviewing people, gathering information, reporting facts and putting together a story — they are a journalist. How they publish is irrelevant. The fact that bloggers are self-published doesn't speak to the issue of what they're doing to produce their content."

Carlson, director of the Interactive Media Lab at the University of Florida in Gainesville, agrees on protections for journalist bloggers but says it is necessary to draw a line between bloggers who are journalists and those who are not. One way to draw the line, Carlson says, is between bloggers who are doing "original reporting" and those who are only "stating opinion" or "regurgitating what others have written."

"You can't necessarily say someone who only does opinion is not a journalist, but often they are not," Carlson continues. "And you can't necessarily say anyone who's doing original reporting is a journalist. But most often they are."

However, Duncan Black, a senior fellow at Media Matters for America and a blogger, says original reporting should not be a prerequisite for a blogger to be treated like other journalists. "What bloggers do fits well within the news media if we broaden [the definition of media] to include the kind of talk shows we find on cable news, public-affairs programs that include news analysis, AM talk radio," he says. "The news media is much broader than people like to think sometimes."

Corporate affiliation should be irrelevant, Black adds. "A press ID from *The New York Times* shouldn't give you special privileges," he says. Rosensteil agrees. "From a journalistic point of view, the technology exists now that you don't need an organization to practice journalism," he says.

Moreover, Cox notes, the mainstream media now are moving rapidly into the blogosphere themselves. "It's not an us [bloggers] versus them [mainstream media] issue," says Cox. "It very much used to be, but now it's gone. When the *New York Times*, *Washington Post*, *National Journal*, CBS News all have bloggers, there's no longer a dichotomy."

BACKGROUND

Before Blogs

Modern-day bloggers trace their antecedents back to Ice Age cave painters and to the political pamphleteers of the early centuries of the print revolution. In U.S. history,

CHRONOLOGY

1970s-1980s *Early days of computer networking; electronic bulletin boards emerge, Internet is born.*

1990s *World Wide Web launched; first weblogs follow.*

1991 First World Wide Web site brought online by British computer scientist Sir Tim Berners-Lee.

1993 Mosaic Web browser simplifies creating Web pages.

1994 Swarthmore College student Justin Hall starts Web-based diary "Justin's Links from the Underground," seen as forerunner of personal blogging.

1996 Matt Drudge migrates gossipy Hollywood-based Drudge Report from e-mail distribution to Web.

1997 Jorn Barger begins publishing "RobotWisdom," coins the word "weblog" to describe process of logging the Web as he surfed.

1998 Drudge Report breaks story of President Clinton's liaison with White House intern Monica Lewinsky.

1999 Pyra Labs creates "Blogger," easy-to-use software for creating blogs. . . . Fewer than 100 blogs known to be in existence.

2000-Present *Blogs number in the millions, but are unread by most Americans.*

2001 Terrorist attacks of 9/11 bring outpouring of conservative, pro-war sentiments on "war blogs."

2002 *New York Times* word maven William Safire devotes July 28 column to origins, usage of "blog" . . . Bloggers Glenn Reynolds (Instapundit) and Joshua Micah Marshall (TalkingPointsMemo) publicize Senate GOP Leader Trent Lott's praise for Strom Thurmond's segregationist presidential campaign in 1948; controversy picked up by mainstream media, forces Lott to relinquish post.

2003 Teen blog site MySpace.com is founded; acquired by Rupert Murdoch's NewsCorp in 2005 for $580 million. . . . Howard Dean uses Internet, blogs to raise funds, mobilize support for 2004 presidential campaign; folds campaign in February 2004 after faring badly in Iowa, New Hampshire.

May 2004 Senate staffer Jessica Cutler fired for writing sexy "Washingtonienne" blog from office computer but gets six-figure book deal from episode.

July 2004 Bloggers credentialed for political party conventions.

September-Novemer 2004 Conservative blogs sharply attack CBS report questioning President Bush's service in Texas Air National Guard; controversy hastens Dan Rather's retirement as news anchor, forces network to acknowledge flaws in report. . . . Bush and Democratic challenger John Kerry both use blogs in presidential campaigns. . . . Media Bloggers Association formed.

January 2005 Iran jails 20 online journalists and bloggers.

February 2005 Gallup Poll shows a third of Internet users read blogs at least occasionally, but nearly two-thirds never do.

May 2005 *Business Week* cover story tells businesses to use blogs for market research, consumer feedback. . . . Ariana Huffington debuts liberal blog HuffingtonPost.com.

March 2006 Federal Election Commission says political blogs not subject to federal campaign finance laws.

April 2006 *Los Angeles Times* columnist's blog on California politics is suspended after he was found to have posted comments on site and elsewhere under an assumed name.

May 2006 Matt Drudge, Ariana Huffington named by *Time* magazine as among world's 100 most influential people. . . . California state appeals court says bloggers entitled to same protection for confidential sources as other journalists. . . . Bloggers tracked by Technorati surpass 42 million. . . . Egypt jails at least six bloggers among other dissidents.

June 26 2010 *The Washington Post* fires blogger David Weigel for previous e-mails attacking conservatives.

July 19-21 2010 Conservative blogger Andrew Breitbart posts edited video, ignites reverse-racism controversy over remarks by Agriculture Department official Shirley Sherrod.

Aug. 23 2010 Blogs report that Philadelphia hits bloggers with fees for running online ads.

Businesses Ignore Blogosphere at Their Peril

The Kryptonite lock company's slogan — "Tough Locks for a Tough World" — refers to the protection its locks offer against "real world" thieves. But the Canton, Mass., manufacturer of high-end bicycle locks learned that cyberspace is a tough world, too, especially for businesses that ignore the blogosphere.

Kryptonite still feels the impact of the September 2004 blogosphere eruption that occurred when someone using the name "unaesthetic" posted on a discussion site the fact that the company's ubiquitous U-shaped lock could be picked with the plastic casing of a ballpoint pen. Within two days, a number of blogs, including the consumer electronics site engadget, had posted a video demonstrating how to perform the trick. Hundreds of thousands of people read about the lock's flaw, and cyclists in chatrooms and blogs expressed their alarm.

Two days later the company promised a tougher line of locks, but bloggers stayed on the case. The blog-monitoring Web site Technorati estimated that 1.8 million Internet users read about the lock's flaws. Finally, 10 days after word initially broke, the company said it would exchange any lock for free.[1] The incident cost the company's parent company Ingersoll-Rand an estimated $10 million.[2]

Donna Tocci, the company's media chief, now checks 30-40 blogs a day for discussions about its products.[3]

"This wouldn't happen today," says Steve Rubel, a senior vice president and author of the blog "Micro Persuasion" at the Edelman public relations firm. "Kryptonite didn't respond fast enough, and it spun out of control."

Love it or hate it, businesses are coming to grips with the blogosphere and learning that when managed well it can help the bottom line — or at least public relations. For instance, when a Manhattan blogger complained that he could not find Degree Sport deodorant in his neighborhood, manufacturer Unilever not only e-mailed him to tell him where he could find it but also sent him a free case of the antiperspirant, Rubel says.

In another example of how blogs can improve customer relations, Microsoft employee Robert Scoble's blog (http://scobleizer.wordpress.com/) was credited with helping reduce external criticism of the company's launch of MSN Space in 2004. Scoble then co-authored *Naked Conversations*, describing how blogs are changing communications between business and customers. Microsoft Chairman Bill Gates wrote admiringly on the book jacket that Scoble was "building a connection" to customers, adding, "Maybe they'll tell us how we can better improve our products."

Everyone who follows business blogs has a favorite story about how they have helped or hurt any given firm, says David Kline, co-author of *blog! how the newest media revolution is changing politics, business, and culture.*

Nevertheless, only a fraction of America's biggest companies have embraced the blog's power so far. As of April 18 of this year, 29 — or only 5.8 percent — of *Fortune* 500 companies were blogging, according to a "wiki" launched by Chris Anderson of *Wired* magazine and Ross Mayfield of Socialtext, a maker of enterprise social software for collaboration.[4] *

But companies ignore the blogosphere at their peril, as Dell computer manufacturer found out. Writer, publisher

*A wiki — the Hawaiian word for quick — is a Web page that readers can edit.

---

their ancestry can be seen in the openly partisan press of the 19th and early 20th centuries, the muckraking journalists of the progressive era and the rambunctious hosts of mid- and late 20th-century talk radio. Now with an inexpensive platform that was available to none of those ancestors, bloggers have a unique ability to disseminate their messages — chatty or substantive, informational or opinionated — in real time, 24/7, to an audience as large and far-flung as a global computer network will allow.[11]

The connection between bloggers and cave painters came to blog expert Dan Burstein on a visit to southwestern France.[12] Burstein writes of learning for the first time that the pictorial decorations went on in some instances for generations or longer. With no written language, the painters and storytellers of prehistory used visual images to describe and comment on their ideas and beliefs on the topics of their day — hunting, initiation rites, sickness, mortality, the afterlife. The automotive and interactive journalism expert Jeff Jarvis complained on his blog (Buzzmachine) that his Dell laptop kept crashing and recounted his fruitless efforts to get Dell customer support to help. His subsequent blog post announcing that he planned to buy an Apple laptop became one of the most trafficked posts for weeks.

"If something is happening on the Internet and you're not aware of it, whether you're a company or a major brand or a government agency, there's a price to pay," says Sue MacDonald, marketing manager at Nielsen Buzzmetrics, which helps companies navigate "consumer-generated media," including blogs. Many firms now check what people are saying about them online, but they do so only on an ad hoc basis.

Yet Kline says when people shop online, it is the customer comments rather than advertising or newspapers that have the most important impact on purchasing decisions. He cites *Edelman Annual Trust Barometer*, a survey of 2,000 opinion leaders in 11 countries conducted by the world's biggest public relations firm. Its most recent survey found that participants believe what "a person like me" says about a company or its products more than what anyone else says. Among U.S. participants this tendency leapt from just 20 percent in 2003 to 68 percent in 2005. [5]

Jason Goldman, product manager for Google's blogging service called Blogger, says that at conferences and other gatherings in the last 18 months, there has been a "groundswell" of people getting specifically involved in helping businesses start their own blogs. "The fact that it has already penetrated close to 6 percent among the last bastion of traditional businesses is rather surprising," he says. The percentage of smaller companies blogging, particularly Internet start-ups, was far higher, he adds.

Kline says blogging will dramatically change the way companies advertise. "Now people can go on their blogs

Word spread through cyberspace like wildfire in 2004 after a blogger mentioned that the famous U-shaped Kryptonite-brand lock could be easily opened with the plastic casing of a ballpoint pen.

and say, I had a lousy experience with a Dell computer, and it has an evident, noticeable impact. In the future, the database miners will be less important than those who can derive relevant meaning from even a small sample of consumers in their own words," he says. "Customers are going to become co-creators in terms of marketing strategy."

[1] See David Kirkpatrick, *et al.*, "Why There's No Escaping the Blog," *Fortune*, Jan. 10, 2005.

[2] Ben Delaney, "Kryptonite on level ground six months after U-lock publicity crisis," *Bicycle Retailer*, April 1, 2005.

[3] See "The Blog in the Corporate Machine — Corporate Reputations," *The Economist*, Feb. 11, 2006.

[4] www.socialtext.net/bizblogs/index.cgi

[5] www.edelman.com/news/ShowOne.asp?ID=102.

blog Inside Line sees the same connection. "People blog because cave paintings are obsolete," a Jan. 10, 2006, post reads.

Cave painting was indeed a limiting medium. Reaching a wider audience awaited the development of written languages and a writing "platform." The Egyptians came up with papyrus around 3000 B.C. Europeans used sheepskin parchment. The Chinese initially used bamboo and silk, but around 200 B.C. developed a technique of

using wood pulp to make what came to be called "paper" when it reached Europe more than 1,000 years later. Despite modern-day derision of "dead tree" media, paper was truly a breathtaking breakthrough: it used an abundant natural resource to produce a communications medium both portable and durable.

Publishing was a labor-intensive process dependent on monks and Talmudic scholars, however, until the development of movable type and the printing press. The Chinese

Teens and 'Gen-Y' Love to Blog

Alongside her photograph and personal information on her MySpace weblog, 19-year-old Jenna from Cross Plains, Tenn., praises her "wonderful" boyfriend Jeremy, adding, "even though he can be a dork sometimes."

A 22-year-old from Salt Lake City wrote on his blog that when he revealed that he was homosexual, his father had kicked him in the groin. "The only people I can really count on in this difficult time is you all," he wrote.

Teens and Internet users who belong to Generation Y — the 18-to-28 age group — are in the vanguard of the blogging revolution, revealing their true loves, rating their teachers, coming out, finding dates, sharing passions and even mourning deaths in public.

"The younger generations have no problem expressing their whole life on their blog," says Mark Jen, a product manager at Plaxo, a company that maintains contact information for more than 10 million Internet users. In fact, 38 percent of Internet users ages 12 to 17 read blogs, while 19 percent say they have created one. Forty-one percent of Generation Y Internet users read blogs and one in five have created one of their own, according to a survey released in December 2005 by the Pew Internet and American Life Project. Blog creation trails off significantly in older age groups, dropping to 9 percent for the 29-40 and 51-59 age groups, 3 percent for the 41-50- and 60-69-year-olds and 4 percent for those 70-plus.[1]

But for young people, blogging has opened the door to a new sense of community, says Jen, 23. For instance, Sara, a 23-year-old from San Francisco, reported finding 42 new "friends" in her first day of MySpace membership.

The enormously popular teen blogging site attracted 48 million visitors in April and was the eighth most trafficked site. Founded in 2003, the site was bought for $580 million in July 2005 by Rupert Murdoch's News Corp.

Teens also use blogs — and flex their blog muscle — in innovative ways. Eight million students around the world use RateMyProfessors.com, which allows college and university students to give frank, anonymous assessments of their teachers. More than 3 million school kids in the United States, Canada, the United Kingdom and Ireland have posted 9.2 million ratings on a sister site, RateMyTeachers.com.

The most rated college is Grand Valley State University in Allendale, Mich., where teachers get marks of good, average or poor — and a red chili pepper if they are "hot." Here, a teacher can learn a student was so bored he counted 137 tiles on the ceiling during a lecture.

Similarly, Facebook.com, a two-year-old online social directory, claims 7.5 million members from more than 2,200 colleges, 22,000 high schools and 2,000 companies and is the seventh-most trafficked site. Two-thirds of the membership visits the site daily, spending an average of 20 minutes viewing photos and profiles of peers or updating their own information.

Bearing in mind recent examples of online predators taking advantage of teens on the Internet, Rep. Michael Fitzpatrick (R-Pa.) has introduced a bill that would restrict minors from accessing commercial social networking Web sites and chat rooms at schools and public libraries.[2] Mobilizing America's Youth, a group that works to increase political participation by the young, opposes the bill, although it agrees with the intent: to protect Internet users. Spokesman Damien Power said Facebook.com allows users to block other users and to report unsolicited messages to site administrators.[3]

---

pioneered movable type beginning in the 11th century. Clay type was used first, then wood and finally metal.

In the mid-15th century German goldsmith Johann Gutenberg combined metal type with a mechanical printing press. The invention spread quickly, and books — once a luxury — became by contemporary standards cheap and plentiful, as did pamphlets, like the anticlerical writings of the English Puritan John Milton in the mid-17th century or the political satire of the Anglo-Irish author

Jonathan Swift in the early 18th. In America, Thomas Paine's pro-independence pamphlet "Common Sense" (1776) sold half a million copies and is widely credited with helping swing popular sentiment toward revolution.[13]

The Industrial Revolution made printing even cheaper in the 19th century, as the United States was developing what was then the world's most efficient and reliable postal system. News was cheap: It was the era of the "penny

However, the ease with which teenagers and young adults "let it all hang out" on their blogs — particularly descriptions of illegal activities like drug or alcohol use — could come back to haunt them. Police regularly trawl MySpace for evidence of crimes both big and small.

Rayann VonSchoech, a community-services officer with the Sacramento Police Department's gang-suppression unit, has bookmarked about 30 MySpace blogs to check for faces matching gang street names or other signs of a looming crime.[4] "I already have a bank full of gangsters," she said. Her colleague Detective Sam Blackmon estimated that the Internet helps provide clues to about 10 percent of the city's gang arrests.[5]

And in Riverton, Kan., five students were arrested in April on suspicion of plotting a school shooting attack after posting a threatening message on MySpace.com.[6]

Marketers have begun to view the popularity of such sites among the youthful market sector as a vast untapped advertising opportunity. But the younger generation is suspicious of advertisers, so companies are cautious.

"We don't tell clients to market *to* teens," says Steve Rubel, a prominent blogger and senior vice president at the global public relations firm Edelman. "We say you should market *with* teens."

He adds, "You need to figure out what their motivations are and help them succeed, and at the same time . . . integrate your brand into that experience."

Georgia State University student Pamela Elder accesses her Facebook.com blog, where she has reconnected with old friends. The two-year-old online social directory claims 7.5 million members from more than 2,200 colleges, 22,000 high schools and 2,000 companies.

---

[1] The Pew survey can be found at www.pewinternet.org/PPF/r/144/report_display.asp.

[2] See Timothy Taylor and Stephanie Woodrow, "Youths to Congress: Don't Block MySpace," *Roll Call*, May 22, 2006.

[3] *Ibid.*

[4] Carrie Peyton Dahlberg, "Many eyes on teens' space; Law enforcement combs popular Web site where youths let it all hang out," *The Sacramento Bee*, May 30, 2006.

[5] *Ibid.*

[6] Marcus Kabel, "Five Students Arrested in Foiled Southeast Kansas School Shooting," *Belleville News-Democrat*, April 20, 2006.

---

newspaper." And with the invention of the telegraph, news could travel even faster.

Throughout this period, U.S. newspapers were highly partisan. "There's nothing that we see on any blog that compares to the scurrilous kind of attacks newspapers would print about politicians in those days," says author Kline. At the turn of the century, journalist-authors like Ida Tarbell, Lincoln Steffens and Upton Sinclair created the model of investigative reporting. President Theodore Roosevelt labeled them "muckrakers," even as he congratulated them for attacking the "grave evils" of the day.

The advent of radio and television made news even cheaper and quicker. Advertising-supported over-the-air broadcasting gradually became a big business — "the biggest of Big Media," as journalist-turned-blogger Dan Gillmor puts it.[14] Broadcasting became too profitable to risk being too controversial. Simultaneously, newspapers generally were moving away from outright partisanship toward an ethos of objectivity and professionalism. In the process, today's bloggers suggest, print and broadcast media alike became more centralized and homogenized — and less interesting.

The era gave rise, however, to a few mavericks who can be viewed as forerunners of today's bloggers, with the best example being I. F. Stone (1907-1989), says media historian Starr. After two decades as a journalist and author, Stone in 1953 started his own publication, *I. F. Stone's Weekly*, and filled it for 18 years with hard-hitting articles often based on close examination of government documents left unread by mainstream reporters.

Talk-radio hosts can also be seen as antecedents for bloggers. Call-in shows date from 1945, but the format exploded in the late 1980s when the Federal Communications Commission's repeal of the Fairness Doctrine eliminated stations' need to ensure balanced viewpoints. Over the next decade the rise of conservative hosts like Rush Limbaugh — and the eventual emergence of a few, less successful liberal counterparts — stemmed from a shared distrust between host and listeners of "the media" and the listeners' ability to voice their opinions on the air.

Meanwhile, a new communications technology was emerging. Rudimentary elements of computer networking dated from the 1960s. The electronic bulletin boards of the 1980s allowed computer users to dial up individual sites for information. Then in the early 1990s came the World Wide Web: a global information space accessible to any Internet-connected computer with the use of click-and-point technology. A new chapter in media history was about to begin.

Birth of Blogs

The first bloggers began blogging in the mid-'90s before the word "blog" had been coined or the technology for widespread use had been developed. The pioneers were computer experts who were and remain little known outside the information-technology community. The advent of easy-to-use software at the end of the decade allowed non-geeks to begin blogging. Then, in the first years of the new century, the Sept. 11, 2001, terrorist attacks showed that the new technology could facilitate national conversation about cataclysmic events while the

toppling of Senate Republican leader Lott demonstrated that bloggers could have real impact on politics and government.[15]

The British computer scientist Sir Tim Berners-Lee brought the first World Wide Web site online on Aug. 6, 1991. He had developed the concept of hypertext in the 1980s as a means of facilitating the sharing and updating of computer-stored information among researchers. In 1989 he saw the potential to join his hypertext markup language (HTML) software with the Internet to allow information-sharing globally. And, as blogger Gillmor notes, Berners-Lee also envisioned two-way communication: the ability to read from *and* to write to documents found on the Web.[16]

Programmers at the National Center for Supercomputing Applications in Champaign, Ill., made the next break-through: the development of Mosaic, the first Web browser to provide a multimedia, graphical user interface to the Internet. The leader of the team, Marc L. Andreessen, went on to found the company that later became Netscape. With Mosaic, Web pages were relatively easy to create, and some early forms of what Gillmor calls "personal journalism" emerged. He counts Justin's Links from the Underground by Swarthmore College student Justin Hall as "perhaps the first serious weblog."

"It was journalism," Hall explained later, "but it was mostly about me."[17]

Credit for naming the practice goes to Jorn Barger, a computer geek from the age of 11 and an active participant in the early 1990s in Usenet, the pre-Web computer communications network. On Dec. 17, 1997, Barger began posting short comments and links on his Robot Wisdom Web site. He coined the term "weblog," which he defined in a September 1999 posting as "a webpage where a weblogger . . . 'logs' all the other webpages she finds interesting." By then, Barger was reporting getting 1,500-2,000 hits a day, the term was being shortened to "blog," and the new phenomenon was being heralded — in the words of tech journalist Jon Katz — as "the freshest example of how people use the Net to make their own, radically different new media."[18]

Pyra Labs, a start-up company in San Francisco founded in 1999 by Evan Williams and Meg Hourihan, provided the last of the initial building blocks: an easy-to-use software dubbed "Blogger." The service was made available, for free, in August 1999 — at a time when blogs may have numbered fewer than 100. As software developer Matthew McKinnon wrote two years later, Blogger allowed anyone with a Web site to set up a blog "in about two minutes" and to update the site any time from anywhere.[19] As word of the free service spread, the number of blogs grew. The software was rewritten in 2002 so that it could be licensed, and the advertising-supported blogspot began to emerge as the dominant software. By then, the number of blogs was estimated at 40,000.[20]

At that point, blogging was also generating its first intramural spat: complaints from early bloggers about the rise of so-called "war bloggers" in the aftermath of the Sept. 11 terrorist attacks. As the U.S.-led invasion of Afghanistan got under way, several hawkish blogs emerged — notably, Glenn Reynolds' Instapundit — to vent indignation and to chronicle and support the military actions. In contrast to the techies' "inward-looking" sites, Reynolds said his and other sites were "outward-looking" — focused on a larger audience.[21] Old-line bloggers flinched at the newcomers' political slant and at the spike in attention, but the visibility was paying off in eyeballs. Reynolds was counting nearly 20,000 visitors a day by mid-2002.

By the end of the year, the broader-focused blogs were being depicted as a new power center, based on their role in forcing Lott to step down as Senate Republican leader. Mainstream media missed the story of Lott's Dec. 5 remarks at first, but the story gained legs thanks to venting from hundreds of bloggers ranging across the political spectrum. "The Internet's First Scalp," the *New York Post* declared in a headline.[22]

Reynolds and liberal counterpart Joshua Micah Marshall demurred. "I think you can exaggerate the role of the blogs in this," Reynolds said, while Marshall took exception to what he called "blog triumphalism."[23]

Whether exaggerated or not, the episode sent a clear warning to journalists and politicians alike: Ignore the bloggers at your peril.

Power of Blogs

With blogging still in its first decade, the number of blogs has skyrocketed along with readership. Bloggers continued to demonstrate their power by helping force the resignations of two media heavyweights in 2005: CBS News anchor Dan Rather and CNN President Eason Jordan. Political candidates also began to use blogs as fund-raising and mobilizing tools — most notably, former Vermont Gov. Howard Dean in his unsuccessful bid for the Democratic presidential nomination in 2004. But the intermingling of journalistic and political roles by some bloggers raised a variety of legal and ethical issues.

The blogosphere's growth has been nothing short of phenomenal. From fewer than 1 million blogs at the start of 2003, the number doubled every six months through early 2006. News coverage of blogs also increased. *The New York Times* used the word in 28 articles in 2002 and 553 articles in 2005. Blog readership also grew rapidly, as the number of adults who have read blogs increased more than fourfold — from 13.2 million in May 2003 to 57 million by January 2006, according to the Pew Internet center. Significantly, more than one out of 10 Internet users have also posted material or comments on other people's blogs.[24]

In 2004 Dean's Internet-driven presidential campaign created a surge of interest in blogs and other online tools among politicians, voters and political journalists. Dean went from a blip on the political radar screen in early 2003 to the presumed Democratic front-runner by the end of the year primarily on the strength of using the Internet to raise more than $40 million from 300,000 donors. At one point his campaign weblog drew 100,000 visitors a day. The excitement about Web-based politics deflated when Dean's Web support failed to materialize at the polls: he ended his campaign on Feb. 18 after losing badly in the Iowa caucuses in January and the New Hampshire primary in early February 2004.[25]

Both President Bush and the eventual Democratic nominee John Kerry did pick up Dean's idea of using blogs as a tool to communicate with supporters and volunteers — but in different formats. An Associated Press Internet reporter described Bush's campaign blog as "flashier," Kerry's more substantive, and noted that Kerry's blog allowed visitors to post comments, while Bush's did not.[26] Bush "didn't get in trouble" for not having an interactive blog, Professor Davis remarks today. "His supporters didn't punish him for it, and he won."

Bloggers did play an important part, however, in helping the president's campaign combat questions that resurfaced late in the campaign about Bush's service in the Texas Air National Guard in the 1960s. The CBS program "60 Minutes II" aired a story on Sept. 8, 2004, claiming that newly discovered documents provided by an anonymous source showed that then-Lt. Bush had received favorable treatment in the Guard and failed to fulfill some service requirements. Rather, a correspondent on the program and then in his 24th year as "CBS Evening News" anchor, reported the story.

An array of conservative bloggers — led by FreeRepublic.com — immediately questioned the authenticity of the documents and accused Rather and CBS of political bias. "You can almost say that conservative bloggers acted as a fire brigade" on the story, says David Perlmutter, a professor of journalism at the University of Kansas who is writing a book on political blogs. Under heavy attack, Rather announced in November that he would step down as anchor in March 2005. Then, after an independent investigation, CBS News conceded in January 2005 that it could not authenticate the documents, fired the story's producer and demoted three other executives connected with the program.

In another episode, CNN President Jordan was forced to resign in February 2005 after comments he made two weeks earlier blaming the U.S. military for the deaths of 12 journalists in Iraq. As with the so-called Rathergate story, conservative blogs publicized the comments as evidence of liberal bias by CNN and eventually dragged mainstream media into covering the story. Jordan's resignation under pressure cheered conservatives but left one leading blogger ambivalent. "I wish our goal were not taking off heads but digging up truth," Jeff Jarvis of buzzmachine.com told *The New York Times*.[27]

Different ethical issues were raised by the role of two political bloggers in South Dakota's hotly contested 2004 Senate race. Senate Democratic Leader Tom Daschle was running neck and neck with Rep. Jim Thune, a Republican strongly supported by national GOP leaders. It turned out that two bloggers, Jon Lauck and Jason Van Beek, who sharply attacked Daschle on their sites, were paid $27,000 and $8,000, respectively, by the Thune campaign, though the campaign did not disclose the payments until after the election. Thune won by about 4,700 votes, and Van Beek now has a full-time job in Thune's Senate office. The campaign insisted at the time that the bloggers were paid for research, not for blogging.[28]

CURRENT SITUATION
Gaining Respect

Bloggers and other Internet sites are savoring two important legal victories that recognize confidential-source protections for online journalists and exempt all unpaid Internet political activity from federal campaign-finance regulation.

In a closely watched trade-secrets case, a state appeals court in California ruled on May 26 that online journalists are entitled to the same protection as other news organizations against being forced to divulge confidential sources. The ruling blocks Apple Computer from learning the identities of individuals who leaked inside information to two bloggers in 2004 about a then unreleased digital-music device the company was developing.[29]

Meanwhile, the Federal Election Commission (FEC) decided on March 27 to extend to bloggers and other online publications the same exemption enjoyed by traditional news media: Bloggers will not be required to disclose their costs of covering federal election campaigns. Under the commission's decision, even overtly partisan blogs organized to support a particular candidate or party need not disclose their expenditures unless actually controlled by the candidate or party.[30]

Blogging advocates praised both decisions. "Bloggers should be treated the same as the media under campaign finance law," says Adam Bonin, a Philadelphia lawyer who represented three liberal bloggers before the FEC.

Media Bloggers Association President Cox calls the California decision "another step up in the ladder of building the case law around blogging."

The Apple case stemmed from the pre-release publication of details of the company's new "Asteroid" device in November 2004 on two Web sites devoted to Apple products: Power Page, published by Pennsylvania blogger Jason O'Grady, and Apple Insider, published by the pseudonymous "Kasper Jade." Apple filed suit in state court claiming the two sites had appropriated valuable trade secrets and then tried to use pretrial discovery to find out who leaked the information.

O'Grady and "Jade" both invoked California's journalist shield law in refusing, but the trial judge said the privilege did not apply because the theft of trade secrets amounted to a crime. On appeal, Apple pressed its argument that the bloggers could not claim protection of the

Is blogging increasing public participation in politics?

YES
Robert Cox
President, Media Bloggers Association

Written for *CQ Researcher*, June 2006

Since blogs first "arrived" on the political scene during the 2004 election, blogging has increased popular participation in politics. Blog readership and blog creation have been growing at a phenomenal rate, with political blogging the most active part of the blogosphere.

The question is not whether blogging has increased political participation but rather will that continue as political professionals strive to co-opt blogging for their own ends. Professor Richard Davis (at right) has rightly warned that those in the past who have heralded a new technology as transforming American democracy have been disappointed. Television was to allow more Americans to engage in the great issues of the day, but in the years since the watershed Kennedy-Nixon debates the long-term trend has been a decline in voter turnout.

It is certainly reasonable to fear that political power brokers will seek to control spin on the blogs, just as they do in the rest of the media. Meanwhile, with Rupert Murdoch's purchase of MySpace and the acquisition of About.com by *The New York Times*, large media institutions are already staking out their online claims.

Blogs are fundamentally different from previous mass-communications technologies like newspapers, radio and television. Because they reside on the Internet and are inexpensive to own and operate, anyone with online access can utilize an infinitely scalable, near-free distribution system to reach a global audience. They not only are interactive but also permit information to flow in multiple directions and to be distributed on multiple levels. More important, as Davis notes, blog reading is "purposive," requiring "affirmative steps" that make it ideal for attracting and organizing citizens willing to actively engage in a political campaign. The "netroots" efforts on behalf of Howard Dean's campaign in 2004 demonstrated the power of blogs as a fundraising tool.

The question is not whether blogs increase political participation — they do — but how that participation will manifest itself in the political process. Politicians now realize that blogs have the potential to be a disruptive force in the political power structure. Professor Davis is right to worry that politicians are taking steps to avoid being disintermediated out of the political process, but squelching bloggers is about as effective as squeezing mercury. Traditional gatekeepers in the political process are fighting a rearguard action as blogging redefines the political landscape, levels the information playing field and gives millions of Americans a voice they never had in our national political dialogue.

NO
Richard Davis
Professor of Political Science, Brigham Young University

Written for *CQ Researcher*, June 2006

Blogs provide another vehicle for political expression. In that sense, they increase political participation. But if political participation is defined more broadly, blogs potentially fall short.

For example, if we mean increased involvement by bloggers in political activities such as voting, donating, communicating with public officials, community service, and so forth, then there is no evidence blogs have performed that function.

And if we mean involving more people who have not previously been involved in politics, then that seems unlikely as well. That's because the political-blog audience consists of the already highly political. According to a recent survey by Harris Interactive, 52 percent of daily, political-blog readers also listen to talk radio at least several times a week and 86 percent watch network or cable news broadcasts. Among the general public, only 37 percent listen to talk radio, and 71 percent watch network news.

But some might say that will change as blog use grows. That argument is based on a premise that fails to consider human behavior. The mere existence of a technology does not change people's interests, attitudes and political behavior. For example, when people go online, they do much the same thing they used to do through other means: write to family and friends, trade stocks, follow sports scores or pay attention to politics. They are not more likely to engage in activities in which they have little interest.

Political blogs are even less likely than the Internet generally to reach citizens who are not politically interested or active. They are a niche of the blogosphere and of the Internet that the less politically interested must search out and find. Why would they do so? Perhaps if they were angry about some governmental decision, they would. But the stimulus would be their anger, not blogs.

The digital divide between rich and poor feared in the 1990s actually became a divide between the politically interested and active — who found e-mail, Web sites, and online discussion a new mechanism for gathering political information and expressing themselves — and the politically less interested, who used the Internet for other things.

Political blogs are part of that digital divide as well. The politically interested will gravitate to them while the majority who see politics primarily as a civic duty, if even that, will go elsewhere.

law at all, but the San Jose-based appeals court disagreed. "The shield law is intended to protect the gathering and dissemination of news, and that is what petitioners did here," Justice Conrad Rushing wrote in the 69-page opinion.

"Bloggers who practice journalism are journalists . . . and therefore are entitled to the same protection afforded to any other journalist. Period," says Cox.

The FEC's decision largely reaffirmed the agency's initial stance to leave Internet political activity essentially unregulated. A federal judge in Washington in 2004 ordered the agency to reconsider the issue in a suit brought by the House sponsors of the Bipartisan Campaign Reform Act (BCRA), the 2002 measure commonly known by the names of its Senate sponsors: Sens. John McCain, R-Ariz., and Russ Feingold, D-Wis.

In its new regulation, the FEC decided federal candidates must disclose expenditures for paid political advertising on the Internet but left all other Internet political communications unregulated. The rules "totally exempt individuals who engage in political activity on the Internet from the restrictions of the campaign-finance laws," FEC Chairman Michael Toner said before the March 27 vote.

For bloggers, the FEC action adds Web sites and any other Internet or electronic publications to the definition of news media in a longstanding exemption from having to report the costs of news coverage, editorials or commentaries. "Bloggers and others who communicate on the Internet are entitled to the press exemption in the same way as traditional media entities," the commission wrote in explaining the rule.

The commission had taken the same stance in an advisory ruling in November 2005, telling the pro-Democratic blog Fire Up that it did not need to disclose its spending as campaign contributions. A coalition of public-interest groups favoring campaign finance regulation had opposed the exemption. "This looked much more like a partisan political organization," explains Paul Ryan, FEC program director for the Campaign Legal Center.

Prominent bloggers on the left and right both praised the FEC's rule. "This is a tremendous win for speech," said Mike Krempasky of the conservative blog RedState .org. Liberal blogger Duncan Black, writing under the pseudonym Artios, said: "This could have been an utter disaster, but it appears to have all worked out in the end."[31]

For their part, the campaign-finance groups say they are satisfied with the FEC's overall position, but Ryan still voices concern about the broad media exemption. "Whenever the FEC opens an exemption, the window for abuse opens," he says.

Blogging at Work

A police union in suburban Washington, D.C., is watching its online message board more carefully these days after some officers were discovered to have posted racist, sexist and anti-immigrant comments on the site.

A *Los Angeles Times* columnist is no longer writing a political blog for the newspaper because he posted comments on the newspaper's Web site and elsewhere on the Web under pseudonyms.

A marine zoologist is out of a job after the Academy of Natural Sciences in Philadelphia fired her for posting comments about her job on her site and on MySpace.com.

Along with all the marvels of blogging come at least a fair share of new problems. Blogging culture invites the posting of information that in the pre-Internet world might have been kept private and messages that might have been left unwritten — or at least undelivered.

Employers and employees are among those working out rules for blogging — mostly by trial and error. The vast majority of companies appear to have no written policies on the subject. But a blogger activist who says he lost out on a job because of one of his postings counts more than 60 other bloggers who have been fired or disciplined for blog-related reasons.

The most famous workplace victim is Jessica Cutler, a twenty-something former staffer for Sen. Mike DeWine, R-Ohio, who was fired in May 2004 for writing up her active sex life under the cyberhandle "Washingtonienne." Cutler thought the anonymous blog would amuse her girlfriends, only to discover that others were not amused after the blog was publicized through another blog: Wonkette, a widely read Washington gossip and politics site.

Cutler landed on her feet, however. She received a six-figure advance to write a thinly fictionalized account of her experiences under the title *The Washingtonienne: A Novel.*[32]

Curt Hopkins, a journalist-blogger (MorphemeTales) and founder of the now-defunct Committee to Protect Bloggers, began counting blog-related job actions in

December 2004 shortly after a public-radio network cited one of his postings in rejecting him for a staff position. By May 2006, Hopkins' list included 61 individuals who had been fired, four who had been disciplined and two, including himself, who were "not hired." Hopkins shut down the blog-protection committee in May for lack of funding.

While no one was fired in the police blog episode, the Montgomery County (Md.) Fraternal Order of Police suffered a black eye in March 2006 when *The Washington Post* disclosed that some officers had anonymously posted offensive comments on the union's password-protected message board. One referred to immigrants as "beaners," and another called a black policewoman a "ghetto" officer. The department responded by restricting access to the site from county computers, while the union promised to monitor the site and remove offensive messages.[33]

The *Los Angeles Times* suspended columnist Michael Hiltzik's Golden State blog in April after he acknowledged posting comments on his own blog and other sites under two assumed names. (The pseudonymous postings were disclosed by another blogger.) The *Times* said it was suspending the blog because Hiltzik had violated ethics guidelines requiring editors and reporters to identify themselves when dealing with the public. Hiltzik continues to write a political column with the same name, however, for the newspaper's print editions.[34]

Meanwhile, the blogosphere is treating marine zoologist Jessa Jeffries as a martyr of sorts after the Academy of Natural Sciences in Philadelphia fired her because her blog (Jessaisms) contained identifiable references to the museum along with racy details about sex and drinking. "Blogger Fired for Actually Having a Life," the widely read Thought Mechanics blog declared in a May 18 posting. Jeffries was unapologetic in her blog post about the firing, but she later told *The New York Times:* "I probably shouldn't have been blogging about work."[35]

Workplace policies on blogging, however, are murky at best. In a survey by the Society for Human Resources Management, only 8 percent of the HR professionals responding said their companies had written policies on the subject. But Jonathan Segal, a Philadelphia employment-law attorney, says it may be too early to try to write detailed policies on employee blogging. "It's so gray, every time you try to write a rule you can come up with a hundred ways that the rules won't work," he says.

For its part, the Electronic Frontier Foundation, a San Francisco-based advocacy group, cautions that more and more bloggers are getting in trouble over the issue and that legal protections for work-related blogging are limited.

"None of this should stop you from blogging," the group says. "Freedom of speech is the foundation of a functioning democracy, and Internet bullies shouldn't use the law to stifle legitimate free expression."[36]

OUTLOOK
'Starting Discussions'

Blogging enthusiasts see the phenomenon as far more than an entertaining hobby or short-lived fad. They see blogs as the dawning of a new media age that will replace top-down journalism and government- and corporate-controlled information with ever more interactive communication and ever more democratic political and economic life.

"Traditional media send messages," the French software executive Loïc le Meur proclaims on his blog. "Blogs start discussions."

Clearly, blogging has yet to reach its potential — in politics, business or culture. Blogs are continuing to increase in number and applications: podcasting and videoblogs are now emerging. "There's lots more innovation and development to be done," says the Pew center's Rainie. "It's very much an unfolding, evolving form."

But a Gallup Poll in February suggests that popular interest in blogging may be leveling off — and at a somewhat low level. Under the headline "Blog Readership Bogged Down," Gallup reports that only 9 percent of Internet users say they frequently read blogs and another 11 percent occasionally. The figures are essentially unchanged from a year earlier.[37]

The number of blogs may itself be misleading, since most are inactive after a couple of weeks. "Most blogs are like diets," says Rosensteil at the Project for Excellence in Journalism. "They're started and then abandoned."

Blogging's influence may also be blunted by its very successes, as the institutions that bloggers are self-consciously challenging adapt the tool for their own uses. Businesses, political candidates and government agencies are learning how to use blogs to promote their products, campaigns or services. It remains to be seen whether they will be transformed by the bottom-up communication that results or whether they will simply learn how to use blogs to manipulate consumer taste and voter behavior.

News organizations are also rapidly adding blogs to their Web sites. "The blogosphere and the mainstream media world are getting blended now and will probably blend more in the future," says Rainie. "The notion that they are separate realms and competing realms will fade."

Blogging has certainly increased the number of voices in the news media and the amount of information and opinion available for news junkies. Independent blogs are making "big media" somewhat more accountable through the fact-checking and agenda-setting functions Rainie cites. At the same time, Rosenstiel says readers take the independent blogs with a grain of salt.

"People who read blogs don't necessarily think of them as accurate," he says. "They view them as interesting opinion, but they don't think of them as The Associated Press. They have a feel for what they're getting."

In addition, some in the "old media" fret that minute-by-minute postings in short bursts have little, if any, lasting value, informational or literary. "Blogging is the closest literary culture has come to instant obsolescence," Washington writer Trevor Butterworth concludes in a lengthy critique in the London-based *Financial Times*. "No Modern Library edition of the great polemicists of the blogosphere to yellow on the shelf; nothing but a virtual tomb for a billion posts. . . ."[38]

Bloggers are also worried about a potential threat to their most valuable resource: unhampered access to the Internet. Some major telephone and cable companies want to charge extra for delivering some high-bandwidth services through their wires faster than others. They say they need the revenue to pay for network infrastructure improvements. But bloggers are part of a coalition that wants Congress to block the idea by requiring non-discriminatory access to the Internet — so-called net neutrality. They argue that the proposed charges would make it harder for "everyday people" to have their voices heard on the Web.[39]

Despite all those reservations and caveats, blogging advocates remain convinced that blogs are an important and lasting tool for self-expression and self-empowerment. "The fact that anybody, anywhere, can create their own media, publish their own opinions and information on the Web — that is not going away," says MacKinnon at Harvard's Berkman Center. "In fact, that is going to become more pervasive."

"Blogging will last," says UCLA's Volokh, "because it taps into one of the most fundamental desires of many humans, which is to express their views — and to get the pleasures both selfish and selfless of knowing that others are listening and — one hopes — being enlightened and helped by the spreading of those views."

Author Kline agrees. "The idea of ordinary people talking to each other about what's important in the world, the ability to reach vast audiences and to maneuver around the official sources of power — that's going to survive," he says. "There's no way this is going to fade, and people are just going to go back and be passive recipients of politics, business, information, products and services. That genie is definitely out of the bottle."

UPDATE

Consider a single blogger's impact on the nation's news diet during one 48-hour period in the summer of 2010.

On the morning of July 19, conservative online political activist Andrew Breitbart posted an inflammatory video on his popular Website. The heavily edited footage apparently showing a black federal official making anti-white comments was picked up that afternoon in the "blogosphere" and then broadcast first that evening by Bill O'Reilly on Fox News, followed by other mainstream media.

Within hours Agriculture Department official Shirley Sherrod was abruptly fired by the Obama administration, and the top White House press spokesman, Robert Gibbs, said Sherrod's speech earlier in the year to the NAACP was a "teachable moment" in the dangers of reverse racism.

The next day, however, from her home in Georgia, Sherrod told reporters that her comments had been taken out of context and were actually intended to invoke racial reconciliation. Cable TV commentators on Fox, including O'Reilly, and other channels retracted their accusations; Agriculture Secretary Tom Vilsack apologized and offered Sherrod her job back; and President Obama himself called Sherrod to make amends (a month later she declined the offer of a new job at Agriculture).

The episode opened "a window on how information and misinformation can careen through the current media ecosystem," wrote media analyst Mark Jurkowitz of the Pew Center for Excellence in Journalism. "Increasingly, supersonic speed predominates, and reaction time shrinks. Online posts come in the middle of the night. Commentary and punditry add velocity to stories even before news reports have sorted them out. Partisan players are increasingly becoming news distributors with ties to cable channels and bloggers who follow them closely."[40]

In just over a decade since bloggers burst on the American scene, they are exhibiting some growing pains that cause some to view them as a mixed blessing. Worldwide, their numbers are now estimated at more than 144 million, publishing 1 million posts per day, according to Blogpulse.[41] But with the arrival of new communications tools, such as Facebook, Twitter, BlackBerry and iPhone, some blogs are losing some readers to competing attractions, according to the Pew Internet & American Life Project.[42]

That's because they have competition for user attention. "Universities are putting student reporting feet on the street, often in concert with citizens or nonprofits," wrote Missouri School of Journalism fellow Michele McLellan. "The nascent Government 2.0 movement uses digital tools to put data in front of citizens and engage them in reporting problems and concerns. Nongovernmental organizations and other nonprofits are jumping into the fray, telling their stories directly to the public and engaging citizens in their work."[43]

Even professional bloggers express befuddlement. "The definition of bloggers has become so blurred now that bloggers write columns and columnists write blogs," says Robert Cox, president of the Media Bloggers Association (MBA), which has seen its membership grow to 2,400 bloggers since it was founded in 2004. "Back in 2003-2005, there were certain silos of communication and not much overlap. All that has changed."

As a form of microblogging, the 144-character Twitter — which is practically a must for celebrities such as basketball star Lebron James and political mavericks such as Sarah Palin — is now being employed by top news anchors Katie Couric, Brian Williams and Diane Sawyer. Baltimore Ravens wide receiver Chad Ochocinco was recently fined for sending messages to fans on Twitter before, during and after games.[44]

After conservative blogger Andrew Breitbart posted an inflammatory video about Agriculture Department official Sherrod, the story was picked up by Fox's Bill O'Reilly and other network news anchors. Later, they retracted their stories.

Getty Images/Ethan Miller

Another sign of the entrenchment of bloggers is that the association has helped win bloggers press credentials to cover federal courts and offers its members an insurance policy for defenses against defamation suits. It boasts a network of 75 attorneys in 20 states.[45]

In the competitive world of blogging, the nation's top 100 bloggers are tracked daily by the Web-based firm Technorati, which also publishes an annual "State of the Blogosphere" data report. (No. 1? *The Huffington Post.*) The 2009 study showed a rise in the proportion of bloggers who blog as part of their work. Seventy percent of part-timers, professional bloggers and self-employed bloggers are blogging more, while hobbyists, citing demands of family, have reduced their blog output, it said. Seventy percent say they are better known in their fields because of their blog. Yet an equal 70 percent cite personal satisfaction as the chief motivator for their blogging. The most popular topics: information technology, news and politics, music, religion, travel, television and film and family issues.[46]

Blogs overseas have demonstrated a serious role for the practice in mobilizing citizen resistance to oppressive governments. On April, 27, 2010, a panel was convened on Capitol Hill to discuss "Bloggers Behind Bars," sponsored by the Center for International Media Assistance. Rep. Adam Schiff, D-Calif., called for worldwide efforts to protect online journalists, who make up more than half of those jailed for news coverage.

The most dramatic example, he said, was in the 2009 Iranian elections, when online citizen journalists were the only source of news after mainstream journalists were expelled from the country.[47] A Web-based group called Global Voices Online recently documented efforts by the government of China to crack down on social media for fear that it is becoming a tool for political subversion. Facebook is now being used as an organizing tool by many of China's regional separatist movements.[48]

Bloggers in the United States have become so much a part of the scene that municipal officials in Philadelphia have begun requiring bloggers to pay either a onetime fee of $300 or an annual $50 fee if the blogger earns income from online ads.[49]

The increasingly hazy line between blogging and journalism was thrown into relief in June when *The Washington Post* asked for the resignation of David Weigel, a 29-year-old blogger the paper had hired to write about political conservatives. A conservative Website known as the Daily Caller had published previously private e-mails from Weigel that mocked well-known conservatives such as Rep. Ron Paul, R-Texas, and blogger Matt Drudge. That led to the revelation of the existence of an exclusive blog, or listserv, called Journolist, launched by *Post* columnist Ezra Klein, on which many Democratic and liberal-leaning journalists were sharing thoughts on politics that they might never have written in their published work. *The Post* acted in response to charges from conservatives that the e-mails showed Weigel was biased as a reporter.[50]

The vast array of bloggers purveying news and commentary has complicated the efforts of press analysts to keep political discussion honest. *PolitiFact.com*, a Pulitzer Prize-winning Website run by the *St. Petersburg Times*, in its early days fact-checked mostly just the statements of government and party leaders. But to keep up in today's political world, its reporters now must chase down and evaluate the moving targets of statements that are made on TV or Twitter and then circulated on blogs.

"We realized that we had created an artificial wall and that talk-show hosts, Websites and pundits were as much a part of the discourse as politicians," said *PolitiFact.com* editor Bill Adair.[51]

Not surprisingly, efforts to organize the varied and often-snarky personalities that populate the nebulous blogosphere have caused friction and bruised some egos. In 2008, when the Media Bloggers Association met with representatives of The Associated Press to negotiate an agreement on bloggers' rights to quote from AP stories, a blogger named Cory Doctorow at popular BoingBoing.net snarled, "The Associated Press has promised to meet with some organization I've never heard of called The Media Bloggers Association to work out the details of its frankly insane proposal to sell licenses to quote five or more words from AP stories. . . . "The Media Bloggers Association substantially consists of one lackluster blogger named Robert Cox," Doctorow continued. "His weblog, Words in Edgewise, and the MBA website, are two halves of the same site. Robert Cox isn't all that interested in blogging per se. What he's really into is self-aggrandizement by representing himself as someone who speaks for bloggers and blogging. An embarrassing number of organizations have fallen for this."[52]

Cox responded to the blast and noted recently that its author later softened his stance. Cox recounts another intra-blogosphere dust-up, this one over whether his Media Bloggers Association was truly the first bloggers group to win press credentials to cover the 2007 trial of former Bush White House national security aide I. Lewis "Scooter" Libby on charges of lying to investigators probing a leak to the press on the identity of CIA operative Valerie Plame Wilson.

The association's victory in gaining courtroom credentials was the culmination of two years of work by Cox in speaking to judges and encouraging them to respect bloggers when they perform the role of journalists, he says. But several other blogging groups, among them Firedoglake.com, also won credentials for the trial, and they attacked Cox for taking credit.[53]

"I take the good with the bad and try to maintain transparency," says Cox, who marvels at his own rise into a media personality through blogging. Such celebrity-making is increasingly difficult on a globe that hosts nearly 150 million blogs. "There was a wave, back in 2003-2005, when some bloggers got famous because they were talented," he says, mentioning "Wonkette" Ana Marie Cox and cooking blogger Julie Powell, author of the book "Julie and Julia," which became the movie about gourmet cook Julia Child. "That world has come and gone."

NOTES

1. See "The People Who Shape Our World," *Time*, May 8, 2006, (www.time.com). For individual entries, see Ana Marie Cox, "Matt Drudge: Redefining What's News," p. 171; Al Franken, "Arianna Huffington: The Woman Who Made a Sharp Left," p. 172. Some background on Drudge and Huffington drawn from Wikipedia (visited May 2006).

2. Pew Internet and American Life Project, "The state of blogging," January 2005; www.pewinternet.org/PPF/r/144/report_display.asp.

3. See Daniel Williams, "New Vehicle for Dissent Is a Fast Track to Prison; Bloggers Held Under Egypt's Emergency Laws," *The Washington Post*, May 31, 2006, p. A10; Tom Zeller Jr., "Internet Firms Facing Questions About Censoring Online Searches in China," *The New York Times*, Feb. 15, 2006, p. C3; Megan K. Stack, "Iran Attempts to Pull the Plug on Web Dissidents," *Los Angeles Times*, Jan. 24, 2005, p. A3.

4. Quoted in Eric Deggans, "Huffington Beats Odds as Blogger," *St. Petersburg* (Fla.) *Times*, May 10, 2006, p. 1A.

5. *Ibid.*

6. Noah Schachtman, "Blogs Make the Headlines," *Wired News*, Dec. 23, 2002.

7. Quoted in David Kline and Dan Burstein, *blog! how the newest media revolution is changing politics, business, and culture* (2005), p. 17.

8. For background, see Kenneth Jost, "Free-Press Disputes," *CQ Researcher*, April 8, 2002, pp. 293-316.

9. www.nationalreview.com.

10. See Anick Jesdanun, "Democrats Credential Bloggers; Republicans Say They Will, Too," The Associated Press, July 9, 2004.

11. For background, see Kline and Burstein, *op. cit.*; Dan Gillmor, *We the Media: Grassroots Journalism by the People, for the People* (2004).

12. Dan Burstein, "From Cave Painting to Wonkette: A Short History of Blogging," in Kline & Burstein, *op. cit.*, pp. xii-xiii.

13. See Emily Eakin, "The Ancient Art of Haranguing Has Moved To the Internet, Belligerent as Ever," *The New York Times*, Aug. 10, 2002, p. B9.

14. Gillmor, *op. cit.*, p. 4.

15. Some background drawn from Wikipedia entries on individuals and computer technologies. For an overview, see Steven Levy, *et al.*, "Living in the Blogosphere," *Newsweek*, Aug. 26, 2002, p. 42.

16. Gillmor, *op. cit.*, pp. 11-12. For a first-person account, see Tim Berners-Lee and Mark Fischetti, *Weaving the Web: Origins and Future of the World Wide Web* (1999). Berners-Lee, who was knighted in 2004, is now director of the World Wide Web Consortium.

17. Gillmor, *op. cit.*, p. 12.

18. Jon Katz, "Here Come the Weblogs," Slashdot.com, May 24, 1999, reprinted in Editors of Perseus Publications, *We've Got Blog: How Weblogs Are Changing Our Culture* (2002). As reprinted, the article carries the date May 24, 2001, an apparent mistake.

19. Matthew McKinnon, "King of the Blogs," *Shift*, summer 2001, linked from "Pyra Labs," *Wikipedia* (visited May 2006).

20. Steven Levy, "Will the Blogs Kill Old Media?" *Newsweek*, May 20, 2002, p. 52.

21. Quoted in David F. Gallagher, "A Rift Among Bloggers," *The New York Times*, June 10, 2002, p. C4.

22. John Podhoretz, "The Internet's First Scalp," *The New York Post*, Dec. 13, 2002, p. 41.

23. Quoted in Mark Jurkowitz, "The Descent of Trent Lott Brings the Rise of Bloggers," *The Boston Globe*, Dec. 26, 2002, p. D1.

24. Total readership from Pew Internet and American Life Project, forthcoming report, July 2006; blog posting data from previous report, January 2005.

25. Some background from Liz Halloran, "The Blogger's Life: Online Deaniacs Vow to Stay Involved," *Hartford Courant*, Feb. 20, 2004, p. D1; Michael Cudahay and Jock Gill, "The Political Is Personal — Not Web-Based," *Pittsburgh Post-Gazette*, Feb. 1, 2004, p. E1.

26. Anick Jesdanun, "Product Review: Bush, Kerry sites lackluster after bar raised in Democratic primaries," The Associated Press, July 15, 2004.

27. Quoted in Katharine Q. Seelye, "Bloggers as News Media Trophy Hunter," *The New York Times*, Feb. 14, 2005, p. C1.

28. See Eric Black, "In New Era of Reporting, Blogs Take a Seat at the Media Table," *The* (Minneapolis) *Star Tribune*, March 9, 2005.

29. The case is *O'Grady v. Superior Court, Calif. Court of Appeal, Sixth District* (May 26, 2006). For coverage, see Howard Mintz, "Apple Loses Case Against Bloggers," *San Jose Mercury News*, May 27, 2006, p. A1.

30. See Federal Election Commission, "Internet Communications," Notice 2006-8, published in *Federal Register*, Vol. 71, No. 70 (April 12, 2006), p. 18589. For coverage, see Adam Nagourney, "Agency Exempts Most of Internet From Campaign Spending Laws," *The New York Times*, March 28, 2006, p. A15; Eric Pfeiffer, "FEC to Leave Alone Web Political Speech," *The Washington Times*, March 28, 2006, p. A6.

31. Both quoted in Thomas B. Edsall, "FEC Rules Exempt Blogs From Internet Political Limits," *The Washington Post*, March 28, 2006, p. A3.

32. See April Witt, "Blog Interrupted," *Washington Post Magazine*, Aug. 15, 2004, p. W12; Jonathan Yardley, "Capitol Hill Siren's Tell-All Fiction," May 24, 2005, p. C1.

33. See Ernesto Londono, "Union's Online Controls Greeted Warily," *The Washington Post*, April 1, 2006, and earlier stories by same writer March 28 and March 31.

34. See Katie Hafner, "At Los Angeles Times, a Columnist Who Used a False Web Name Loses His Blog," *The New York Times*, April 24, 2006, p. C1.

35. Anna Bahney, "Interns? No Bloggers Need Apply," *The New York Times*, May 25, 2006, p. G1.

36. See Electronic Frontier Foundation, "Legal Guide for Bloggers," April 20, 2006.

37. "Blog Readership Bogged Down: Audience Skews Slightly Young," Gallup News Service, Feb. 10, 2006. The results were based on a telephone survey of 1,013 randomly selected adults Dec. 5-8, 2005; the margin of error is plus or minus 3 percentage points. See also "Bloggy, We Hardly Knew Ye," *Chicago Tribune* (editorial), Feb. 22, 2006, p. C16; for a reply, see Eric Zorn, "Post This: Blogs' Demise Highly Exaggerated," *Chicago Tribune*, Feb. 23, 2006, p. C5.

38. Trevor Butterworth, "Time for the Last Post," *Financial Times*, Feb. 18, 2006, *Weekend Magazine*, p. 18.

39. For opposing views, see *Hands Off the Internet*, www.handsoff.com, and www.SavetheInternet.com. For background, see Marcia Clemmittt, "Controlling the Internet," *CQ Researcher*, May 12, 2006, pp. 409-432.

40. Mark Jurkowitz, "The Reconstruction of a Media Mess," Pew Center for Excellence in Journalism, July 26, 2010.

41. See www.blogpulse.com. See also "The blogosphere haystack: 144 million blogs," *Pingdom*, Aug. 4, 2010.

42. "2010 State of the Media," Pew Project for Excellence in Journalism and Pew Internet & American Life Project, www.stateofthemedia.org/2010/.

43. Michele McLellan, "Community Journalism: A Response to Academic Research and a Look Ahead," talk delivered to Pew Project for Excellence in Journalism, Feb. 8, 2010.

44. See Matt Vensel's blog "Virtual Vensanity" for Aug. 26, 2010, http://weblogs.baltimoresun.com/entertainment/bthesite/vensel/2010/08/the_nfl_should_ochocinco_tweet.html.

45. Laura Oliver, "Media Bloggers Association creates blogger insurance scheme," *Online Journalism News*, Sept. 19, 2008, www.journalism.co.uk/2/articles/532383.php.

46. See http://technorati.com/blogging/article/day-2-the-what-and-why2/#ixzz0xXSjuX3x.

47. "Quick Link," Reporters Committee for Freedom of the Press, April 27, 2010.

48. Marta Cooper, "China: Social Media as Political Subversion Tool," *Global Voices Online*, July 29, 2010, http://globalvoicesonline.org/2010/07/29/china-internet-cass/.

49. Rob Pegararo, "Philly's Blogger Fee Turns into Blog Fodder," *The Washington Post*, Aug. 25, 2010, p. A14.

50. Howard Kurtz, "Washington Post Blogger David Weigel Resigns After Messages Leak," *The Washington Post*, June 26, 2010, p. C1.

51. David Carr, "Journalists, Provocateurs, Maybe Both," *The New York Times*, July 25, 2010, p. B1.

52. Cory Doctorow, "BoingBoing," June 19, 2008.

53. Alan Sipress, "Too Casual To Sit on Press Row?" *The Washington Post*, Jan. 11, 2007.

BIBLIOGRAPHY

Books

Armstrong, Jerome, and Markos Moulitsas Zuniga, *Crashing the Gates: Netroots, Grassroots, and the Rise of People-Powered Politics, Chelsea Green*, 2006.
Liberal bloggers Armstrong (MyDD) and Moulitsas (DailyKos) present strategies for revitalizing progressive politics and "revolutionizing" the Democratic Party.

Davis, Richard, *Politics Online: Blogs, Chatrooms and Discussion Groups in American Democracy, Routledge*, 2005.
A professor of political science at Brigham Young University calls online political discussion "a new force in American politics," examines the kind of people who participate and evaluates its potential as a tool for democratic governance.

Editors of Perseus Publishing, *We've Got Blog: How Weblogs Are Changing Our Culture, Perseus Publishing*, 2002.
This collection of 34 first-person accounts and essays from bloggers includes an eight-page glossary and two-page list of "helpful" sites in building your own blog and understanding weblog culture.

Gillmor, Dan, *We the Media: Grassroots Journalism by the People, for the People, O'Reilly Books*, 2004.
A former business columnist for the *San Jose* (Calif.) *Mercury News* and now president of the Center for Citizen Media writes with conviction about "journalism's transformation from a 20th-century mass-media structure to something profoundly more grassroots and democratic."

Kline, David, and Dan Burstein, *blog! how the newest media revolution is changing politics, business, and culture, CDS Books*, 2005.
The authors provide overviews and more than 30 interviews with or commentaries by major bloggers covering the impact of blogs on politics and policy, business and economics, and media and culture. Appendices list most popular blogs as of May 2005 and the authors' recommended blogs by subject matter. Kline, a journalist, and Burstein, a journalist and venture capitalist, are also co-authors of *Road Warriors: Dreams and Nightmares Along the Information Highway* (Dutton, 1995).

Reynolds, Glenn, *An Army of Davids: How Markets and Technology Empower Ordinary People to Beat Big Media, Big Government, and Other Goliaths, Nelson Current*, 2006.
Conservative blogger Reynolds (Instapundit) argues that technology is evening out the balance of power between the individual and the organization.

Scoble, Robert, and Shel Israel, *Naked Conversations: How Blogs Are Changing the Way Businesses Talk With Customers, John Wiley*, 2006.
Business blogger Scoble and former public relations executive Israel use 50 case histories to argue that blogging is an efficient and credible method of business communication. Includes overview of blogging culture internationally and suggestions for how to blog successfully in a crisis.

Articles

Bai, Matt, "Can Bloggers Get Real?" *The New York Times Magazine*, May 28, 2006, p. 13.
The writer questions whether blogs and other online political tools will fundamentally change the nature of U.S. politics.

Baker, Stephen, and Heather Green, "Blogs Will Change Your Business," *Business Week*, May 2, 2005, p. 56.
The cover story — written in the form of blog postings over a five-day period — advises businesses to consider blogs as an invaluable tool for market research and consumer feedback.

Butterworth, Trevor, "Time for the Last Post," *Financial Times*, Feb. 18, 2006, *Weekend Magazine*, p. 16.
The writer debunks blogging's "evangelists," insisting most blogs are "overblown, boring and don't make a penny."

Perlmutter, David D., "Political Blogs: the New Iowa?" *The Chronicle of Higher Education*, **May 26, 2006, p. 38.**
The article raises questions about the role of blogs in the next presidential election. Perlmutter, who recently joined the faculty of the University of Kansas School of Journalism and Mass Communications, also publishes a political-analysis blog: www.policybyblog.squarespace .com.

Rosen, Jeffrey, "Your Blog or Mine?" *The New York Times Magazine*, **Dec. 19, 2004, p. 19.**

Blogs are transforming "the boundaries between public and private," according to Rosen, a journalist and law professor at George Washington University.

Reports and Studies

Pew Internet and American Life Project, **"The state of blogging," January 2005 (www.pewinternet.org/ PPF/r/144/report_display.asp).**
The four-page data memo shows blog readership increasing despite most Americans' unfamiliarity with the practice. An updated report is to be published in July 2006.

For More Information

Berkman Center for Internet and Society, Harvard Law School, Baker House, 1587 Massachusetts Ave., Cambridge, MA 02138; (617) 495-7547; http://cyber.law. harvard.edu. A research program investigating legal, technical and social developments in cyberspace.

Electronic Frontier Foundation, 454 Shotwell St., San Francisco, CA 94110-1914; (415) 436-9333; www.eff.org. A nonprofit working to protect digital rights; represented two of the Web sites involved in the Apple case.

Media Bloggers Association; (928) 223-5711; http:// mediabloggers.org. A nonpartisan organization dedicated to promoting blogging as a distinct form of media and helping to extend the power of the press, with all the rights and responsibilities that entails, to every citizen.

Pew Internet and American Life Project, 1615 L St., N.W., Suite 700, Washington, DC 20036; (202) 419-4500;

www.pewinternet.org. Explores the impact of the Internet on families, communities, work and home, daily life, education, health care and civic and political life.

Project for Excellence in Journalism, 1850 K St., N.W., Suite 850, Washington, DC 20006; (202) 293-7394; www .journalism.org. A Columbia University Graduate School of Journalism initiative aimed at raising journalism standards.

Reporters Committee for Freedom of the Press, 1101 Wilson Blvd., Suite 1100, Arlington, VA 22209; (703) 807-2100; www.rcfp.org. A nonprofit providing free legal assistance to help journalists defend their First Amendment rights.

Society of Professional Journalists, 3909 N. Meridian St., Indianapolis, IN 46208; (317) 927-8000; www.spj.org. Dedicated to the perpetuation of a free press as the cornerstone of democracy.

5

Online Privacy

Patrick Marshall and Charles S. Clark

Cellphones are increasingly being used to provide location information, such as where to find the nearest pizza or the cheapest gasoline. Law enforcement agencies are also turning to service providers to obtain location information on subjects of investigation, raising concern among privacy advocates that Americans' privacy rights could be violated.

CQ Press/Olu Davis

From CQ Researcher,
Nov. 6, 2009.
Updated August 30, 2010.

Could this happen to you? You return home from vacation to find your apartment has been burglarized. In your snail mail is a notice from your health insurer canceling your policy. And when you check your e-mail your minister is asking why you recently purchased a book about devil worship.

Privacy experts say such things happen countless times a day because of new electronic tools that allow Internet service providers, advertisers, hackers and others to track consumers' Web searches, site visits, e-mails and social networking sites.

For instance, burglars reading your Facebook page could easily find out when you are going on vacation. Even if you don't include your home address, a criminal may easily be able to find the information on your profile page. Your health insurer may have canceled your insurance after receiving information from a marketing firm whose online survey you just completed in hopes of winning a new iPod. And when you bought the devil worship book out of curiosity online, the information about the purchase was automatically posted to your Facebook friends, including your minister.

"With social networking, people are leaving trails of digital DNA sprinkled about everywhere in the world," says Tim Sparapani, director of public policy at Facebook.

But the danger isn't just limited to social networking sites like Facebook, say privacy advocates; for example:

• A Dartmouth University professor said he retrieved tens of thousands of medical files — including names, addresses and Social Security numbers — from a peer-to-peer network, or system of linked computers.[1]

Internet Users Welcome Privacy Policies

Most Internet users — especially older people — are uncomfortable when Web sites use data about their online activities, but when privacy and security measures are put in place, a majority of users feel comfortable.

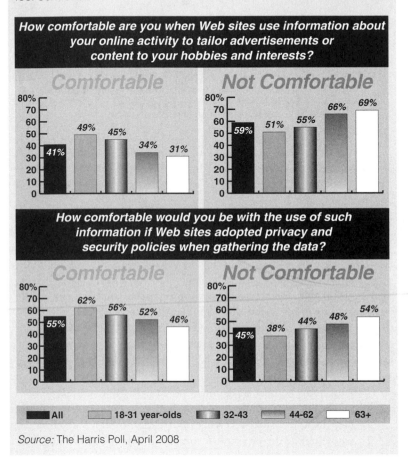

Source: The Harris Poll, April 2008

photographs and personal contact details.[4]

But most online privacy intrusions never receive public attention, despite the growing number of incursions that have come to light in recent years.

"With the advent of personal Web sites, blogs, social networks and Twitter, people are sharing information about themselves that would certainly make their grandparents blush," Richard Bennett, publisher of *BroadbandPolitics.com*, told lawmakers on Capitol Hill in April. "Stories abound about young people who've posted drunken party pictures of themselves while they were in college finding the embarrassment often costly when they apply for jobs and have to explain their antics to Google-savvy recruiters. The Internet is a harsh mistress, and much of what happens there stays there, seemingly forever."[5]

Avoiding social networking sites is not, however, a guarantee of privacy. Internet service providers (ISPs) and search engine providers can learn a good deal about customers by tracking the searches they make.

Search engines, indeed, offer a deep mine of data. In fact, according to one count, Americans performed more than 13 billion searches in September alone.[6] The search engines typically record not only the terms searched for but also the date, time and location of the computer performing the search. While search engine companies generally "anonymize" records of searches, that is no guarantee of complete anonymity.

In addition, advertisers and their agents are able to track the Web activities of users by the use of "cookies" — small text files that are deposited on users' computers when they visit a site.

Finally, service providers — as well as hackers, government agencies and anyone else who can tap into the

• The wife of a senior British intelligence official inadvertently revealed sensitive information in postings to her Facebook site.[2]

• An investment firm employee inadvertently exposed information about clients, including Social Security numbers, when he logged into a peer-to-peer network to share music and movie files.[3]

• A graphic designer in Seattle used Craigslist to pose as a woman seeking sexual encounters and then posted all 178 responses he got to an open Web site, including flow of Internet traffic — can also employ "packet analysis" to examine the content of users' unencrypted communications across the Internet.

It's no surprise that these technologies are extremely popular with Internet advertisers. In fact, the highest-profile current threat to online privacy, according to most privacy advocates, is a new practice called "behavioral targeting" of advertising. By tracking users' actions on specific Web sites and their movements across many sites, advertisers develop user profiles and then target advertising to individual users based on their profiles.

A user might, for example, visit an airline site looking for flights to New York City, then might search for opera CDs. An advertising service following that user's movements might then deliver ads to the user's browser offering tickets to the Metropolitan Opera.

While some users might find such targeted ads helpful, others may feel that having their Web activities tracked and recorded is intrusive. Even those who don't mind the targeted advertising may not like the idea that their Internet activities could potentially be reported to other parties. For example, would users about to apply for health insurance want the insurer to know that they had recently been searching for "symptoms of colon cancer"?

Indeed, when Charter Communications, the nation's fourth-largest cable company, announced in the spring of 2008 that it was preparing to deliver just such advertising services in conjunction with a company called NebuAd, complaints from consumers and privacy advocates

Ten Ways to Protect Your Facebook Privacy

Facebook users cannot control all the photos and videos of themselves that show up on other people's Facebook pages, but they can adjust the privacy and invisibility settings on their own profiles. If you are a Facebook user, here are ways to protect your privacy:

1. Use Friend Lists You can create groups of friends by type and send messages to each group. Friends can be in more than one group, and different groups can have different privacy settings applied to them.

2. Remove Self from Facebook Search Results By default, Facebook makes your presence visible to people in your network. You can change your privacy settings, however, so that only certain groups, such as your social friends, can see your information.

3. Remove Self from Google Facebook displays your profile picture, a list of your friends, a link to add you as a friend, a link to send you a message and a list of your fan pages in search engines. By changing your privacy settings, you can control the visibility of your public search listing.

4. Avoid Photo, Video Tag Mistakes You can be fired at work for incriminating photos and videos, or even suffer damage to relationships. You can, however, keep tagged photos private or make them visible only to some friends.

5. Protect Your Photo Albums People often turn off tagged photo visibility to certain friend lists, yet keep their photo albums public. If you want your photos to be invisible, you must adjust your privacy settings for each album.

6. Prevent Stories From Appearing in Friends' News Feeds You can hide your relationship status completely, or you can avoid making things uncomfortable if your status does change by preventing friend notification. You can prevent friend notification for other stories, as well.

7. Protect Against Unpublished Application Stories When you add an application, a news feed item is often immediately published in your profile. You should check your profile to ensure that no embarrassing notification has been posted, or avoid using applications entirely.

8. Make Contact Information Private Many people make contact information public, such as phone numbers and e-mail addresses. If you want that information kept private, or you start receiving messages from strangers, you can create custom privacy settings for each contact listed. Again, you can allow certain friend lists to see certain contact information.

9. Avoid Embarrassing Wall Posts You may use Facebook for business, but not all of your friends will. You can customize the visibility of your wall postings and control which friends post to prevent work colleagues from seeing embarrassing recaps of the weekend.

10. Keep Friendships Private You may like to show off that you have lots of friends, but your friends may not want to live public lives. It is often a good idea to turn off your friends' visibility to others so that others do not visit your profile and selectively pick off your friends, such as those relevant to them for marketing purposes or other reasons.

Source: Nick O'Neill, "10 Privacy Settings Every Facebook User Should Know," *All Facebook*, Feb. 2, 2009, www.allfacebook.com/2009/02/facebook-privacy/

prompted congressional hearings. Apparently as a result of fallout from the hearings, NebuAd lost so many clients that it went out of business.

While Charter dropped its plan, others are picking up the idea. A recent study by Datran Media, an advertising consulting group, found that 65 percent of marketers currently use or plan to use behavioral targeting.[7]

"The private sector as a whole has tremendous technical means and tremendous economic incentives to collect as much granular data as they can about as many customers as possible," says Jay Stanley, director of public education at the American Civil Liberties Union. "That kind of information about people is money. And in a capitalist system people don't leave money lying around unpicked."

Of course, advertisers aren't the only ones interested in users' online activities. Users' privacy is under even more significant threat from the federal government, according to Stanley. "The National Security Agency is monitoring our telecommunications," he says, including Internet communications.

In addition, he notes, the government has easy access to a broad swath of the data being collected by service providers. "While the private sector is collecting all this information because of its own incentives," says Stanley, "the legal protections against the government swooping in and getting it are precisely what have been loosened over the past decade." Stanley cites in particular provisions of the USA Patriot Act regarding warrantless searches of electronic data.[8]

Recent polls show that advocacy groups aren't the only ones concerned about Internet privacy. According to the *Consumer Reports* National Research Center, 72 percent of American adults polled in July 2008 were concerned that their online behaviors are being tracked and profiled by companies.[9] In addition, 93 percent of respondents believe Internet companies should ask for permission before using personal information.

"I do think users are starting to feel a little bit out of control," says Ari Schwartz, vice president of the nonprofit Center for Democracy and Technology.

There have been several unsuccessful attempts in recent years to legislate stronger protections for online users' data. In the current Congress, the highest-profile effort is being led by Rep. Rick Boucher, D-Va., who has promised to introduce legislation aimed at regulating data collection by advertisers and service providers.

As privacy advocates, advertisers and consumers debate the privacy issue, here are some of the questions being asked:

Should advertisers' collection of data on Web users be regulated?

Advertisers — working with ISPs, search engine providers and individual Web sites — are turning to ever more powerful tools to gather information about users so that they can more accurately target their ads. There are, however, very few checks on what advertisers and service providers can do with the data.

"Users have little idea how much information is gathered, who has access to it or how it is used," Marc Rotenberg, executive director of the Electronic Privacy Information Center (EPIC) and a professor at Georgetown University Law Center, told Congress last spring.[10] "This last point is critical because in the absence of legal rules, companies that are gathering this data will be free to use it for whatever purpose they wish — the data for a targeted ad today could become a detailed personal profile sold to a prospective employer or a government agency tomorrow."

In fact, in most cases the only constraints on service providers in their collection and use of personal data are their own privacy policy statements. According to Peder Magee, senior staff attorney in the Federal Trade Commission's Division of Privacy and Identity Protection, if a company's practices violate its published promises, "that would be a deceptive claim and something we could take some action against."

Privacy advocates warn, however, that some service providers don't offer promises about privacy at all. "As long as you don't actually promise anybody any privacy — and companies have gotten very good at writing privacy policies that contain all kinds of warm, ringing tones about how they care for your privacy without actually making any legal commitments — then they don't have to deliver any," says Stanley at the American Civil Liberties Union.

As Stanley notes, even sites and service providers that do offer privacy statements generally do so in the form of rarely read, long and difficult-to-understand documents buried under an obscure link on a Web site. As a result, many if not most users are unaware of the extent of data being gathered about them and the uses to which it may be put.

With or without their knowledge, "people are giving information to a Web site in order for that site to provide them with a service," says Stanley. "They don't expect that Web site will then turn around and share the information with six other sites, combine the information to create a profile and give it to an advertiser who will decide whether you're rich or poor and give you different opportunities as a result."

Most users are also unaware that their Internet searches are recorded and can be used for profiling. "Internet search records are very, very intrusive records," says Stanley. "The things that you do searches for indicate your hopes and fears, what you're thinking about, what you may be reading, diseases that you have and diseases you fear you might have, things you believe about other people."

Advertisers justify collection of user data on two grounds. First, they argue that advertising is critical to keeping the Web vibrant. "The great majority of . . . Web sites and services are currently provided to consumers free of charge," Charles Curran, executive director of the Network Advertising Initiative, an industry group, told a congressional hearing last June.[11] "Instead of requiring visitors to register and pay a subscription fee, the operators of Web content and services subsidize their offerings with various types of advertising. These advertising revenues provide the creators of free Web content and services — site publishers, bloggers and software developers — with the income they need to pay their staffs and build and expand their online offerings."

Second, advertisers argue the collection of user data helps advertisers better serve consumers. "Targeted advertising is extraordinarily important for everybody," says Dan Jaffe, vice president of government relations for the Association of National Advertisers. That, he says, is because the more information advertisers have about users the fewer irrelevant ads will be delivered to those users.

Conversely, Jaffe says, restrictions on behavioral targeting won't cut down on advertising. "A lot of people seem to think that if they can stop behavioral advertising that they will somehow stop advertising," he says. "Quite

the contrary. Instead, you'll see an explosion of untargeted ads. You'll essentially increase the amount of spam because spam is, in effect, untargeted advertising."

Rather than legislated restrictions on advertising practices, the advertising industry argues that self-regulation — including full disclosure through clear privacy statements and procedures for users to opt out of selected data-collection programs — should be sufficient to protect users' privacy interests.

Berin Szoka, director of the Center for Internet Freedom, a project of the Progress & Freedom Foundation, a "market-oriented" think tank in Washington, agrees. "I think industry can do this on its own," says Szoka. "We should want companies to really make disclosures robust so that people really understand what they're doing." Then, he says, leave it up to the Federal Trade Commission to deal with companies that violate their privacy agreements. "They should be going out and finding the truly bad actors in industry and bringing enforcement actions against them," Szoka urges. "If they need more resources, we can talk about that."

Szoka adds that user education is another important part of the solution. "What we should be doing here is trying to educate users about what is going on online and empowering them to make decisions for themselves," he says. "If you really are very concerned about your privacy online, you have a very simple tool. You can go into your browser and use the basic cookie controls to opt out of browsing altogether, or site by site. You can create your own white lists or black lists. I would like to see those tools become much more powerful."

Privacy advocates, however, are very skeptical of self-regulation. "While we remain hopeful that advertising models based on non-personally identifiable information can be made, there are still too many instances where companies, particularly where there is no regulation, fail to fulfill their responsibilities," Rotenberg of the Electronic Privacy Information Center (EPIC) told lawmakers last spring.

"Second, even if these privacy techniques are shown to be reliable, it will still be necessary to enact legislation to place the burden on the advertising company to prevent the reconstruction of user identity," he added. "Without this statutory obligation, there would be no practical consequence if a company inadvertently disclosed personal

A Glossary of Common Internet Terms

Behavioral Targeting — A type of targeted advertising in which advertisers glean information from user data to tailor ads to user interests, limiting irrelevant ads.

Cloud — A metaphor for the Internet, based on how the Internet is depicted in computer network diagrams. Cloud computing services provide business applications online that are accessed from a browser, while the software and data are stored on servers.

Cookie — A message given to a browser by a server, which is then sent back to the server each time the browser requests a page. Identifies users and prepares customized Web pages for them.

Cookie controls — Some kinds of cookies facilitate tracking of Internet users or store identifying information. Cookie controls let users decide which cookies can be stored on their computers or transmitted to Web sites.

Deep-packet inspection — The examination of contents of Internet transmissions using "packet analysis" software. In addition to content transmitted by users, such as passwords or e-mails, each packet in a transmission contains the address of its origin and destination and information that connects it to the related packets being sent.

GPS — The Global Positioning System is a network of satellites and software that provides positioning, navigation and timing services to worldwide users. Many cellphones now include GPS receivers and software that allow the delivery of location-based services to users.

Location-based services — software programs that employ GPS to deliver a variety of information related to users' current location, such as routing or information about nearby points of interest, such as stores or restaurants.

Privacy mode — Browsers typically retain visited Web sites, downloaded files, terms searched, data — including passwords — typed into online forms, and cached versions of files locally on users' computers. Privacy mode reduces local storage of this information, providing increased privacy on shared computers.

Web browser — A software application used to locate and display Web pages, such as Internet Explorer and Mozilla Firefox.

Web server — A computer program, such as Apache, that delivers Web pages to browsers as well as other data to Web-based applications.

Source: "Browser Privacy Features: A Work in Progress," Center for Democracy and Technology, August 2009, www.cdt.org/privacy/20090804_browser_rpt_update.pdf; "Definitions," Webopedia, Oct. 29, 2009, www.webopedia.com/.

information or simply changed its business model to true user-based profiling."

Are social networking sites doing enough to protect users' privacy?

Privacy advocates maintain that social networking sites present special challenges for privacy protection because the sites by design encourage users to offer and share personal information.

According to Facebook's Sparapani, the information-sharing nature of social networking sites is actually a plus for privacy awareness, in the sense that when people post data they know it is being shared. "Rather than having information randomly collected about you," says Sparapani, "you know what is being collected about you because we're telling you forthrightly. You can then go claim that data and put your own stamp on it."

Critics note, however, that users may not be aware that the data they provide is available not only to their designated friends but also to advertisers, albeit with personal identifiers removed. And many are not aware that when they access any of the applications made available on Facebook — from quizzes and games to movie guides — by default the application developers have access not only to the users' data but also to that of friends of the users.

"Consciously or unconsciously you're in a marketing environment," says Lillie Coney, EPIC's associate director. "If you have a pet, you might be more inclined to give to an animal rescue group. Is that fair to use a consumer? Did you know that what you are seeing is being influenced by the communications you share with others who are your intimate friends in a social networking context? Should that be used in a way to sell you something?"

Coney also worries that the collection of data on social networking sites could lead to "differential marketing," in which not only the products but also the prices offered to users vary depending upon their characteristics. "Are you being presented items at prices that are based on your ability to pay rather than the quality of the item?" she wonders. "They can change the price depending on your profile."

In response to concerns voiced by users and privacy advocates, many social networks — including MySpace and Facebook — have recently introduced extensive enhancements to user privacy controls protecting what information on a user's site is made available to different parties. Users can, for example, prevent applications from having access to personal data.

"Some people want to share everything about themselves at all times with everybody," says Sparapani. "Other people don't want to share much with anybody at all. And everyone else falls in between. What Facebook has done is not just provide privacy controls, it is actually for the first time giving people at every level of the spectrum abilities to do exactly what they want or don't want with their data."

What's more, Sparapani emphasizes that when Facebook does share users' data with third parties, it is always stripped of personally identifiable data.

"We sell ad space, and we agree to serve ads to demographics that you tell us to target," says Sparapani. "But we never turn around and give you data other than to say, yes, your ads were served to these following groups of people with these demographic characteristics. It's a really important distinction."

Facebook also has taken steps to protect users from application developers who might abuse user data. Users

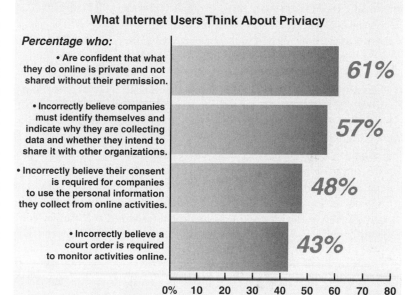

Many Internet Users Ill-Informed About Privacy

More than 60 percent of Internet users are confident that their online activities are private and cannot be shared without their permission. A similar percentage, though, incorrectly thinks Internet companies are mandated to disclose their intentions for collecting data. And about half incorrectly believe that consent is required for companies to use personal information collected from users.

What Internet Users Think About Priviacy

Percentage who:

- Are confident that what they do online is private and not shared without their permission. — **61%**
- Incorrectly believe companies must identify themselves and indicate why they are collecting data and whether they intend to share it with other organizations. — **57%**
- Incorrectly believe their consent is required for companies to use the personal information they collect from online activities. — **48%**
- Incorrectly believe a court order is required to monitor activities online. — **43%**

0% 10 20 30 40 50 60 70 80
Percentage

Source: Consumer Reports

can now block applications entirely or block them from accessing personal data.

Also, says Sparapani, "We do spot-checks of applications." Facebook staff review applications to see what data they are gathering and whether it is relevant to their apparent purpose. "We also have built the platform such that no application can access the most sensitive information that you have on your profile, such as contact information."

Coney acknowledges that Facebook has made significant strides in improving privacy controls and statements. "It is very important that companies are making an effort," she says. "It is important that they recognize that privacy is a major issue with their consumers."

At the same time, Coney says the efforts aren't enough. "A lot of these sites give an impression that they are private," she says. "But the privacy notices are so complicated. I know they're written with concern about liability exposure, but they have to be simpler."

Sparapani contends that the best protection is an educated user base. And he praises the capabilities of the majority of Facebook users. "Our users are really quite savvy as a group," he says. "Our users are the best police force out there. They know when an application doesn't do what it says it does, or when it does more than it should, and they feel free to report us, and then we initiate a review of that specific application."

Many users, however, are not so savvy, says Coney, noting, "That's why we have regulatory agencies that stand up for the consumers."

While agreeing that educating users is a crucial step, Coney argues that broader protections for personal information are needed. "We also need to see a uniform foundation for privacy protection established," she says. "This requires the regulatory agencies such as the Federal Trade Commission to establish a regulatory framework that companies have to operate in, and it requires Congress to establish laws that are not technology centric but that are based on collection and use of personally identifiable information."

Do federal privacy policies regarding the Internet need to be updated?

Calls for changes in federal policies regarding privacy on the Internet come primarily on two fronts: use of cookies on federal Web sites and revision of the Electronic Communications Privacy Act of 1986 (ECPA), the primary federal legislation regulating non-commercial aspects of Internet activity.

Issued in 2000, current federal cookie policy prohibits federal agencies from using cookies and other tracking technologies on federal Web sites. "There is an exception to that, which is used quite rarely: If the department or agency head makes a finding that there's a compelling need to use a cookie, the agency or department can do so," says a senior Office of Management and Budget (OMB) official, who agreed to be interviewed without being named. For example, the official said, Web sites operated by the National Aeronautics and Space Administration and the National Institutes of Health have received such exemptions.

Last June, however, the OMB began seeking comments to the following proposed changes in this policy:

Federal Web sites would be allowed to employ Web tracking technologies as long as they post clear and conspicuous notice on the Web site, provide a clear and understandable means for users to opt-out of such tracking and do not limit users' access to information if they opt-out of the tracking.[12]

The suggestion has alarmed privacy advocates. "This is a sea change in government privacy policy," Michael Macleod-Ball, acting director of the Washington legislative office of the American Civil Liberties Union (ACLU), said in a press release in August. "Without explaining this reversal of policy, the OMB is seeking to allow the mass collection of personal information of every user of a federal government Web site. Until the OMB answers the multitude of questions surrounding this policy shift, we will continue to raise our strenuous objections."

According to the OMB official, the policy change is not a done deal. "There are no actual proposed changes in the sense that anything is hardwired to be changed," he says. While he acknowledges that cookies carry potential privacy concerns, he says "making certain that people's privacy is protected in an extremely robust way is going to be a paramount concern of this administration, should any changes be proposed."

At the same time, he said, "it may be the case that there are ways in which judicious use of cookies on government Web sites can enable the Web sites to be more interactive, more robust, richer in terms of content and features and capabilities, so that they can really enable government to work better for people. That is the animating goal here."

While most privacy advocates oppose changes to existing cookie policies on federal Web sites, most advocacy groups are calling for major changes to ECPA on the grounds that the 1986 legislation is seriously out of date and no longer adequately protects sensitive data.

"This very important law, which I think in many ways does effectively protect people's privacy online, has understandably become outdated as the pace of technological change has increased," says Kevin Bankston, a senior attorney at the Electronic Frontier Foundation. "There are at this point fundamental questions about what ECPA protects that are unanswered and maybe are unanswerable without additional congressional guidance."

According to Bankston, nothing more pointedly demonstrates how out of date ECPA is than its provisions regarding e-mail. "E-mail is a technology that actually existed in 1986, and ECPA was drafted with that in mind," he says. "And yet there still critical questions about how ECPA applies to e-mail."

Under ECPA, for example, an electronic communication that has been in electronic storage with an electronic storage provider for 180 days or fewer requires a warrant if the government wants to access it. "The reason 180 days is required is because of differences in the past technology," says Bankston. "Back in 1986, when you dialed into your e-mail service and you downloaded your e-mail, it was erased off the server. So if you had left your e-mail there for six months, the fair assumption was that you had abandoned it and therefore it was not deserving of special protection."

What's more, says Bankston, a number of emerging technologies aren't specifically treated under ECPA. The issue of how ECPA applies to the government getting data from Internet search logs is, he says, "completely unsettled."

While Bankston and other privacy advocates call for reforms in ECPA, no party is actively opposing such reform. Many privacy advocates, however, believe that the Department of Justice would prefer to see the current law remain as it is. "I think it is fair to say that they may be resistant," says Jim Dempsey, vice president for public policy at the Center for Democracy and Technology. "To some extent, the Justice Department is doing a good job of manipulating the ambiguities and the loopholes in the statute now."

While he did not directly respond to Dempsey's charge of manipulating ambiguities and loopholes in ECPA, a Department of Justice official says, "We've been looking for places where there are gaps and trying to resolve issues. We've also been working within the structure created by Congress, which tried to be technology neutral to some extent in passing the statute. Where there are interpretive gaps, we are presenting that to the courts. And there is opportunity, of course, to have the courts interpret the statute.

"I wouldn't say ECPA is out of date," added the official, who asked that his name not be used. "I would say there are concepts in it where Congress might have had a technology in mind when it was legislating and that

Rep. Rick Boucher, D-Va., (left), chairman of the House Subcommittee on Communications, Technology and the Internet, says he will introduce legislation this fall to protect online privacy. Rep. Cliff Stearns, R-Fla., favors consumer education efforts and industry self-regulation and warns against overregulation.

technology is no longer in place. The courts have then tried to adapt to newer technologies that replaced it."

Nor has Congress actively taken up the issue of ECPA reform in recent years. According to Dempsey, "Up until now the issues have been discussed and debated only among the true ECPA nerds. It is a relatively small community of people who know about the statute, who understand the statute and who see how it works, so up until now the issue has not received a lot of public prominence."

BACKGROUND
Tracking Technologies

From 1967, when the Internet was born, until the mid-1990s, privacy was a non-issue. There was no advertising, no security measures apart from log ins, no spam and, until 1989, no graphic interfaces — no icons, images, windows, etc.

It was not until 1994 that the first tracking tool — the "cookie" — was introduced by Netscape Communications to check on whether visitors to the Netscape Web site had been there before. Early advertisers also found uses for cookies. When users downloaded pages from a Web site that included an advertisement or other content from

C H R O N O L O G Y

1980s-1990s *Internet service providers (ISPs) and advertisers develop tools for tracking user visits and online behaviors.*

1986 Electronic Communications and Privacy Act (ECPA) protects transmissions of electronic data by computers.

1994 First Internet tracking tool — the "cookie" — is introduced by Netscape Communications to check users' visits to its Web site.

1995 DoubleClick Web advertising company begins using cookies to track Internet users' Web visits.

1996 Internet Engineering Task Force identifies cookies as a potential threat to privacy. The next year the group calls for third-party cookies — those that feed data to a party other than the visited Web site — to be disabled in Web browsers. Microsoft and Netscape — the two major browser makers — reject the recommendation.

1998 Children's Online Privacy Protection Act of 1998 restricts the collection for commercial purposes of personal information about children under age 13.

1999 Network Advertising Initiative, launched by 12 advertising companies, begins developing standards for Internet advertising. . . . Federal Trade Commission holds its first workshop on behavioral targeting in Internet advertising.

2000s *Federal government begins to look more closely at legislation and regulation to protect Web users as Internet service providers, advertisers and federal agencies get more sophisticated in user tracking.*

2000 Clinton administration sets strict rules on the use of cookies on federal Web sites. . . . FBI introduces Carnivore program for monitoring Internet users' activities.

2001 USA Patriot Act amends ECPA to allow the FBI to access data by simply issuing "National Security Letters" to ISPs, rather than obtaining a warrant.

2005 A disgruntled employee reveals on her blog that Kaiser Permanente had inadvertently posted private patient information on its Web site. The health-care provider is ultimately fined $200,000 by the state of California.

2006 Department of Justice asks federal judge to force Google to turn over user-search queries as part of an investigation of violations of online pornography laws; Google successfully resists the subpoena. . . . America

Online makes the records of 20 million subscriber searches available to Internet researchers; some users are identified, underscoring the potential for privacy incursions.

2007 Facebook's Beacon advertising campaign uses information gathered from users' activities on other Web sites that are partnering with Facebook. After public criticism, Facebook changes the program to track users' activities only if they specifically opt-in to the program. . . . Sen. Patrick Leahy, D-Vt., introduces Personal Data Privacy and Security Act of 2007, aimed at enhancing criminal penalties and increasing reporting requirements. The bill does not come to a vote in the full Senate. . . . Ask.com announces that it will allow users to control whether their search terms are saved by the search service, a move applauded by privacy advocates. . . . *The Washington Post* reveals that federal officials are routinely asking courts to order cellphone companies to furnish real-time tracking data so they can pinpoint the whereabouts of drug traffickers and other suspects.

2008 Charter Communications, an ISP, and NebuAd, an advertising company, announce plans to analyze subscribers' Internet traffic and then tailor ads to users whose profiles indicate a match of interests; congressional lawmakers hold hearings and pressure the companies to abandon the project. . . . A federal judge in Pittsburgh declines prosecutors' attempts to obtain people's cellphone tracking information without a warrant.

2009 House Subcommittee on Communications, Technology and the Internet holds hearing on behavioral targeting by Internet advertisers. . . . Office of Management and Budget proposes loosening federal restrictions on use of cookies on federal Web sites. . . . National Archives and Records Administration concedes it sent a defective hard drive back to a vendor before erasing the health records of as many as 70 million veterans. . . . Canada's privacy commission reports that Facebook violates Canadian privacy laws in four areas and gives the site 30 days to change its policies.

April 14, 2010 CLEAR technical online ad standards released by advertising industry.

May 4, 2010 Rep. Rick Boucher, D-Va., unveils bill to protect Internet privacy of consumers.

May 25, 2010 Facebook founder and CEO Mark Zuckerberg announces simplification of the site's privacy protection settings.

July 22, 2010 Rep. Bobby Rush, D-Ill., introduces bill to protect online privacy.

Is Data Storage 'in the Cloud' Safe?

Privacy advocates warn there is no legal protection.

Back in the early days of the Internet, users stored their personal information on floppy discs and the hard drives of their computers.

That's all changed now. Increasing numbers of users are storing data on the Internet — or "in the cloud" — and using cloud applications, such as Google Apps, or cloud data storage like Microsoft LiveMesh. The convenience is obvious: Once data is stored online, it can be accessed from any Internet-connected computer.

But privacy advocates warn that the legislation protecting the privacy of users' data hasn't changed to keep up. As a recent story on National Public Radio noted, while the checkbook sitting in your desk at home is protected by the Fourth Amendment from being accessed by government agents without a warrant, that protection may not apply to data you keep in an online checking account.[1]

And since the data is stored remotely it may be difficult for users to even know how vulnerable it is. Is the third-party server holding the data reliable? Is the data encrypted, or is it susceptible to theft by hackers? Are there assurances the storage company will not share the data with others? What if the company shuts down the service, or the government asks the company for access to a customer's stored data or a party to a lawsuit demands the data?

Privacy advocates warn, for example, that some cloud service providers claim to "support" various security technologies — such as data encryption — when those technologies may not be enabled by default (automatically) and may require the user to request them.

Indeed, in June 38 researchers and academics in computer science, information security and privacy law signed a letter to Google asking the company to follow through on protecting the data of users of its cloud applications by turning on the supported HTTPS Web-encryption technology.[2] Google engineer Alma Whitten replied, "We're currently looking into whether it would make sense to turn on HTTPS as the default for all G-mail users," as well as for users of other Google cloud applications.[3]

While no major problems have occurred thus far with cloud storage, privacy advocates say clear, legal protections for stored data don't exist. In fact, according to a recent report by the World Privacy Foundation, data stored in the cloud may have more than one legal location, with differing legal consequences depending upon the location.

"A cloud provider may, without notice to a user, move the user's information from jurisdiction to jurisdiction, from provider to provider or from machine to machine," the report notes. "The legal location of information placed in a cloud could be one or more places of business of the cloud provider, the location of the computer on which the information is stored, the location of a communication that transmits the information from user to provider and from provider to user, a location where the user has communicated or could communicate with the provider, and possibly other locations."[4]

The foundation cautions users that the application of current privacy law to the data stored in the cloud is "unpredictable," in that the courts, without clear direction from Congress, are applying the laws inconsistently. What's more, it warns, "The government is not the only entity that might seek to obtain a user's record from a cloud provider. A private litigant or other party might seek records from a cloud provider rather than directly from a user because the cloud provider would not have the same motivation as the user to resist a subpoena or other demand."

—Patrick Marshall

---

[1] Martin Kaste, "Online Data Present A Privacy Minefield," "All Things Considered," National Public Radio, Nov. 4, 2009, www.npr.org/templates/story/story.php?storyId=114163862.

[2] http://files.cloudprivacy.net/google-letter-final.pdf.

[3] http://googleonlinesecurity.blogspot.com/2009/06/https-security-for-web-applications.html.

[4] Robert Gelman, "Privacy in the Clouds: Risks to Privacy and Confidentiality from Cloud Computing," World Privacy Forum, Feb. 23, 2009, p. 7.

the advertiser's server, a "third-party cookie" could also be included. That enabled advertisers not only to determine when their ads were viewed but also to detect what other sites the user visited where that cookie was also present.

Initially, cookies attracted little public notice. Users were not informed when cookies were deposited on their computers, and Web browsers did not have tools for blocking cookies. It wasn't until the *Financial Times* of London published an article about cookies in February 1996 that the general public knew about cookies. By that time, a working group of the Internet Engineering Task Force, an international standards group, identified cookies — and especially third-party cookies — as a potential threat to user privacy.

While the task force recommended that third-party cookies not be allowed, or at least be blocked by browsers by default, both Netscape and Microsoft Corp. — makers of the two dominant browsers — declined to follow the recommendation.

But, while cookies may present risks for user privacy, they also offer convenience and a richer Web experience. For example, cookies can be used to allow automated logins to Web sites or to deliver content that is customized according to user preferences. And Web site managers can use the information in cookies to improve the design and navigation of sites by seeing how users traverse pages.

While there is no federal law governing the use of cookies on nongovernmental Web sites, the Clinton administration in 2000 set strict rules on cookie use at federal Web sites following disclosures that the White House Office of National Drug Control Policy had used cookies to track users visiting its site.

Search engine logs represent another rich source of user data. The search engine technologies that concern privacy advocates, however, were developed relatively late in the game to enhance security and the user experience.

The first software tool for searching the Internet was a program called Archie. Created in 1990, it simply sought out and downloaded directory listings of files on public FTP (file transfer protocol) sites. Archie did not index or display the contents of the files.

The Web's first actual search engine — Aliweb — debuted in November 1993. Unlike today's search engines, which send out "robots" to visit Web sites and generate an index of contents, Aliweb relied on Web site administrators to submit links to index files.

The first program developed to "crawl" the Web to find sites and index them for searching was JumpStation, which appeared in December 1993, but it indexed only titles and headings rather than the entire contents of pages.

Beginning in 1994, several search engines appeared that performed full-text indexing of Web sites. It wasn't until 2000, however, that a clear winner — Google — emerged in the race to become the dominant search engine. Google introduced page ranking, which allowed users to more quickly and reliably retrieve Web sites of interest, using search terms. By 2008, Google accounted for more than 82 percent of search engine traffic worldwide.

The key concern privacy advocates have about search engines is the electronic logs that they keep of users' searches. According to Google, the logs are primarily generated to help in improving the service. By examining search activity coming from a specific Internet Protocol (IP) address — and each computer on the Internet is assigned a unique IP address — the company can detect problems developing on the network.

"The ability on Google's side to look at what is happening from a particular IP address over time is the kind of thing that we often look at to prevent abuse or to do certain kinds of machine learning on," says Alma Whitten, a Google software engineer. More specifically, says Whitten, Google engineers will monitor the logs to look for patterns that may tip off the presence of "denial of service" attacks. And engineers use the logs in an effort to improve the algorithms that make searches possible.

Advertisers Self-regulate

As early as 1995, the pioneering Web advertising firm DoubleClick began using cookies to track users on the Web. At the same time, some in the advertising industry also realized that while tracking technology offered opportunities for marketing, it also represented a challenge to consumer confidence.

"Back in the early 1990s, the few people trying to use [the Internet for marketing] were being flamed [criticized] because a lot of people on the Internet claimed that it should be a marketing-free zone," recalls Jaffe, at the Association of National Advertisers. "We said back then that if this was going to be an effective medium, adequate concern about consumer privacy issues had to be one of the pillars it was built on."

In fact, most efforts to ensure privacy protections with respect to marketing on the Internet have been accomplished through self-regulation with the assistance and oversight of the Federal Trade Commission (FTC). The one legislative exception to this is the Children's Online Privacy Protection Act of 1998, which placed restrictions and requirements on the collection for commercial purposes of personal information of children under the age of 13.[13]

The Network Advertising Initiative (NAI), a nonprofit industry group formed by 12 companies, was created in 1999 to work with the FTC to develop a set of principles to govern Internet advertising efforts. The principles basically required NAI member companies to post a notice on all Web sites served by their networks informing users the advertiser may place a third-party cookie on their computers. In addition, members were required to offer an opt-out tool for users who didn't want targeted ads from NAI members, and to refrain from merging personally identifiable information with Web browsing data without users' opt-in.

The FTC convened a town hall forum with industry representatives in 2007 to discuss the need for further regulation of online adverting activities. After the forum, the NAI issued revised guidelines in December 2008 that expanded members' commitment to provide security for data and also required:

• Consumer opt-in for "sensitive" information used with behavioral targeting, such as health conditions or treatments, and location information;

• Parental consent to use non-personally identifiable data to target behavioral advertising to children under age 13, and

• An annual in-house compliance review.

Similar standards were adopted by another industry group, the Interactive Advertising Bureau, in 2008.

While efforts at self-regulation may have provided some assurances to the public, they have not slowed the use of tracking cookies or newer tracking technologies, such as deep-packet inspection, by advertising firms and service providers. (*See glossary, p. 122.*)

The limitations on self-regulation became clear to the public and to Congress in 2008, when Charter Communications, an Internet service provider, and

CQ Press/Screenshot (both)

Government and Private Industry Sites

Federal agencies are prohibited by federal policies from using "cookies" and other tracking technologies on their Web sites. However, some sites, including those operated by the National Institutes of Health (top), have received exemptions. Proposed changes in federal policies regarding the Web have alarmed privacy advocates, who say the changes would "allow the mass collection of personal information of every user of a federal government Web site." In response to concerns voiced by users and privacy advocates, many social networks — including Facebook (bottom) — have recently introduced extensive enhancements to user privacy controls protecting what information on a user's site is made available to different parties.

NebuAd, an advertising company, announced plans to perform deep-packet inspection on subscribers' Internet traffic. By examining users' activities on the Web, the companies planned to tailor ads and target them to users whose profiles indicated a match of interests.

Congressional hearings resulted in the plans being dropped. But while some legislators argued that the proposed practice violated existing wiretap and privacy laws, no legislation resulted that might clarify the legality of deep-packet inspection.

Some analysts on Capitol Hill tie the prospect for privacy legislation to growing public awareness and concern. "It's clear that the technology exists to monitor where consumers go and what they do on the Internet. It's also clear that a lot of companies are looking to monetize it," Jessica Rosenworcel, senior communications counsel for the Senate Commerce panel, said after the hearings last spring. "What is less clear is what consumers are aware of and what they're comfortable with."[14]

Federal Tracking

Congress has generally taken a hands-off approach to Internet privacy issues, except for the Electronic Communications Privacy Act of 1986. ECPA basically extended federal restrictions on wiretaps of telephone calls to protect transmissions of electronic data by computers. Title II of the act, the Stored Communications Act, protects communication held in storage, specifically e-mails, though with less stringent protections than are accorded under Title I, which protects transmissions. Under Title II, if an unopened e-mail has been in storage for 180 days or less, the government must obtain a search warrant to access it.

ECPA's protections were weakened by the USA Patriot Act of 2001, which allowed the FBI to access data by simply issuing so-called National Security Letters to ISPs, which allow FBI investigators to obtain information without a warrant.

"So once the private companies gather and store the information, it is there to be plucked by the government with very little judicial oversight," says the ACLU's Stanley. "Basically, the Patriot Act took judges out of the equation."

While Congress has shown reluctance since 1986 to weigh in on online privacy issues — even to bring the provisions of ECPA up to date with respect to changes in Internet technologies — the executive branch has made repeated efforts to expand its capabilities to monitor Internet activity.

The FBI introduced its Carnivore program in 2000 to conduct Internet surveillance — purportedly under the guidance of ECPA. The software, which was apparently a tool for deep-packet analysis, attracted such negative coverage in the media that the name was changed to DCS1000. The bureau apparently abandoned Carnivore in 2005 in favor of other commercially available monitoring tools.

In 2002, the U.S. Defense Advanced Research Projects Agency proposed developing an Internet surveillance system — "Total Information Awareness" — that would monitor content across the Internet. The project apparently was dropped after the U.S. Senate voted for restrictions on its development in 2003.

That same year, the Bush administration announced plans to build an Internet monitoring center to detect and respond to attacks on key systems. The Global Early Warning Information System was to be developed under the National Communications System, a Defense Department agency.

The Department of Justice has repeatedly taken Google to court in an effort to gain access to search records. In 2005, for example, the DoJ filed a motion in federal court to force Google to comply with a subpoena for the text of search "strings" entered into the search engine over a one-week period. The court granted part of the request, but denied the government access to users' specific search strings.[15]

The next year the Department of Justice again asked a federal judge to force Google to turn over user search queries as part of an investigation of violations of online pornography laws. Google successfully fought the subpoena.[16]

In April 2008 the FBI called for legislation that would allow federal law enforcement agencies to monitor Internet traffic for "illegal activity."[17]

CURRENT SITUATION
Action in Congress

Internet privacy for consumers is attracting some attention in Congress.

In April the House Energy and Commerce Subcommittee on Communications, Technology and the Internet, chaired by Virginia Rep. Boucher, held hearings on consumer privacy. And in June the House Energy and Commerce Subcommittee on Commerce, Trade and Consumer Protection, chaired by Rep. Bobby Rush, D-Ill., held hearings specifically on behavioral targeting of online advertising.

Is Your Smartphone Keeping Tabs on You?

Advertisers and police tune in, but civil libertarians worry.

Global positioning system (GPS) chips in cellphones and mobile navigation devices have turned location-based services into a booming industry. Already some cellphone applications and auto GPS devices tell you where to find pizza close by, or the cheapest gasoline.

Indeed, according to *The Wall Street Journal*, location-based services will be a $13-billion-a-year business by 2013, compared to $515 million last year.[1]

But it's not just advertisers who are interested in accessing cellphone and vehicle location information. Law enforcement agencies are increasingly turning to service providers to obtain location information on subjects of investigation.

The laws applying to such actions, however, are not clear. "Federal officials are routinely asking courts to order cellphone companies to furnish real-time tracking data so they can pinpoint the whereabouts of drug traffickers, fugitives and other criminal suspects, according to judges and industry lawyers," noted *Washington Post* reporter Ellen Nakashima. "In some cases, judges have granted the requests without requiring the government to demonstrate that there is probable cause to believe that a crime is taking place or that the inquiry will yield evidence of a crime."[2]

"The question of what legal process the government needs to follow to track your cell phone is hotly disputed in front of magistrate judges across the country," says Kevin Bankston, an attorney with the Electronic Frontier Foundation.

Bankston says his group only became aware of the issue in 2005, mainly because such government actions generally are kept secret. "Typically, we don't know what is going on at that level," he explains. "It all occurs under seal. Unless something comes out at a criminal trial, we don't know what they're doing."

Under the circumstances, says Bankston, "The only solution is Congress — it could step in and provide clear rules for cellphone tracking."

Some privacy advocates also point to the potential for abuse of location information from "other" parties, such as stalkers and domestic abusers.

In recent congressional testimony, Leslie Harris, president of the Center for Democracy and Technology, called for three measures, the first two of which would require congressional action:

• The disclosure of precise location information in a commercial context must only be made with specific, informed, opt-in consent in which a user has the ability to selectively disclose locations only to trusted parties. As Congress contemplates enacting baseline consumer privacy legislation, such a requirement could easily be part of a broader framework governing sensitive consumer data.

• The standards for government and law enforcement access to location information must be amended to make clear that a probable-cause warrant is required for the government to obtain location information.

• Location-based services and applications should follow technical standards that give users clear control over the use of their location information and that require the transmittal of privacy rules with the location information itself.[3]

— Patrick Marshall

---

[1] Amol Sharma and Jessica E. Vascellaro, "Companies Eye Location-Services Market," *The Wall Street Journal*, Nov. 21, 2008, http://online.wsj.com/article/SB122722971742046469.html.

[2] Ellen Nakashima, "Cellphone Tracking Powers on Request, Secret Warrants Granted Without Probable Cause," *The Washington Post*, Nov. 23, 2007, www.washingtonpost.com/wp-dyn/content/article/2007/11/22/AR2007112201444.html.

[3] Statement before House Energy and Commerce Subcommittee on Communications, Technology and the Internet, April 23, 2009.

Boucher and Rush have made clear that the two subcommittees are working closely together in conducting hearings. "There are currently no federal laws specifically governing behavioral advertising nor do we have a comprehensive general privacy law," Rush noted in opening the June hearings. "As members of Congress, we have anticipated for some time that this hearing would be highly informative and very valuable in helping us

Should Congress regulate online behavioral advertising?

YES

Jeff Chester
Executive Director, Center for Digital Democracy

From testimony before House Subcommittee on Communications, Technology and the Internet, June 18, 2009

Some in the online ad industry appear to suggest that any legislative attempt to place consumers in charge of their online data would undermine the economic role of the Internet media. But I believe that by legislatively creating a system where consumers can be assured that their data are protected and transactions are structured to further empower them, trust and confidence in our online marketplace will grow and thrive. I firmly believe that we can protect privacy and also see the online marketplace and medium prosper.

Behavioral targeting and related technologies may provide "marketing nirvana," as one company explained, but it leaves consumers unaware and vulnerable to an array of marketing communications that are increasingly tied to our financial and health activities.

[Advertisers'] privacy policies are an inadequate mechanism that fail to protect the public. As documented in a recent University of California-Berkeley School of Information study on online privacy, privacy policies are difficult to read; the amount of time required to read them is too great; they lead consumers to falsely believe their privacy is protected; there [aren't] meaningful differences between policies, leaving consumers with no alternatives; and consumers aren't really aware of the "potential dangers."

The FTC [Federal Trade Commission] has been largely incapable of ensuring American privacy is protected online. Staff has been reined in from more aggressively pursuing the issue, primarily to ensure that industry self-regulation remains as the agency's principal approach.

The FTC needs to have additional resources, especially so it can better protect consumers from digital marketing transactions involving their financial and health data. Congress should press the FTC to be more proactive in this arena.

The failure to adequately regulate the financial sector greatly contributed to the worst economic crisis since the Great Depression. Regulation isn't a dirty word. It's essential so consumers and businesses can conduct their transactions with assurance that the system is as honest and accountable as possible.

The uncertainty over the loss of privacy and other consumer harms will continue to undermine confidence in the online advertising business. That's why the online ad industry will actually greatly benefit from privacy regulation. Given a new regulatory regime protecting privacy, industry leaders and entrepreneurs will develop new forms of marketing services where data collection and profiling are done in an aboveboard, consumer-friendly fashion.

NO

Berin Szoka
Director, Center for Internet Freedom
Adam Thierer
Director, Center for Digital Media Freedom
Progress & Freedom Foundation

From "Online Advertising and User Privacy: Principles to Guide the Debate," September 2008

To the extent that effective, self-help privacy tools exist, they provide a means of solving policy problems that is not only "less restrictive" than government regulation but generally more effective and customizable as well. Why settle for one-size-fits-all solutions of incomplete effectiveness when users can quite easily and effectively manage their own privacy?

Fortunately, a wide variety of self-help tools and "technologies of evasion" are readily available to all users and can easily thwart traditional cookie-based tracking, as well as more sophisticated tracking technologies, such as packet inspection.

The "free" Internet economy is based on a simple value exchange: Users get access to an ever-expanding collection of content and services at no cost from Web sites that are able to generate revenue from "eyeballs" on their pages by selling space on their sites to advertisers, usually through ad networks. The smarter that advertising, the more free content and services it can support.

As users face an increasingly clear choice between (1) getting content and services for free supported by behavioral advertising and (2) paying to receive those same services and content without tracking or even without ads altogether, policy makers will finally see whether users are really as bothered by profiling as the advocates of [online behavioral advertising] regulation insist. Given the ongoing and widespread replacement of fee- or subscription-supported Web business models with ad-supported models, it seems likely that the vast majority of consumers will continue to choose ad-supported models, including profiling.

Indeed, if smarter online advertising will not fund the Internet's future, what will? As both the desire for "free" services and content and the need for bandwidth expand, [online behavioral advertising] has the potential to offer important new revenue sources that can help support the entire ecosystem of online content creation and service innovation, while also providing a new source of funding for Internet infrastructure and making ads less annoying and more informative.

But looming legislative and regulatory action could stop all of that by replacing the current regime — in which the FTC merely enforces industry self-regulatory policies — with one in which the government preemptively dictates how data may be collected and used.

answer the question that everyone seems to ask: Is federal privacy legislation necessary, or should companies be trusted to discipline and regulate themselves?"

Boucher has been more assertive in his view that legislation is necessary. "I think that as far as they go the voluntary codes that have been adopted within the industry are constructive," Boucher told *CQ Researcher*. "They represent a step forward. The problem is that not every Web site will be a part of that voluntary commitment." As a result, Boucher has promised to introduce legislation during the current Congress, promising that it will be bipartisan.

While Democrats on both subcommittees seem generally more inclined toward regulating online advertisers, Republicans seem to prefer self-regulation. Nevertheless, comments by committee members during the hearings suggest there is room for bipartisanship. "It is still a little bit of a Wild West out there [on the Internet], and I think it is time that Congress begins to look at and try to bring some law and order to that particular Wild West area," Rep. Joe Barton, R-Texas, said.[18]

Rep. Cliff Stearns, R-Fla., said he favored consumer education efforts and warned the hearing against over-regulation. "Consumers' online activities provide advertisers with valuable information upon which to market their products and their services," Stearns said. "Collecting this type of information for targeted advertising is very important because it simply allows many of these products and services to remain free to consumers. Without this information, Web sites would either have to cut back on their free information and services or would have to start charging a fee. Neither result is good for the consumers."[19]

Stearns added that "Overreaching privacy regulation could have a significant negative economic impact at a time when many businesses in our economy are struggling, so let us be very careful on these issues before we leap to legislative regulatory proposals."

While the privacy of consumer data is receiving increasing attention, government access to users' online data is drawing relatively little attention, although many privacy advocates say government access is potentially the greater threat.

Federal monitoring programs tend to have a lower profile because they generally take place behind the scenes, say privacy advocates. Internet monitoring by the super-secret National Security Agency and other intelligence organizations, of course, is classified information and rarely subjected to public scrutiny. And even cases involving the Department of Justice are rarely in the spotlight.

"At some level the Justice Department retains control over the cases that emerge into the public light," says the Center for Democracy and Technology's Dempsey. "A lot of recipients of government orders are generally prohibited from disclosing their existence. And they don't necessarily want to disclose the order because they don't want to scare their customers.

"The companies grapple with these issues quietly behind the scenes, in negotiations with the Justice Department," Dempsey continues. What's more, privacy advocates note, the Justice Department has near complete control over the cases it chooses to litigate. "The Justice Department will drop charges or decide not to use the evidence against anybody in a case that might be going against them," says Dempsey. "So the Justice Department gets to go public with the issues only in the context of drug trafficking, child abuse and terrorism — those cases the deptartment prefers to talk about."

Accordingly, some privacy advocates believe that one of the most important reforms needed in the Electronic Communications Privacy Act is requirements for reporting. "Right now the government can bend the rules and make really outrageous arguments," says Bankston of the Electronic Frontier Foundation. "Because the proceedings are sealed, and there's no adversary there to point out when the government is overreaching, they can in fact get powers that were not given to them by Congress for years at a stretch before they are found out. This problem could be addressed if Congress were to require reporting."

Privacy advocates note that privacy threats occur in part because legislative and regulatory policies generally seem to trail behind the capabilities of emerging technologies.

"Our courts have not kept up with technology and have not kept up with the needs of privacy," says the ACLU's Stanley. "When the Fourth Amendment was written, most of people's lives took place in the home. Your medical life, your correspondence, your financial records were in the home. And the founding fathers recognized the need for privacy and put in strong protections for privacy in the home. But much of our lives are now stored on the servers of international corporations. And yet we have not extended privacy to cover that."

One solution to that problem suggested by some privacy advocates is adoption of an information-centric approach to privacy, rather than the current technology-centric approach.

"We're interested in getting a comprehensive privacy law," says Schwartz of the Center for Democracy and Technology. "Right now, we have laws protecting medical privacy and video rental records. But we don't have the general overarching privacy law that some other countries do."

Advertisers Press Ahead

While Internet service providers have apparently acceded to pressure from Congress to refrain from monitoring users' Internet activity, search engine companies and advertisers are moving ahead. Most notably, Google last March launched its own behavioral targeting program, "AdSense." The program tracks Web visits and search terms in order to build a profile of users' interests. Google is then able to display targeted ads when a user visits a participating Web site.

To avoid the complaints that ultimately sank NebuAd, Google allows users to opt out of the program and to view and edit the categories they are assigned to by Google based on their Web site visits.

"Because we're very aware that people might have privacy concerns about this, we've put a great deal of effort into being very transparent about how this will work," says Google software engineer Whitten.

"On any of those ads where we're doing this there is a link across the bottom, and if the user clicks on that they get taken to a page where Google explains how this works and gives them the opportunity to view the interest categories that Google has associated with their cookie and offers to let them opt out of the whole thing," explains Whitten. "We've made sure that all of the categories involved are very innocuous." According to Whitten, the categories include such interests as cooking, travel and sports. More personal and intrusive topics, such as cancer and political affiliations, are not included.

Schwartz at the Center for Democracy and Technology praises Google's decision. "We're targeted in so many ways and in so many categories" by advertisers, he says. "There's discussion about what kind of information is sensitive. You hear less concern about that when Google makes the categories they are targeting available. It doesn't solve every problem to make them available and let you change them, but it helps."

Microsoft is reportedly also working hard on developing behavioral targeting tools, though the company declined comment.

And some social networking sites have moved into providing behavioral targeting services for advertisers. In 2007 Facebook introduced its Beacon advertising campaign, which uses information gathered from a user's activities on other Web sites that are partnering with Facebook. If, for example, consumers purchase books at Amazon.com, an item about those purchases might appear on their page. Facebook did offer an opt-out to users, but the service nevertheless attracted so much criticism that the company scaled back Beacon in several important ways. First, and most significantly, Beacon now only works with users who choose to opt in to the program.

At the same time that major advertising companies and service providers are refining and developing behavioral targeting programs, they are working closely with each other and with the Federal Trade Commission to develop self-regulation standards for the rapidly emerging capabilities. And not coincidentally, both the FTC and a coalition of advertisers this year released reports on self-regulation of behavioral-targeted advertising programs.

On Feb. 12, the FTC issued its report, citing as one of the primary reasons the fact that "staff recognized that existing self-regulatory efforts had not provided comprehensive and accessible protections to consumers. Accordingly, in issuing the proposed principles, staff intended to guide industry in developing more meaningful and effective self-regulatory models than had been developed to date."[20]

The four broad principles are:

- **Transparency and control:** Companies should provide "meaningful disclosures" about the practice and choice about whether to allow it.

- **Security and data retention:** Companies should provide reasonable data security measures and should retain data "only as long as necessary for legitimate business or law enforcement needs."

- **Material changes:** Before a company uses data in a manner that is "materially different" from promises made when the company collected the data, it should obtain "affirmative express consent" from the consumer.

• **Sensitive data:** Before using data about children, health or finances, companies should obtain affirmative express consent.

The report noted that the FTC had received many objections from industry representatives about proposals requiring companies to receive affirmative, express consent before using data in a materially different manner and before collecting sensitive data.

Nevertheless, the commission vote to approve the report was unanimous. However, in a concurring statement included in the report, Commissioner Jon Leibowitz warned advertisers, "Industry needs to do a better job of meaningful, rigorous self-regulation, or it will certainly invite legislation by Congress and a more regulatory approach by our commission. Put simply, this could be the last, clear chance to show that self-regulation can — and will — effectively protect consumers' privacy in a dynamic, online marketplace."

Several months after the FTC issued its report the coalition of advertisers released its own, identically titled report.[21] Moreover, the industry principles are nearly identical with the FTC's, except regarding consent required for collecting sensitive data or making material changes in the use of data. While the FTC calls for requirements that users must actively "opt-in," the industry group would see an individual's refraining from opting out of the system as sufficient.[22]

For now, the FTC is taking a wait-and-see approach to attempts at self-regulation. "We felt when we released the principles that companies need to do a much better job," says senior staff attorney Magee. "Since our principles came out, we have seen some positive steps by business. But we probably haven't had enough time to see the full impact of them and how some of these self-regulatory programs are going to be operationalized and what it is going to mean to consumers.

"It's a good start. But how long we support that approach and how long Congress holds off on legislating remains to be seen."

OUTLOOK

'A Number of Issues'

Chairman Boucher of the House Subcommittee on Communications, Technology and the Internet intends to introduce legislation this fall to regulate behavioral targeting in online advertising.

"There are a number of issues that we will seek to address," says Boucher. "Fundamental to all the protections we're proposing will be a requirement that any Web site that collects information from Internet users have a clear statement on the Web site of what information is collected and provide to the Internet user the opportunity to opt out of having any information collected."

Boucher adds that there would be further requirements for more sensitive data, such as financial and medical data as well as any information about children.

But Boucher also intends to offer advertisers a "safe harbor." If advertisers follow a specified set of "best practices," their data collection would be subject only to opt-outs by consumers. Opt-ins, which advertisers argue are much more difficult to obtain from consumers, would not be required.

"We're looking at a growing list of possible practices that would fit within that category and trying to make some determination at this point as to where the line is drawn," says Boucher. "That is a work in progress. We've not drafted a bill yet. We're still at the information-collection stage on this question . . . and we may ultimately decide to leave that determination to the Federal Trade Commission."

For its part, the advertising industry continues to warn against relying on legislation for regulating online advertisers. "A lot of people ask, 'Why not have legislation to solve the problem?'" says Jaffe at the Association of National Advertisers. "Because locking in policy in an area that is changing as rapidly as this is risky. Where technology is changing rapidly, almost inevitably legislation stands in the way of innovation and misses the target and is overly rigid."

Some members of Boucher's subcommittee during the April hearing also expressed hesitation about regulating the online advertising industry. "As we move forward towards privacy legislation, we must empower consumers to make their own privacy-related decisions," said Florida Rep. Stearns, the subcommittee's ranking Republican. "Only the consumer knows how he or she feels about the information that is being collected, the parties doing the collecting and the actual purpose for which the information will ultimately be used. Congress cannot and should not make that decision for them."[23]

Privacy advocates, for their part, would like to see something even broader than what Boucher has in mind. While some interest groups are calling for a comprehensive privacy law that focuses on people's data rather than the technology used to collect it, others argue the law should give citizens an advocate when it comes to privacy.

"This is an area where you need privacy guardians who have some power and who are dedicated to privacy issues to monitor and regulate," says the ACLU's Stanley. "The European Union and most every industrialized country have privacy commissioners who have the power to do that."

As for providing protections from government monitoring of online data, privacy advocates concede that progress will be slow. "On the Electronic Communications Privacy Act front, I do believe that the civil liberties organizations and industry are coming close to reaching a consensus position to put before Congress," says Bankston of the Electronic Frontier Foundation.

But that's only the beginning of the process, says Dempsey at the Center for Democracy and Technology. "It will be a long effort, and actually achieving legislation will require "a long and cautious process," he says. "We have to educate the members of Congress. We have to, to a certain extent, educate the public."

UPDATE

As Facebook prepared to click in its 500-millionth member this summer, the giant of social networking in May humbled itself before its global audience by simplifying its controversial privacy controls. The existing jumble of some 150 different options for protecting personal online data had drawn outcries from consumers, privacy advocacy groups, and Congress. "We probably should have been more sensitive to this issue beforehand," said Facebook founder and CEO Mark Zuckerberg.

Critics were encouraged but will continue to seek new government protections. "Facebook is trying to change privacy on the Internet, and users are pushing back," said Marc Rotenberg, executive director of the Electronic Privacy Information Center, one of several groups that have filed complaints about Facebook's privacy practices with the Federal Communications Commission (FCC). "This is about who controls the disclosure of data. Facebook cannot make that decision for users."[24]

Fresh challenges to personal privacy posed by the accelerating digital revolution have continued to multiply. In late July, *The Wall Street Journal* stirred up a fuss with an exposé revealing that the 50 most heavily used Websites in the country had each remotely installed an average of 64 tracking tools on the millions of computers of users who had visited them. The destinations include such prominent sites as MSN.com, AOL.com, Answers.com, Yahoo.com and Careerbuilder.com.[25]

In a swift response, Reps. Ed Markey, D-Mass., and Joe Barton, R-Texas, co-chairs of the House Bipartisan Privacy Caucus, sent letters to the 15 Website owners demanding details on the types of tracking devices and the nature of the personal data collected. And an investigation by the House Energy and Commerce Committee was demanded by an alliance of consumer groups, among them the Center for Digital Democracy, Consumer Action, Consumer Watchdog, U.S. PIRG and the Privacy Rights Clearinghouse.

The motives for the Website owners, their business partners and their advertisers to use consumer-tracking software are no mystery. Behaviorally targeted advertisements based on Web users' prior site visits are more than twice as effective in generating revenue for advertisers, according to a study by a former Federal Trade Commission (FTC) consumer-protection chief released in March by the Network Advertising Initiative (NAI), an industry online-standards group based in Kennebunkport, Maine.[26]

And it isn't just private-sector electronic eyes that are scrutinizing citizens' online presence. The FBI and the CIA increasingly are scouring blogs, social-networking sites, Web forums and chat rooms in the course of law enforcement and security investigations, according to documents recently obtained under the Freedom of Information Act by the Electronic Frontier Foundation (EFF).

"Government investigators are collecting a wealth of information through the Internet in general and outside of the law enforcement context," wrote EFF blogger Tim Wayne. "It is also a good reminder that while social networks and other Websites have privacy settings, the Internet does not."[27]

The question of whether the federal government should step in to protect privacy rights for Internet users has been rising up the agenda of congressional committees and executive branch agencies.

"Regulation reining in online consumer data collection has reached a tipping point," says Jeff Chester, executive director of the Center for Digital Democracy. "There is bipartisan support for enacting sensible safeguards that protect consumer privacy and limit what information can be collected, especially when it comes to sensitive areas like finance, health and family data. The FTC is drilling deep down into the issue — and will likely push for greater consumer control. The Obama administration knows it has to strike the correct balance between fostering a robust online economy and protecting consumers." Industry "will have to adapt to new federal rules of the digital road," he adds.

Businesses and free-market advocates continue to resist a federal framework, preferring continuing efforts by industry at "self-regulation" of online activity. In April, the NAI and the Interactive Advertising Bureau released a set of technical standards that enhance notice to consumers about the use of online ads. Called CLEAR (Control Links for Education and Advertising Responsibly), the specifications will allow advertisers and ad networks to begin offering a clickable icon in or near online ads that directs users to additional information about online behavioral advertising and choices about the ads.

Philosophical opponents of federal intervention cite the benefits to consumers of the free flow of information and note that notions of privacy differ among individuals. "The debate here isn't whether government should get involved in protecting online privacy, but how," says Berin Michael Szoka, a senior fellow at the Progress & Freedom Foundation and director of its Center for Internet Freedom. "Most lawmakers seem to believe the answer is sweeping, new legislation that imposes restrictive default settings for the collection and use of data. But they pay only lip service to the costs to consumers of such a crackdown, especially in boosting the advertising revenues that fund free content and services from *The New York Times* to social-networking tools."

His group believes the FTC should use its existing authority against unfair or deceptive trade practices and to educate consumers about how to "take charge" of their privacy.

In response to widespread criticism, Facebook founder and CEO Mark Zuckerberg announced in May that the social-networking behemoth would simplify its controversial and complicated privacy controls.

With the "future of the Internet" at stake, Szoka adds, "Congress should ask the FTC to study systems by which sites and data collectors can translate their legalistic privacy policies into code that can be automatically interpreted by privacy tools in browsers, so users can make easy, effective choices about online privacy in a way that recognizes the value exchange of getting free content in return for sharing data about their interests to make advertising profitable for ad-supported Websites."

Helping average Internet users navigate the net is precisely what Sen. John D. Rockefeller, D-W.Va, said on July 27 when he opened a hearing on Internet privacy at the Senate Committee on Commerce, Science and Transportation. "The consumer I am concerned about is not a savvy computer whiz-kid. I am not talking about a lawyer who reads legalese for a living and can delve into the fine print of what privacy protections he or she is getting," he said. "I am talking about a 55-year-old coal miner in West Virginia who sends an e-mail to his son in college. I'm talking about a 30-year-old mother who uses her broadband connection to research the best doctor she can take her sick toddler to see. I'm talking about a 65-year-old man who just signed up for a Facebook account so he can view photos of his grandson, and reconnect with old friends."

Questions posed by Rockefeller included how much consumers know about online data sharing and how they can avoid scams. "What are consumers getting in exchange for this information sharing?" he asked.

In the House, Rep. Rick Boucher, D-Va., unveiled long-promised legislation in draft form in May. "Our legislation confers privacy rights on individuals, informing them of the personal information that is collected and shared about them and giving them greater control over the collection, use and sharing of that information," said Boucher. "Online advertising supports much of the commercial content, applications and services that are available on the Internet today without charge, and this legislation will not disrupt this well-established and successful business model. It simply extends to consumers important baseline privacy protections."

A similar bill introduced on July 22 by Rep. Bobby Rush, D-Ill., would require marketers to provide detailed disclosures to all consumers describing their information-collection practices. Consumer "opt-out" consent would be required for the collection and use of "covered information," and express affirmative consent — or "opt in" — would be required before a company could share covered information with third parties. Marketers would be required to provide consumers with access to the information that has been collected from or about them. Under Rush's proposed Best Practices Act, the FTC would be required to set up a so-called safe harbor program for companies that wish to self-regulate. Firms that voluntarily pledged to follow the new privacy policy would no longer have to obtain user consent to share information.[28]

In addition to Congress and the FTC, the Commerce Department is viewed by many privacy activists as a key agency for a positive federal action. Commerce is at the "intersection of privacy and innovation" and should take a lead role as a "global privacy advocate," the Center for Democracy and Technology said in a June 25 paper. "Our comments ask the [Department of Commerce] to reaffirm that consumers' trust in the security and privacy of online transactions is a major reason for American business success."[29] The online advertising community opposes any major Commerce initiative.

As the debate on regulation continued, the Privacy Rights Clearinghouse in June published the "Top Eight Things You Shouldn't Give Social Networking Sites." Its no-no's include access to your e-mail account; your work e-mail address; your exact date and place of birth; your browsing history; your vacation plans; public posts with your address, phone number and e-mail address; embarrassing or compromising photos; and money.[30]

NOTES

1. See www.tuck.dartmouth.edu/faculty/publications/forum/johnson.html.

2. Sarah Lyall, "On Facebook, a Spy Revealed (Pale Legs, Too)," *The New York Times*, July 6, 2009, p. A1.

3. Brian Krebs, "Justice Breyer Is Among Victims in Data Breach Caused by File Sharing," *The Washington Post*, July 9, 2008, p. A1.

4. Matthias Schwartz, "Malwebolence," *The New York Times*, Aug. 3, 2008, p. MM24.

5. Testimony before House Energy and Commerce Subcommittee on Communications, Technology and the Internet, April 23, 2009.

6. www.comscore.com/Press_Events/Press_releases/2009/10/comScore_Releases_September_2009_U.S._Search_Engine_Rankings.

7. See www.reuters.com/article/pressRelease/idUS148003+27-Jan-2009+MW20090127.

8. For background, see the following *CQ Researcher* reports: Kenneth Jost, "Civil Liberties Debate," Oct. 24, 2003, pp. 893-916; Kenneth Jost, "Government Secrecy," Dec. 2, 2005, pp. 1005-1028; Marcia Clemmitt, "Privacy in Peril," Nov. 17, 2006, pp. 961-984.

9. See www.consumersunion.org/pub/core_telecom_and_utilities/006189.html.

10. Statement of Marc Rotenberg, executive director, EPIC, and adjunct professor, Georgetown University Law Center, before House Energy and Commerce Subcommittee on Communications, Technology and the Internet, April 24, 2009.

11. Statement of Charles Curran, executive director, Network Advertising Initiative, before House Energy and Commerce Subcommittee on Commerce, Trade, and Consumer Protection and Subcommittee on Communications, Technology and the Internet, June 18, 2009.

12. http://blog.ostp.gov/category/cookie-policy/.

13. For background, see Marcia Clemmitt, "Cyber Socializing," *CQ Researcher*, July 28, 2006, pp. 625-648.

14. Adrianne Kroepsch, "Deeper Ad Probes Sound Web Alarm," *CQ Weekly*, May 11, 2009, p. 1076.

15. See http://epic.org/privacy/gmail/doj_court_order.pdf.

16. See www.google.com/press/images/ruling_20060317.pdf.

17. See http://news.cnet.com/8301-10784_3-99 26899-7.html.

18. Preliminary transcript of the hearing available at: http://energycommerce.house.gov/Press_111/20090618/transcript_20090618_ct.pdf.

19. *Ibid.*

20. "Self-regulatory Principles for Online Behavioral Advertising," Federal Trade Commission, February 2009, p. 11.

21. "Self-regulatory Principles for Online Behavioral Advertising," American Association of Advertising Agencies, Association of National Advertisers, Council of Better Business Bureaus, Direct Marketing Association, Interactive Advertising Bureau, July 2, 2009.

22. *Ibid.*, p. 10.

23. "House Energy and Commerce Subcommittee on Communications, Technology and the Internet Holds Hearing on Communications Networks and Consumer Privacy: Recent Developments," CQ Congressional Transcripts, Congressional Hearings, April 23, 2009.

24. Miguel Helft and Jenna Wortham, "Facebook Bows to Pressure Over Privacy," *The New York Times*, May 26, 2010.

25. Julie Angwin and Tom McGinty, "Sites Feed Personal Details to New Tracking Industry," *The Wall Street Journal*, July 30, 2010. See the series "What They Know" at http://online.wsj.com/public/page/what-they-know-digital-privacy.html.

26. "Network Advertising Initiative," press release, March 24, 2010, www.networkadvertising.org/pdfs/NAI_Beales_Release.pdf.

27. Tim Wayne, "Government Uses Social Networking Sites for More Than Investigations," Electronic Frontier Foundation, www.eff.org/deeplinks/2010/08/government-monitors-much-more-social-networks.

28. Drake Lundell, "Congress to Crack Down on Facebook," *The Kiplinger Letter*, Aug. 13, 2010, www.kiplinger.com/businessresource/forecast/archive/congress-to-crack-down-on-facebook.html.

29. "Department of Commerce at the Intersection of Privacy and Innovation," Center for Democracy and Technology, June 25, 2010.

30. Privacy Rights Clearinghouse, posted June 4, 2010. See www.privacyrights.org/8-social-networking-privacy-tips.

BIBLIOGRAPHY

Books

Bahadur, Gary, et al., *Privacy Defended: Protecting Yourself Online*, Que, 2002.
A user-friendly book by network security experts explains why Internet users should care about online privacy and security.

Chander, Anupam, et al., eds., *Securing Privacy in the Internet Age*, Stanford University Press, 2008.
Essays by experts in the field focus primarily on legal standards and litigation of Internet-related privacy issues.

Holtzman, David H., *Privacy Lost: How Technology is Endangering Your Privacy*, Jossey-Bass, 2006.
A former chief scientist at IBM's Internet Information Technology group covers virtually every aspect of online privacy, from the technologies that enable incursions to legal standards to the impact on personal life.

Solove, Daniel J., and Marc Rotenberg, *Information Privacy Law*, Aspen, 2003.
Coauthor Rotenberg, president of the Electronic Privacy Information Center, surveys the full range of privacy issues, not just online privacy. Includes extensive discussion of key statutes and regulations.

Articles

Burstein, Aaron J., "Amending the ECPA to Enable a Culture of Cybersecurity Research," *Harvard Journal of Law & Technology*, Vol. 22, No. 1, fall 2008.
Burstein argues there is a need to provide an exemption in the Electronic Communications Protection Act (ECPA) to allow researchers to perform cybersecurity studies and programs.

Clifford, Stephanie, "Fresh Views at Agency Overseeing Online Ads," *The New York Times*, Aug. 5, 2009, p. B1.

The article examines the pros and cons of Federal Trade Commission efforts to strengthen its oversight of online advertisers.

Griffith, Eric, "How to Reclaim Your Online Privacy," *PC World*, Feb. 1, 2009.

Griffith offers a wealth of practical tips on how to configure your computer to protect your privacy while you're on the Internet.

Kopytoff, Verne, "Paying Attention to Online Privacy: Google lawyer says the entire concept is changing as technology marches forward," *The San Francisco Chronicle*, Dec. 30, 2007, p. D1.

A lawyer for Google discusses how technology is changing peoples' views on privacy.

Studies and Reports

"FTC Staff Report: Self-Regulatory Principles For Online Behavioral Advertising," Federal Trade Commission, February 2009.

The Federal Trade Commission examines behavioral targeting of online advertising as well as the advertising industry's efforts at self-regulation.

"Privacy Online: Fair Information Practices in the Electronic Marketplace, A Report to Congress," Federal Trade Commission, May 2000.

The FTC called for legislation ensuring consumer online privacy, a call Congress has not yet answered.

"Self-regulatory Principles for Online Behavioral Advertising," American Association of Advertising Agencies, Association of National Advertisers, Council of Better Business Bureaus, Direct Marketing Association, Interactive Advertising Bureau, July 2, 2009.

While this report carries the same title as an FTC staff report that preceded it by six months, it reaches somewhat different conclusions. Specifically, the advertisers call for opt-out protections for consumers' sensitive data, while the FTC staff calls for opt-in to be required for advertisers to access sensitive data.

Dixon, Pam, "The Network Advertising Initiative: Failing at Consumer Protection and at Self-Regulation," World Privacy Forum, fall 2007.

This report looks in detail at online advertisers' efforts at self-regulation and finds them wanting.

Gellman, Robert, "Privacy in the Clouds: Risks to Privacy and Confidentiality from Cloud Computing," World Privacy Forum, Feb. 23, 2009.

Gellman provides a detailed discussion of the legal questions surrounding user data stored by third parties.

Landesberg, Martha K., *et al.*, "Privacy Online: A Report to Congress," Federal Trade Commission, June 1998.

The FTC's first in-depth look at online marketing and its impact on consumer privacy explores whether the advertising industry is capable of self-regulation.

Szoka, Berin, and Adam Thierer, "Online Advertising & User Privacy: Principles to Guide the Debate," Progress & Freedom Foundation, September 2008.

The authors argue in favor of behavioral targeting and recommend regulation only as a last resort.

For More Information

American Civil Liberties Union, 125 Broad St., 18th Floor, New York, NY 10004; www.aclu.org. Provides education and legal support for civil liberties issues.

Association of National Advertisers, 708 Third Ave., 33rd Floor, New York, NY 10017; (202) 296-1883; www.ana.net. Provides information, advocacy and lobbying efforts for the advertising industry.

Center for Democracy and Technology, 1634 Eye St., N.W. #1100, Washington, DC 20006; (202) 637-9800; www.cdt.org. Advocates and informs on privacy, copyright and openness to keep the Internet "open, innovative and free."

Center for Digital Democracy, www.democraticmedia.org. "Works to promote an electronic media system that fosters democratic expression and human rights."

Electronic Frontier Foundation, 454 Shotwell St., San Francisco, CA 94110-1914; (415) 436-9333; www.eff.org. EFF defines itself as "the leading civil liberties group defending your rights in the digital world."

Electronic Privacy Information Center, 1718 Connecticut Ave., N.W., Washington, DC 20009; (202) 483-1140; www.epic.org. Provides information as well as lobbying and advocacy efforts on a wide range of privacy issues.

Network Advertising Initiative, 62 Portland Road, Suite 44, Kennebunk, ME 04043; (207) 467-3500; www.networkadvertising.org. An industry organization formed to develop standards for online advertising.

Privacy Rights Clearinghouse, 3100-5th Ave., Suite B, San Diego, CA 92103; (619) 298-3396; www.privacyrights.org. An advocacy group and clearinghouse that assembles a great deal of information from varied sources on privacy issues.

Progress and Freedom Foundation, 1444 I St., N.W., Suite 500, Washington, DC 20005; (202) 289-8928; www.pff.org. Describes itself as "a market-oriented think tank that studies the digital revolution and its implications for public policy."

6

Press Freedom

Peter Katel

Courtesy Christopher Elliott

Travel blogger Christopher Elliott refused to comply with a Department of Homeland Security subpoena prompted by his posting of a confidential security directive that followed the attempted bombing of a U.S. jetliner on Christmas day. Journalism experts worry about the beleaguered news industry's ability to protect press freedom amid questions about who qualifies as a legitimate journalist.

From *CQ Researcher*,
February 5, 2010.

Journalist Christopher Elliott and his wife had just started giving their children their baths one evening a few days after Christmas when there was an unexpected knock at the door of their home in Washington. The early-evening visit was from a Department of Homeland Security (DHS) investigator bearing a subpoena for Elliott, who runs an independent, consumer-oriented Web site about travel.

DHS was demanding that Elliott turn over "all documents, e-mails, and/or faxsimile [sic] transmissions" involving his receipt and posting of a restricted Transportation Security Administration (TSA) security order.[1]

Elliott had posted the directive on his blog on Dec. 27, two days before the agent arrived. The document showed that, in response to the attempted Christmas Day bombing of a Northwest Airlines flight, TSA was stepping up security on United States-bound flights from abroad. News articles citing passengers and TSA personnel had already reported additional pre-boarding searches and a requirement that passengers remain in their seats for the last hour of a flight.[2]

Now, thanks to Elliott and another Web-based writer, the new measures weren't being paraphrased or interpreted but spelled out directly by TSA. "I broke no laws," Elliott says, noting that the directive carried no secrecy classification, though he acknowledges that airline employees and other direct recipients are prohibited from disclosing the document. "DHS didn't even tell me to take it off my Web site; they just wanted my source."

Elliott wasn't the only subpoena target. That same December evening, DHS agents called at the home of another travel blogger,

Traffic Increases on News Web Sites

The number of visitors to the nation's top 10 news Web sites increased an average of 23 percent from 2007 to 2008. Yahoo! News had the highest number of visitors; CBS News saw its viewership increase more than 50 percent.

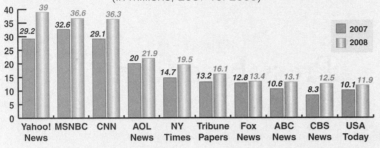

Average Monthly Unique Visitors to Top Web Sites
(in millions, 2007 vs. 2008)

Source: Project for Excellence in Journalism analysis of comScore, Inc., data.

Steven Frischling, who had posted the TSA directive on his "Flying With Fish" blog. Frischling, a commercial photographer, complied the next day, turning over his computer. With that, TSA dropped its subpoena for Elliott and notified Frischling that no more information was sought from him.[3]

Law-enforcement demands that journalists name confidential sources, or supply other information gathered in reporting, raise questions about how much freedom the Constitution's free-press guarantee requires. The Supreme Court ruled in 1972 that journalists don't enjoy a special privilege against testifying, though judges have ruled for reporters in many such cases — at least until the past decade. "Shield" laws in 37 states and Washington, D.C., give journalists some protection against supplying evidence, and a federal shield bill passed the House last year and is pending in the Senate. (See "Current Situation," p. 158.)[4]

The congressional legislation largely was prompted by a 2007 case in which reporter Judith Miller of *The New York Times* spent 85 days in jail for refusing to disclose intelligence information. She finally complied after saying her confidential source released her from her pledge to protect his identity.[5]

If Miller's eventual testimony gave other prosecutors hopes of success in forcing information from journalists,

the rise of independent blogging has also expanded the field of potential subpoena targets, many of whom may not have the legal backing that news-organization employees typically enjoy.

The ever-expanding universe of the Web is home to old-line media organizations and news-oriented start-ups of both the nonpartisan and highly partisan kind, as well as individuals — specialists and amateurs alike — who offer news, commentary, documents and more.

On the one hand, the migration of media to the Internet is threatening to extinguish news on paper and on television — hitting old-line media companies in the pocketbook and weakening their ability to wage free-press fights. Yet these same companies have jumped to the Web, benefiting news consumers, who can also dive into the limitless outpouring of news from all over the world collected and disseminated by means that didn't even exist in recent memory — cellphone cameras, Twitter and social-networking sites. (*See sidebar, p. 154.*)

Indeed, "citizen journalists" almost instantly reached the Web from earthquake-ravaged Haiti. And President Obama made it known that he followed on-the-ground Twitter reports on the upsurge of protests that followed Iran's presidential election last year that were disseminated on the *Atlantic* magazine's Web site by blogger Andrew Sullivan, one of the first paper-based journalists to turn to full-time blogging.[6]

Travel blogger Elliott also boasts old-school journalism credentials: reader advocate for *National Geographic Traveler* and columnist for *The Washington Post* and MSNBC. In keeping with his journalism training, Elliott refused to turn over anything and immediately called his own lawyer and The Reporters Committee for the Freedom of the Press. He says the *Post* and his other outlets said they'd stand behind him.

A smaller news organization might have abandoned him. "There might be a circumstance in which we would refuse to comply with a court order, but we are a small company and could not afford a protracted legal action," an anonymous editor wrote to a media-law specialist tracking the volume of subpoenas at newsrooms nationwide.[7]

The study, based on a detailed survey, counted 3,062 subpoenas — 332 of them in federal cases — issued to the 761 respondents in 2006 alone, reported study author RonNell Andersen Jones, a law professor at Brigham Young University Law School in Provo, Utah. In 2001, the Reporters Committee made a similar survey and counted 823 subpoenas, 9 percent of them in federal proceedings. The data aren't strictly comparable, but Jones concluded they show a marked increase in subpoenas demanding confidential information.[8]

Added to the financial burdens weighing down newspapers and other traditional media, the legal pressure is giving rise to a mood approaching despair. "I've been going to media law conferences for a long time," says Jones, a onetime newspaper reporter and law clerk for former Supreme Court Justice Sandra Day O'Connor. "In the last year or so there's been a lot of dialogue about how we sustain some of the most important things we do in the face of widespread bankruptcy and collapse."

Since the early 2000s, traditional news media have been engulfed in a business crisis whose end seems nowhere in sight. As newspapers and TV news lose readers and viewers, advertisers (now also suffering from the recession) are leaving as well. For example, newspaper ad revenue plummeted by 26 percent — from $46.7 billion to $34.7 billion — from 2005 to 2008 alone and continued falling last year. (*See graph, p. 146.*)[9]

Long-established regional newspapers that closed in the last two years include the *Seattle Post-Intelligencer*, which now exists in much reduced form online; the *Albuquerque Tribune*; and the *Rocky Mountain News* of Denver. And the year ended with rounds of substantial news cuts at major news organizations including The Associated Press and *New York Times*. Early this year, CBS News began layoffs of about 90 people, including star producers.[10]

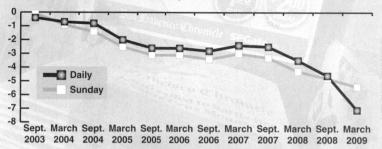

Decline in Print Circulation Continues

Daily and Sunday newspaper circulation declined by 7.1 percent and 5.4 percent, respectively, between September 2008 and March 2009, reflecting accelerating circulation declines since 2003.

Decline in Daily and Sunday Newspaper Circulation by Six-month Period, 2003-2009

■ Daily
□ Sunday

| | Sept. 2003 | March 2004 | Sept. 2004 | March 2005 | Sept. 2005 | March 2006 | Sept. 2006 | March 2007 | Sept. 2007 | March 2008 | Sept. 2008 | March 2009 |

Source: "State of the News Media," Pew Project for Excellence in Journalism, 2009

Big media companies, meanwhile, are enjoying vastly expanded Web audiences, but they're haunted by an inescapable reality. "The advertising model has collapsed," says Edward Wasserman, a journalism professor at Washington and Lee University in Lexington, Va., and former executive business editor of *The Miami Herald.* Newspaper and TV executives widely agree that news companies will never earn from Web advertising what they used to make in print and broadcast ad revenue.

Among journalists whose jobs have disappeared, some have joined the Web-based start-ups, usually nonprofit and donor-funded, that have cropped up around the country, such as *ProPublica* and the *Texas Tribune.* Others have launched their own online enterprises. As for young people starting out, the old model of graduating from journalism school and finding a job at a news organization may be dying.

Alan Mutter, an adjunct journalism professor at the University of California, Berkeley, often advises job-searching recent graduates. "I tell them, 'You can be a journalist by saying you're a journalist and starting to commit journalism.' It's utterly gratifying when you find people who do. One started a blog penetrating the intricacies of the university's financing."

In any case, add new J-school graduates with blogs to the ranks of those who might benefit from a federal shield law, depending on how it defines "journalist." Some lawmakers are complaining that the legislation's present definition is too broad. "For those of us who have been around for a while and have watched the change in journalism, there's always been a standard for legitimacy — that's the future of journalism," Sen. Dianne Feinstein, D-Calif., said at a December session of the Senate Judiciary Committee. "Here there is no standard for legitimacy."[11] (*See "At Issue," p. 159.*)

Few would disagree that old journalistic norms are under siege. But travel journalist Elliott has no doubt about the standards that led him to seek out and post the TSA security order. "It was a directive that TSA should have told everybody about — what to expect on an inbound flight," he says. "But they didn't. The document had been widely disseminated; every airline had it, every airport had it. It was information that the public needed to know."

Here are some of the key questions about press freedom being asked:

Can media companies afford free-press battles?

Fear and uncertainty grip traditional media companies large and small. News of layoffs, bankruptcies and debates over how to rebuild a new business model have been constant in recent years. In this climate, the once-powerful news industry is now seen by many as too burdened by its own problems to actively defend press freedom. To be sure, notes Lucy Dalglish, executive director of The Reporters Committee for Freedom of the Press, major media companies still leap to the legal barricades on important cases, such as subpoenas involving journalism students at Northwestern University's Medill School investigating a possible miscarriage of justice. (*See "Current Situation," p. 158.*)

But the layoffs have been extensive. From November 2009 to early January alone, major developments included: Layoffs of 90 employees by The Associated Press; a cutback of 100 news staffers at *The New York*

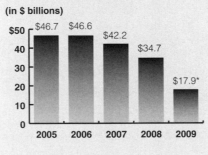

Newspaper Ad Revenue in Free Fall

Total newspaper advertising revenue dropped 26 percent from 2005 to 2008, and early figures indicate an even more dramatic decline for 2009.

Newspaper Advertising Revenue, 2005-2009

(in $ billions)

Year	Revenue
2005	$46.7
2006	$46.6
2007	$42.2
2008	$34.7
2009	$17.9*

* Through Sept. 30, 2009

Source: Newspaper Association of America

Times; a bankruptcy reorganization by MediaNews Group, a chain with 54 daily newspapers in 11 states, plus TV and radio stations; planned layoffs of at least 400 news division employees from several magazines at Time Inc., whose publications include *Sports Illustrated* and *Fortune.* Overall, an estimated 15,000 newspaper employees (not all of them journalists) lost jobs last year.[12]

Somewhat more encouraging, major Web news sites launched or announced during the same period included the not-for-profit *Texas Tribune*, which said it raised nearly $4 million in start-up money; *Peer News*, founded by eBay founder and chairman Pierre Omidyar to cover news in Hawaii; and the *Connecticut Mirror*, a foundation-funded site focusing on government and policy.[13]

But as old media fight to stay afloat and new ventures try to find their way, freedom-of-the-press efforts seem to be diminishing.

"To the extent that press and government are at odds with each other, it seems there is an endless supply of government lawyers now, and fewer media lawyers, and fewer causes that the media can afford to champion," says Michael A. Giudicessi, a lawyer for the *Des Moines Register*, one of the Midwest's leading papers. "If there's a meeting [of public officials] being closed, if a document is being withheld, the government understands it can turn to staff lawyers and say, 'Find us an excuse to keep it confidential,' " says Giudicessi. "But news executives have to ask themselves, 'Do I keep a reporter on staff for another year, or fight an access case?' " In fact, Giudicessi was formerly a staff lawyer for the paper.

However, says conservative activist and publisher Andrew Breitbart, of *Breitbart.com*, the news media — which he views as a left-liberal political group — isn't coming to the aid of right-leaning entrepreneurs like him.

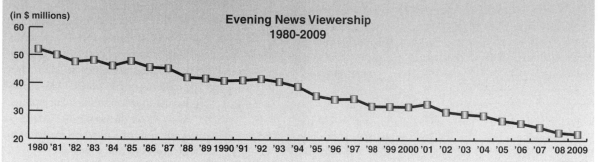

TV News Audiences Are Plummeting

The number of viewers of TV evening news is less than half as large as it was 30 years ago, despite population increases of nearly 3 million per year.

Evening News Viewership 1980-2009

Source: "The State of the News Media," Project for Excellence in Journalism analysis of Nielsen Media Research data, 2009.

Breitbart was sued after posting a video shot by conservative political activists James O'Keefe and a female associate, posing as a pimp and a prostitute in a sting aimed at the liberal Association of Community Organizations for Reform Now (ACORN). The two were pretending to solicit advice on how to set up a prostitution business. "The lawsuit against me, as a publisher, was a stab in the heart of press freedom," Breitbart says. "But there has yet to be a MSM [mainstream media] entity to come to our defense, to say that ACORN is wrong to sue the journalists or me."

Breitbart argues that traditional news organizations don't consider him to be a journalist because, unlike them, he's open about his political agenda. "Maybe the media can pretend that nobody noticed" the ACORN lawsuit, he says.

Dalglish says Breitbart might well have been able to avail himself of the group's pro-bono assistance. "He hasn't called. If he's out there trying to independently present information," says Dalglish, a former journalist and media lawyer, "and has no financial interaction with political candidates of any type, then he probably is committing journalism."

Former business editor Wasserman of Washington and Lee University says the media have been complaining of reduced resources for decades. "I've been in the media since the early '70s, and they've always complained about inadequate resources even when they were absolutely minting money and had unchallenged monopolies in broadcasting," he says.

In the present climate, though, Wasserman agrees that a weakened press means a more timid journalism. "There's less money for reporting, certainly less for litigation and less to go after those more adventurous and expensive stories that require litigation to get documents freed up," he says.

But the University of California's Mutter, a former top editor at the *Chicago Sun-Times* and the *San Francisco Chronicle* and ex-CEO of three Silicon Valley firms, argues that the digital technology that helped explode the news media's old business model also creates entirely new avenues for making information public. "One reason I believe there is going to be a lot of press freedom is that it's impossible to suppress people, even in totalitarian countries," he says.

Wide availability of cell-phone videos showing Iranian security forces repressing demonstrators is one example, Mutter says. "Even in China, people can route around government censorship," he says.

Are independent bloggers entitled to free-press protections?

In journalism's ancient past — say, 20 years ago — a working journalist by definition was affiliated with a newspaper or magazine or a radio or TV station, or perhaps a specialized newsletter. Virtually everyone in the

Journalists Say Protection of Sources Declined

Nearly 70 percent of the journalists surveyed felt they had less support from the courts in protecting their sources in 2006 than in 2001. Less than 3 percent said more protection was provided.

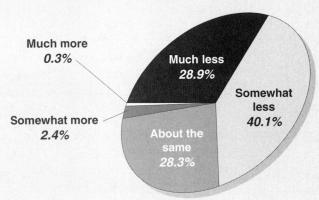

Perceived Protection of Media Sources by Courts, 2006
(compared to 2001)

Much more 0.3%
Somewhat more 2.4%
Much less 28.9%
About the same 28.3%
Somewhat less 40.1%

Source: RonNell Andersen Jones, "Media Subpoenas: Impact, Perception, and Legal Protection in the Changing World of American Journalism," *Washington Law Review*, September 2009

business had formally or informally learned the basics — get all sides of a controversy, attribute quotes to the people who made them, verify information and don't allow yourself to be used as a platform for libel.

At least one veteran of old-school training argues that the instant quality of Web publishing makes some long-established journalism standards obsolete — even the one about not spreading rumors. In late January, journalist and Web entrepreneur Michael Wolff bragged on his *Newser* site that he had posted on Twitter.com — a new, much-discussed short-form message site for social networks — the unverified rumor that media mogul Rupert Murdoch might be preparing to sell two of his London newspapers. "A very short while ago, this would have been unpublishable," he said. But in the instant-news world, "We'll know together" if the rumor is true.[14]

The late David Shaw, the *Los Angeles Times'* influential media critic, deplored such conduct. "Many bloggers — not all, perhaps not even most — don't seem to worry much about being accurate," Shaw wrote. "They just want to get their opinions — and their 'scoops' — out there as fast as they pop into their brains. . . . The knowledge that

you can correct errors quickly, combined with the absence of editors or filters, encourages laziness, carelessness and inaccuracy."[15]

Commenting on a lawsuit filed against two Web publications by Apple Computers, Shaw argued that bloggers weren't entitled to constitutional free-press privileges, such as protection by a "shield" law against having to reveal sources. Such protections — on the books in 37 states — were designed for "the media as an institution," Shaw wrote.

Anticipating Shaw's arguments by a few months, Garrett Graff, now editor of *Washingtonian* magazine, countered some of them. Most bloggers don't even consider themselves journalists, Graff wrote, but added, "Over the coming months and years there will be an ever-increasing number of bloggers who are doing reporting and news gathering, and there will be many times when a blogger breaks news simply because there are 8 million of them writing — far more than there are journalists in the U.S."[16]

And Graff wrote, "As a society we have to err on the side of giving out journalism's protections of free speech and a free press more widely than not. . . . As soon as someone, whether it's a judge or the White House or a panel of 'real' journalists, becomes the arbiter of 'journalism' we're all in trouble."[17] In 2005, at age 23, Graff became the first blogger admitted to a White House press briefing.[18]

The Apple case centered on the firm's demand for the sources used by two Web publications that disclosed details about a new Apple product. A trial judge ruled in Apple's favor on the grounds that the sites had disclosed trade secrets. But an appeals court rejected Apple's claim that the sites weren't practicing bona fide journalism and said the state shield law — enacted in 1974, before the Web existed — protected them against naming sources.[19]

In effect, the appeals court was applying what media-law specialists call a "function test." By that standard, anyone who does what journalists do — find information, analyze and perhaps comment on it and disseminate their work — is performing the work of the free press and should be treated accordingly when authorities demand sources' identities. But Dalglish of the Reporters Committee says that not everyone with a Web site can meet that standard.

She asks, "Do you as a citizen, or as a journalist, want anybody at all who's been subpoenaed to testify to a grand jury to go home and write something on their home computer and then say they can't be subpoenaed?"

People untrained in journalism who make an effort to practice the craft on their sites can easily run afoul of problems that have also bedeviled experienced reporters, argues Wasserman of Washington and Lee University. Although he supports a functional definition of journalism, he adds, "You'd like to think that people doing this are exercising a measure of care."

For instance, Wasserman notes that journalists often have to negotiate situations in which their sources attempt to manipulate them. He posits a plausible scenario for a business writer: "A short-seller approaches you with nasty information about a CEO's divorce, and it's just wonderful stuff and it's solid, and you know they want to discredit the guy and make lots of money" by selling the company's stock short when it declines. The reporter's dilemma: write the piece, knowing he is being used as part of a business strategy, or walk away from a hot story.

Ethical pitfalls aside, thousands of people with no background on how to deal with sources' agendas, and no editors to guide them, arguably are practicing some form of journalism on the Web. As "citizen journalism" grows, its practitioners include people posting information about zoning issues to a neighborhood site, or rescue workers providing information on the Web about disaster victims after hurricanes and earthquakes.

With the citizen journalist trend unlikely to slow down, argues Mary-Rose Papandrea, a professor at Boston College Law School, the idea of limiting free-press protection only to journalists — however defined — is obsolete. "Americans increasingly obtain their information and insights into important issues through the Internet and through bloggers in particular," she writes.[20]

With virtually everyone empowered to transmit news, information and opinion, Papandrea writes,

everyone who does so should have a limited right to refuse to testify about their sources. Eyewitness testimony about a crime, or evidence of an imminent national security threat, wouldn't be shielded, she says. "Given that the institutional press no longer has a monopoly over the dissemination of information to the public, all those who disseminate information to the public must be presumptively entitled to invoke the privilege's protections."[21]

Is the era of mass-market objective journalism coming to an end?

In late January, not long after his undercover sting at ACORN offices, videographer O'Keefe was arrested at the New Orleans office of Democratic Sen. Mary Landrieu. O'Keefe and two of his three companions, both dressed as phone repairmen, were charged with entering a federal building for the purpose of "interfering" with the senatorial office's phone system.[22]

O'Keefe later wrote that "as an investigative journalist" he'd been trying to check on whether the senator's office phones were working. Constituents critical of her support for the administration's health care bill had reported trouble getting their calls through, he said. "On reflection, I could have used a different approach," he acknowledged.[23]

The conservative activist may be an extreme case. But provocateurs, on both the left and the right, have long existed on the margins of traditional, nonpartisan journalism.

Today, the opening up of the media universe has also provided a platform for press critics of all stripes to decry errors or bias in news organizations that proclaim adherence to objective journalism.

Among the major examples of the fury that media faults can whip up, veteran anchorman Dan Rather's premature departure from CBS News in 2004 followed discoveries made by conservative Web sites.[24]

That same year, *The New York Times* came under scathing criticism from the left — criticism to which the paper eventually bowed. In a front-page 1,200-word explanation — a tacit apology — the paper conceded fundamental weaknesses in a series of pre-Iraq War articles that made a strong case for the existence of weapons of mass destruction in Iraq. The weapons — which turned out not to exist — became the official justification

Senate Judiciary Committee members Charles Schumer, D-N.Y., left, and Dick Durbin, D-Ill., disagree over proposed legislation to create a journalists' "shield" law. Durbin says the bill's definition of a journalist is so broad as to be meaningless, but Schumer and others who support the legislation contend the courts would weed out those undeserving of being shielded.

for the U.S.-led invasion. "Accounts of Iraqi defectors were not always weighed against their strong desire to have Saddam Hussein ousted," *The Times* said of principal sources.[25] Many of those articles had been written by Judith Miller.

Yet for all the outrage directed at mainstream media by critics on the right and the left, the most-visited news sites on the Web provide reporting of the standard, objective kind. Yahoo! News, MSNBC, CNN and AOL ranked at the top in 2008, the Pew Research Center's Project for Excellence in Journalism found. They were followed by *The New York Times*, which got 19.5 million unique visitors a month in 2008 (and 15.4 million in December 2009).[26]

The non-newspaper sites ranked ahead of *The Times* —Yahoo! News, MSNBC, CNN, and AOL News — all provided news in the nonpartisan, mainstream mode. "The majority of news that is produced with the largest audience, in traditional platforms and online, is still produced by institutions that adhere to traditional values of reportorial verification and independence," says Tom Rosenstiel, director of the Pew journalism center.

Rosenstiel acknowledges that the appeal of partisan journalism is growing. "There is no doubt that there is more of that content than there was," he says. "But the role of the growing partisan media appears at the moment to get a news institution that is somewhat

friendly — like a cable news outlet — to grab a story and have it leap into the mainstream."

Breitbart, the right-of-center Web publisher, used that launch process to publicize O'Keefe's covert ACORN videos. Breitbart immediately alerted star Fox News commentator Glenn Beck, who ran excerpts. Fox News then covered the story heavily, with the mainstream media following days later.[27]

"My sites are trying to go from simply acting as media critic and saying, 'Let's report stories, let's get rid of the middleman,'" Breitbart says. "You can be 'Deep Throat' and you can be Woodward and Bernstein." (Breitbart, however, says he didn't know in advance about the Landrieu office attempt.)

Breitbart's main site, a news aggregation service, includes many links to dispatches by The Associated Press and other wire services that follow strict rules of nonpartisan coverage. "For those who aspire to it, [objectivity] is an admirable goal," he says. "But those adherents are few and far between. The left media, such as *The New York Times*, used objective journalism as a front for pushing the media to the left."

What Breitbart sees as a purely ideological contest may owe more to business imperatives that favor sites which draw identifiable demographic groups.

"Highly targeted advertisers want editorial content that's already tagged for the buyers they want to get," says Wasserman of Washington and Lee University, contrasting the Web model to old-style newspaper advertising aimed at the public in general. "A lot of people are tearing their hair out over that issue."

Nevertheless, Wasserman argues that a strong market still remains for reporting that strives for political neutrality. "You still have tremendous strength in these national franchises — *The Times*, the *Wall Street Journal*, *USA Today*," he says. "These are publications people go to because they trust them to get the facts basically right and to have pretty good judgment about what's important and what's not."

Still, even resolutely nonpartisan news sites can be driven into trends they would once have resisted by the Web's business imperatives: to draw as many "unique users" as possible to a site. "We are seeing an enormous tilt in what is defined as news — an enormous tilt towards entertainment," says editor-turned-tech entrepreneur Mutter, citing major news organizations' attention to the Jay Leno-Conan O'Brien uproar at NBC, and earlier wall-to-wall coverage of pop star Michael Jackson's death.

Moreover, Mutter says, the Web-enabled habits of readers are hitting hard at the old model of neutral coverage that people of all persuasions can read. "We are seeing more and more people subscribing only to things that comport with their interests. If you're anti-Israel, you only want to read anti-Israel blogs. That's quite terrifying. In a day when there was a comparatively limited number of media outlets, most were sort of balanced and ecumenical, especially in the modern era."

BACKGROUND

Shifting Boundaries

Attempts to restrict press freedom began soon after the 1791 ratification of the Bill of Rights.[28]

In 1798, Congress passed the Sedition Act, which defined as criminal "any false, scandalous, and malicious" writing about the president (but not the vice president), Congress or the U.S. government.

Officially, justification for the law was an imminent war with France (which never went beyond undeclared hostilities). In reality, the Federalist-controlled Congress aimed to crack down on its Democratic-Republican opponents, including Thomas Jefferson, the vice president.

Of the 10 people arrested under the Sedition Act, at least three were journalists. The law expired in 1801, ending any chance of a Supreme Court decision on its constitutionality.

In a larger sense, passage of the controversial act reflected a post-independence view of the press. Before the American Revolution, pamphlets and newspapers that attacked colonial authorities earned applause from the future Founding Fathers. That attitude changed once they were in power.

Jefferson, before he became president, wrote, "Were it left to me to decide whether we should have a government without newspapers, or newspapers without a government, I should not hesitate to prefer the latter." His perspective changed in the White House. "The man who reads nothing at all," he wrote after taking office, "is better educated than the man who reads nothing but newspapers."[29]

The impulse to restrict newspapers when they criticized the government arose again during the Civil War. As the conflict raged, Union generals, but not President Abraham Lincoln, halted publication of about 300 newspapers on grounds that they'd published anti-war or anti-administration writings.

But the next major war saw another president, Woodrow Wilson, call for systematic repression of the speech and writings of radicals and pacifists who opposed U.S. entrance into World War I. Congress obliged with the Espionage Act of 1917, which made it a crime to "promote the success of" enemy forces or to "willfully obstruct the recruiting or enlistment service."[30]

A year later, Congress went even further with the Sedition Act of 1918, which made it a crime to criticize the U.S. government, Constitution or military.

After the war, courts began to hear challenges to convictions under the sedition law and similar state statutes, as well as other laws designed to curb dissident writings. Two landmark U.S. Supreme Court decisions proved critical in setting new press-freedom standards.

In 1925, *Gitlow v. New York* established that the First Amendment applied in states as well as to the federal government. For that reason, press-freedom scholars call the decision an advance. But it did uphold the conviction under state law of a Communist Party founder who wrote a pamphlet advocating revolution. "A State may punish utterances endangering the foundations of organized government and threatening its overthrow by unlawful means," the court said.[31]

Six years later, the high court took a bigger step toward protecting freedom to publish. In a case arising from political accusations — freighted with anti-Semitism — leveled against a Minneapolis police chief, the court rejected a state prohibition on "malicious, scandalous or defamatory" publications.[32]

Chief Justice Charles Evans Hughes, author of the 5-4 majority opinion in *Near v. Minnesota*, swept aside the state's argument that it banned only publications that couldn't prove their allegations. Decisions on whether allegations or comments were illegally defamatory should be made after publication, the court said.

Changing Profession

In the Republic's early days, newspapers and magazines were used as political weapons. But the rise of technology

1950s-1980 *Television grows in influence as U.S. confronts major challenges.*

1954 TV newsman Edward R. Murrow challenges red-baiting Sen. Joseph R. McCarthy, R-Wis., contributing to McCarthy's downfall.

1963 Press coverage of violence against civil rights protesters arouses widespread indignation, support for legislation. . . . President John F. Kennedy demands that *The New York Times* withdraw a Vietnam correspondent whose reporting challenges Pentagon's inflated success stories.

1968 News reports of North Vietnam's failed but powerful Tet Offensive help turn public opinion against war.

1971 *New York Times* begins publishing "Pentagon Papers." . . . Supreme Court refuses to block articles, ruling government hadn't proved national security threat.

1972 Supreme Court rules that reporters are required to obey subpoenas for information, including confidential sources. . . . Justice Lewis F. Powell writes separately that courts should balance need for testimony against free-press rights.

1973 *Washington Post* and other papers uncover Watergate scandal, building new respect for news media.

1980 Supreme Court rules that the press and public must have access to criminal trials except under limited circumstances.

1981-1990s *News media fall in opinion polls as talk radio hosts step up criticism, and Internet sites begin to offer news alternatives.*

1981 In a harbinger of scandals at other papers, *Washington Post* loses Pulitzer Prize awarded for a bogus story about an 8-year-old heroin addict.

1987 Federal Communications Commission repeals "Fairness Doctrine," allowing the emergence of talk radio, which becomes a largely conservative alternative to the mainstream media.

1996 Fox News begins building audience by nurturing conservative hosts.

1998 Pioneer Internet news entrepreneur Matt Drudge shows new Web's power by breaking news of President Bill Clinton-Monica Lewinsky scandal.

2000s *Old media revenues decline dramatically as news consumption on the Web skyrockets, and court decisions turn against journalists.*

2002 Senate Republican Leader Trent Lott of Mississippi loses his leadership post after a liberal news Web site reports his praise for the segregationist policies once championed by Sen. Strom Thurmond, R-S.C.

2003 Influential federal Judge Richard Posner cites 1972 Supreme Court decision in ruling that reporters enjoy no shield against subpoenas.

2004 Conservative bloggers uncover flaws in a report by longtime CBS News anchor Dan Rather about President George W. Bush's youthful military service; Rather is later forced out.

2005 Garrett Graff becomes first blogger accredited to White House news briefing.

2006 Newsroom executives report that subpoenas for reporters have risen substantially.

2007 *New York Times* reporter Judith Miller testifies in federal court after spending 85 days in jail for refusing to name source. . . . Videographer Joshua Wolf is freed after a record 226 days in jail for refusing to hand over video of San Francisco anti-war protest.

2008 Newspaper ad revenue drops 26 percent from 2005.

2009 Newspaper industry cuts 50,000 jobs since mid-2008. . . . House passes federal shield bill for journalists facing subpoenas; Senate Judiciary Committee approves another version of bill but continues debating who should be covered. . . . Homeland Security Department issues subpoenas for two travel bloggers; subpoenas withdrawn after blogger complies.

2010 Conservative media activist James O'Keefe is arrested with three others at Democratic Sen. Mary Landrieu's New Orleans office as they attempt an undercover video operation.

helped the development of fact-based journalism. In 1846, newspapers began using the newly invented telegraph to receive news and helped organize a cooperative news service, The Associated Press. Telegraph transmission was costly, and member newspapers had differing political orientations, so AP reporters sent stripped-down, factual dispatches.[33]

In the early 20th century, magazine journalists took fact-based reporting in a new direction: investigative journalism. *McClure's* magazine led the charge, running exposés on topics such as the anti-competitive business tactics of John D. Rockefeller's Standard Oil Co., corruption in city and state governments and child labor. President Theodore Roosevelt derisively called the crusading reporters "muckrakers," which they took as a badge of honor.

During this period, some newspaper industry leaders sought to raise reporting standards. Journalism should attain the "rank of a learned profession," newspaper magnate Joseph Pulitzer said in endowing the Columbia University School of Journalism, which began operating in 1912.[34]

In the early 1920s, the newly formed American Society of Newspaper Editors (ASNE) continued the trend toward professionalism, adopting a code that demanded impartiality: "News reports should be free from opinion or bias of any kind."[35]

As efforts to separate objective newspaper reporting from opinion-mongering and sensationalism continued, a new source of information emerged. In the late 1920s, radio networks began delivering news along with the entertainment they'd been featuring since earlier in the decade.

The professional rivalry may have mattered less to newspaper publishers than the appearance of their first major competitor for advertising dollars. By 1939 radio had 27 percent of advertisers' dollars — up from only 4 percent in 1927. Newspapers accounted for 38 percent — down from 54 percent. Magazines — 35 percent in 1939, down from 42 percent in 1929.

Nevertheless, advertising was so massive, especially during the post-World War II economic expansion, that the market proved big enough for most players. After a sharp drop-off during the war, the number of mass-market daily newspapers remained basically stable from 1945 to 1976, barely increasing from 1,744 to 1,756.

Journalistically, "objectivity" had established itself firmly by the 1950s. During the war, however, journalists and the government worked as comrades-in-arms, with censorship essentially voluntary. And the media ran dispatches from the government's Office of War Information without challenging their accuracy.

That history may have fostered an atmosphere of acceptance in reporting public officials' statements, especially on the most politically explosive issue of the day, communism. Notably, many news organizations covered Sen. Joseph R. McCarthy's campaign to unmask alleged Communists in government by merely reporting his allegations, even as he announced wildly varying numbers of alleged infiltrators.[36]

Some journalists worried at the time that they were backing down. "We are all very much more careful about what we write, what we say, what we join, than we used to be because we all start from the premise that whatever we do may be subject to damaging criticism from the extreme right," *New York Times* editorial writer John B. Oakes wrote to a colleague in 1953.[37]

Adversarial Journalism

While newspapers generally held back, the star of the newest medium — television — took on McCarthy. In 1954, as host of the news program "See It Now," Edward R. Murrow declared that McCarthy was promoting a climate of suspicion that gave "considerable comfort to our enemies."[38]

Murrow said privately that he was only following the lead of the handful of forthright print reporters. But he contributed to McCarthy's political decline, demonstrating TV's mass-communication power.

In 1950, only 13 percent of households had televisions. By 1960, televisions sat in 87 percent of American households.[39]

But for all the power of TV broadcasts — such as the dramatic, round-the-clock live coverage following the assassination of President John F. Kennedy — most TV news reports gave only the basics. Newspapers remained essential reading for detail and background.

In the early 1960s, sustained coverage of the violence directed at civil rights activists played a crucial part in building support for anti-discrimination and voting rights legislation. Not surprisingly, segregationists depicted the press (including

'Citizen Journalists' Spread News About Quake

In Iran, savvy protesters use Bluetooth, Twitter.

Citizen journalists using social-media technology sprang into action after the earthquake in Haiti and amidst savage political repression in Iran.

Hotel Oloffson manager Richard Morse sent what almost certainly was the first "citizen journalist" report from Port-au-Prince after the earthquake: "were ok at the oloffson. internet is on !! no phones ! hope all are okay. alot of big building in PAP are down," Morse wrote on his Twitter.com account.[1]

He sent it at 5:23 p.m. on Jan. 12, noted Shashi Bellamkonda, a social-media expert for Network Solutions. The U.S. Geological Survey registered the earthquake began at 4:53 p.m.[2] The Associated Press correspondent in Port-au-Prince sent his first urgent "NewsAlert" only minutes before Morse, at 5:11 p.m.: "A strong earthquake has hit the impoverished country of Haiti where a hospital has collapsed."[3]

Cell-phone calls were going through only intermittently, but tweets — which use less bandwidth on wireless networks — turned into one of the major sources of information in the immediate aftermath of the catastrophe.

"People are praying in groups . . . others are looking for relatives . . . no phone service . . . no electricity," Morse wrote. "I'm told that parts of the Palace have collapsed . . . the UNIBANK here on Rue Capois has collapsed . . . people are bringing people by on stretchers . . . two helicopters have flown over head an hour ago but nothing since then. . . ."

The evocative details had journalists pressing for more: "Mainstream reporters were relying on social media for details," the *Columbia Journalism Review* reported on Jan. 13. The magazine noted that *The New York Times'*

news blog put out a call to people with digital connections to or from the island nation: "Any readers who are in Haiti or in touch with people there are encouraged to . . . share first-hand accounts with us."[4]

Twittering, Facebook messaging and texting reinforced traditional media rather than replacing it. "I needed the media; I was glued to CNN," says Valda Valbrun, principal of Walkersville Middle School in Frederick, Md., whose 82-year-old Haitian-born father had moved back to Haiti after retiring. "The coverage they did was spectacular. Then I did go to Twitter, because I saw that people were able to do that."

But as days passed with no word from her father, Valbrun started using Facebook to communicate with friends who had their own connections to Haiti. "And I used CNN to post my father's picture," she said, praising the network's Web page of missing people. As it turned out, he survived the disaster and was able to return to the United States.

In the holy city of Qum last December, Iranian journalist Nazila Fathi of *The New York Times* reported from her home in exile in Toronto, demonstrators at the funeral of anti-government leader Grand Ayatollah Hossain Ali Montazeri deployed a tool that many Americans may not know about. "Long ago, Iranian dissidents discovered that Bluetooth can link cellphones to each other in a crowd," Fathi wrote. "And that made 'Bluetooth' a verb in Iran: a way to turn citizen reportage instantly viral. A protester Bluetooths a video clip to others nearby, and they do the same. Suddenly, if the authorities want to keep the image from escaping the scene, they must confiscate hundreds or thousands of phones and cameras."[5]

---

some crusading Southern papers, such as the *Atlanta Constitution* and the *Delta Times-Democrat* of Greenville, Miss.) as an ally of the movement it was covering.

Overseas, another conflict was developing over news reports from Vietnam. In the early 1960s, Kennedy summoned *New York Times* publisher Arthur Ochs Sulzberger to the White House to demand that he withdraw correspondent David Halberstam, whose reporting challenged official reports of progress.

Sulzberger ignored Kennedy's demand, and subsequent events vindicated the skeptical reporters, whose key sources were junior officers and officials. However, some press

critics still argue that distorted reporting, notably of the 1968 Tet Offensive, turned public opinion against the war.[40]

The seeming disconnect between official optimism and reality in Vietnam drove domestic journalists to scrutinize government ever more rigorously. What some called "adversarial" coverage reached a high point in 1973 with the uncovering of the Watergate scandal, led by *Washington Post* reporters Bob Woodward and Carl Bernstein. After the unprecedented resignation of President Richard M. Nixon, journalists grew in public and judicial esteem as watchdogs over government.

Ever since protests began during the election of President Mahmoud Ahmadinejad, videos and Twitter feeds from Iran have been retransmitted abroad via blogs and social networks. "By following blogs and the cellphone videos seeping out of Iran," Fathi wrote, "in some ways I could report more productively than when I had to fear and outwit the government."[6]

But citizen journalism has its limits, especially in Iran. The government's security services show plenty of technological savvy as well. Exiles' social networks are heavily penetrated by government agents, *The Wall Street Journal* reports, leaving democracy activists abroad open to e-mailed threats.

Some exiles visiting the homeland have encountered unpleasant surprises. "One 28-year-old physician who lives in Dubai said that in July he was asked to log on to his Facebook account by a security guard upon arrival in Tehran's airport," *The Journal's* Farnaz Fassihi reported. "At first, he says, he lied and said he didn't have one. So the guard took him to a small room with a laptop and did a Google search for his name. His Facebook account turned up, he says, and his passport was confiscated. After a month and several rounds of interrogations, he says, he was allowed to exit the country."[7]

— *Peter Katel*

Iranians take pictures with cameras and cellphones in Tehran during the August 2007 hanging of two men convicted of killing a prominent judge.

AP Photo/Vahid Salemi

[1] Redistributed on "Corbett," listserv on Haitian affairs maintained by Bob Corbett of St. Louis, Mo.

[2] Shashi Bellamkonda, "Haiti Earthquake: Twitter reports on the ground from Haiti give early picture of calamity," Jan. 17, 2010, www.examiner.com/x-33257-DC-Social-Media-Marketing-Examiner-y2010m1d17-Twitter-reports-on-the-ground-from-Haiti-give-early-picture-of-calamity.

[3] The Associated Press, APNewsAlert,0020,www.breitbart.com/article.php?id=D9D6F7A00&show_article=1.

[4] Quoted in Curtis Brainard, "'New' Media Crucial in Aftermath of Haitian Earthquake," *Columbia Journalism Review*, Jan. 13, 2010,

www.cjr.org/the_ observatory/new_media_crucial_in_aftermath.php.

[5] Nazila Fathi, "The Exile's Eye," *The New York Times*, Jan. 17, 2010, "Week in Review," p. 1.

[6] *Ibid.*

[7] Farnaz Fassihi, "Iranian Crackdown Goes Global," *The Wall Street Journal*, Dec. 3, 2009, http://online.wsj.com/article/SB125978649644673331.html.

"A skyrocketing reputational status . . . led some judges and scholars to suggest that daily newspapers and television news operations should be revered as a fourth branch of government," writes press-law scholar Jones of Brigham Young University Law School.[41]

Judicial respect had been building for some time. The Supreme Court's landmark 1964 *New York Times v. Sullivan* decision shielded the press from libel suits by public officials. Only in cases of "actual malice," in which a news organization published a statement knowing it was untrue, or with "reckless disregard of whether it was false," could justify a libel claim against a news organization.[42]

Subsequently, the high court extended the *Sullivan* standard to public figures who don't hold public office. A modified version of the rule was applied to libel suits by private individuals.

The Supreme Court's next major press-freedom decision protected publication of secret government information. In 1971, *The New York Times* began publishing a series of articles based on the leaked "Pentagon Papers," a massive, secret Defense Department history of the Vietnam War.

Lower courts granted the Nixon administration's demand to halt publication. But the Supreme Court

Journalism Schools Adapting to Changing Times

But teaching the basics still gets top billing.

In the fast-changing world of journalism, reporters and editors have no choice but to change with the times. The same goes for journalism schools.

With the industry increasingly embracing more personal forms of journalism — not to mention shifting from print to the Web — journalism schools are changing their curricula as well. While traditional news reporting still dominates the curricula, J-schools are putting more emphasis on new media and advocacy and opinion journalism.

Journalism should "have a greater ambition than simply reporting facts without analysis or context," Nicholas Lemann, dean of the Columbia University Graduate School of Journalism, wrote in *The Chronicle of Higher Education.*[1] Ironically, amid the shrinking news industry, journalism schools are thriving. The question is, how are they changing to accommodate the professionally dynamic but financially beleaguered field?

Susanne Shaw, a professor of journalism at the University of Kansas and executive director of The Accrediting Council on Education in Journalism and Mass Communications, says the numerous changes in the journalism industry are causing many schools to consider changing their curriculum. However, she thinks the focus is more on multimedia — including Web-based video and audio — than on advocacy journalism. The university currently has just one class dedicated solely to commentary and opinion writing, as does the University of Kentucky, though it covers such writing in other classes too, Shaw says.

"Most schools, I think, are trying to include courses to prepare students to do it all," Shaw says, instead of focusing more on just advocacy journalism.

Tom Warhover, chairman of the print and digital news faculty at the University of Missouri School of Journalism — the nation's first J-school — says that despite the emergence of blogs and other new electronic opportunities for citizen journalists, the journalism industry as a whole is not abandoning old-fashioned, straight-news journalism for advocacy.

Nonetheless, Warhover deems advocacy and opinion writing important and says Missouri also offers an editorial-writing class. Moreover, Missouri is considering a new curriculum track dedicated to opinion and advocacy journalism, he says. Students need those skills in order to have the flexibility to go down any journalistic path they choose,

J-School Grads Heading for Web Jobs

The percentage of journalism graduates writing and editing for the Web increased by 35 percent from 2006 to 2007 and nearly tripled from 2004 to 2007. Overall, about 56 percent of J-school grads were doing Web editing and writing; more than a quarter of the graduates were designing Web pages.

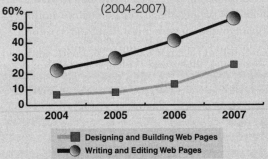

Percentage of Journalism Graduates in Web-Related Journalism Jobs (2004-2007)

Legend:
- Designing and Building Web Pages
- Writing and Editing Web Pages

Source: "Annual Survey of Journalism & Mass Communication Graduates," Project for Excellence in Journalism, Cox Center at the University of Georgia

especially if it leads to the "open range of the Internet," or to the increasingly popular world of nonprofit organizations.

"Teaching advocacy in that realm is a really interesting and burgeoning possibility," he says.

Above all, Shaw says, students must acquire solid journalism skills. "The bottom line is you've got to be a good writer, and know how to ask the right questions," she says.

— *Julia Russell*

---

[1] Nicholas Lemann, "Opinion and Ideas," *The Chronicle of Higher Education,* Nov. 15, 2009, www.lexisnexis.com.proxy-um.researchport.umd .edu/us/lnacademic/results/docview/docview.do?docLinkInd=true &risb=21_T8456847691&format=GNBFI&sort=BOOLEAN&startDo cNo=1&resultsUrlKey=29_T8456847699&cisb=22_T8456847696&tree Max=true&treeWidth=0&csi=171267&docNo=1.

reversed the ruling, saying the government hadn't proved the articles harmed national security, which could justify prior restraint.[43]

Tide Turns

After the Pentagon Papers, however, another case muddied the press-freedom issue. The high court ruled 5-4 in 1972 that journalists weren't shielded from subpoenas seeking their notes and testimony in criminal cases.

But Justice Lewis F. Powell softened the blow. In a separate concurring opinion, Powell agreed that in the case at hand, journalists who had reported information from anonymous sources enjoyed no privilege against testifying. But in future cases, he concluded, courts should strike "a proper balance between freedom of the press and the obligation of all citizens to give relevant testimony with respect to criminal conduct."[44]

Powell didn't specify how to balance those interests. But at a time of high esteem for the press, his opinion gave media lawyers a tool to persuade judges to block subpoenas.[45]

For many years thereafter, the press enjoyed de facto protection, but Judge Richard A. Posner, an influential member of the 7th U.S. Circuit Court of Appeals in Chicago, brought the long spell to an end in 2003. Relying on the Supreme Court's full 1972 decision — not on Powell's concurrence — Posner pointed out that no precedent existed for applying "special criteria" to journalists trying to resist subpoenas.[46]

Thereafter, reporters challenging orders to testify endured major defeats. The most prominent case involved subpoenas for reporters in the 2007 trial of Lewis "Scooter" Libby, a top aide to Vice President Richard B. Cheney who was eventually convicted of perjury in a case that grew out of leaked intelligence secrets. *Times* reporter Miller spent 85 days in jail for defying a subpoena to testify. She gave in, she said, because her source, Libby, released her from a confidentiality agreement.[47]

Other reporters summoned in the Libby trial gave evidence after they or their companies made deals with prosecutors to limit their testimony. Elsewhere, in San Francisco, prosecutors demanded that two *San Francisco Chronicle* reporters name their source for a major story about steroids in baseball. (They refused, but the source finally came forward.) The same year, freelance videographer Joshua Wolf was released after a record 226 days in federal custody for refusing to turn over all his video of violence at a street demonstration in San Francisco.

He was freed after agreeing to post the material on the Web.[48]

The change in the legal climate coincided with declining regard for journalists and the media industry's sinking fortunes. By 2009, public opinion had hit a 24-year low, with 63 percent of Americans finding a pattern of media inaccuracy and 60 percent claiming political bias in news reports.[49]

Some pinpoint the decline's beginning to 1987, when the Federal Communications Commission (FCC) dropped the Fairness Doctrine, established in 1949, which required broadcasters to present controversial issues of public importance and to do so fairly. *[50]

Repeal of the Fairness Doctrine enabled political talk radio to emerge as an important political force. Rush Limbaugh, a pioneer of the format, made biting criticism of the "mainstream media" a major part of his conservative take on issues. When media tycoon Rupert Murdoch's News Corp. founded Fox News Channel in 1996, directed by former Republican political strategist Roger Ailes, its mostly conservative lineup of commentators echoed Limbaugh's denunciations of so-called liberal media.[51]

As a cable channel, Fox didn't come under FCC jurisdiction. But its overall approach makes clear its debt to Limbaugh and — some observers say — to the end of the Fairness Doctrine. "TV's Fox could not get away with its shameless shilling for the [Bush] White House if the Fairness Doctrine were still in place," liberal radio commentator Ian Masters of KPFK in Los Angeles argued in 2003.[52]

Liberal talk radio, however, draws smaller audiences. Some conservatives saw the recent collapse of Air America — a liberal talk-radio syndication service — as a major development. Bill O'Reilly, a popular, conservative Fox News commentator, called Air America's closing evidence of "the collapse of the far-left media." Air America veterans cited bad business management and noted that some of its stars have gone on to successful radio careers on their own, and in the case of comedian and former host Al Franken, to the U.S. Senate.[53]

In any event, the appearance of the Web and its repercussions for the news business have proved far more consequential than the talk-radio surge. The first event to make that point also showed that the Internet could extend the reach of one individual worldwide. That individual, Matt Drudge, runs the *Drudge Report*, a constantly

---

* The Fairness Doctrine differs from the Equal Time rule, which deals only with political candidates.

updated page of news links and occasional reporting. In 1998, he reported that *Newsweek* had killed a detailed story on President Clinton's affair with a former White House intern, soon identified as Monica Lewinsky. Drudge's report touched off the political firestorm that led to Clinton's impeachment.

"This story has done for the Internet what the Gulf War did for CNN and what the Kennedy assassination did for television in general," said Michael Kinsley, then editor of *Slate*, a pioneering Web-based magazine. (When it started up in 1996 *Slate* occasionally reached 10,000 readers a day; now it gets about 1.3 million a day.)[54]

By 2000, news organizations had concluded that having a Web presence was indispensable. But the disconnect between a Web site's power to vastly expand a news organization's reach, and its inability to build revenues to match, was already plain. "Except in a few cases, the idea that anyone will make money from selling news on the Web is laughable," Barry Parr, a business analyst with International Data Corp., told the *Los Angeles Times*.[55]

But independent sites, especially those with clear political identities, did build readership — and showed their power. In 2002, Josh Marshall's then one-man Web operation, the Democratic-oriented *TalkingPointsMemo*, scooped the mainstream press by reporting the significance of a comment by then-Senate Majority Leader Trent Lott of Mississippi praising the Jim Crow-era policies once championed by Sen. Strom Thurmond. (Lott lost his Republican leadership post.)[56]

Two years later, conservative blog sites set the stage for veteran anchor Dan Rather's premature departure from CBS News in 2004. Contributors to *Free Republic*, *Power Line* and *Little Green Footballs* (whose political orientation has since shifted), highlighted suspicious features of documents that Rather cited to back up a story that young George W. Bush had used family political connections to land a safe spot in the Texas Air National Guard to avoid serving in Vietnam. The documents later turned out to have been created years after they were dated, as the bloggers had argued.[57]

CURRENT SITUATION

Shielding Everyone?

A bill recently approved by the Senate Judiciary Committee would create the first federal shield law for journalists facing demands to testify in court or turn over material to law enforcement agencies.

Backers of the Senate legislation say their bill wouldn't extend the privilege to just anybody who, in today's Web-enabled world, blogs, tweets, or uploads video to YouTube and finds him or herself facing a federal subpoena.

But some committee members criticize the bill as it now reads, arguing it would cover everybody, even a leafleter in a Senate office building hallway. "This definition is no definition at all," Sen. Richard Durbin, D-Ill., said during a Dec. 10, 2009, meeting of the panel. "It is so broad as to be meaningless."[58]

But fellow Democrats who support the legislation contend that the courts would weed out those undeserving of being shielded.

"We're talking really about bloggers here," Sen. Arlen Specter, D-Pa., the bill's main sponsor, said during a debate that included mention of the liberal *Huffington Post* Web site, which includes posts by dozens of bloggers. "I would give them the benefit of the coverage."

Specter and other bill supporters won the argument, passing the bill after voting down an amendment to restrict the bill's coverage proposed by Sen. Dianne Feinstein, D-Calif., with support from Durbin.

Whatever definition committee members finally settle on, the bill wouldn't automatically confer immunity from subpoenas. A judge could order that a potential witness give evidence that was ruled to be necessary to prevent or lessen threats to national security. Nor would protection be granted for eyewitness evidence of a crime.

Arguments on those issues have been resolved.

But staffers and outside experts say that given Durbin's position as assistant majority leader, the bill will not come to the floor until he's satisfied with the definition of who would be covered. "He wants a sense of professionalism," says Dalglish of The Reporters Committee for Freedom of the Press, who is active in the crafting of a modified definition. The committee is concerned that reporters covering news via the Internet not be excluded.

The definition issue was expected to be resolved as early as the first week in February. Shield backers were counting heads in the Senate in early February. With backers having included a prominent Republican, Sen. Lindsey Graham of South Carolina, Dalglish was not expecting a partisan fight.

Should the proposed "shield" bill protect independent bloggers and all freelance journalists?

YES
Sen. Charles E. Schumer, D-N.Y.
Chairman, Committee on Rules and Administration

From remarks before Senate Judiciary Committee meeting and afterwards, Dec. 10, 2009

Journalism is changing. But I do not believe we should define [who merits protection] by the medium. People can do bad things on paper and good things on paper, bad things electronically and good things electronically. I've been subject to the brickbats of bloggers, but what they say shouldn't matter. We shouldn't look at whether people are saying bad things. That doesn't change what kind of privilege they have if they are protecting information.

Maybe it will happen — maybe once every three years — that the press secretary of one of us gets confidential information and then disseminates it. But the idea that every press secretary or every leafleter is going to invoke the [shield] privilege — it's not going to happen. It's only in a rare instance that you're disseminating confidential information and someone wants you to disclose it.

We've struck the right balance between national security concerns and the public's right to know. And it's important to remember that even if someone is a covered person, they don't automatically get protection. There is a [court] balancing test. Certainly a leafleter would not meet the balancing test. This bill does not give a huge privilege to everyone.

The [defeated] amendment proposed by Sen. [Dianne] Feinstein [D-Calif.] and Sen. [Richard] Durbin [D-Ill.] would require that a freelance journalist be able to demonstrate they've been under contract for six months of the past two years, and that a covered person gather information by direct interviews or by making direct observations of events.

Legitimate people who deserve this protection wouldn't even be allowed in. The definition excludes those who comment on public events, but who don't necessarily go into the field; mainstream columnists for established newspapers would be excluded. Journalists whose story results from a review of Freedom of Information Act documents would not be covered. Freelance journalists — in today's economy it is less and less likely that a freelance journalist would be able to demonstrate they've been under contract for six months of the past two years. If I am a journalist and I write a column, but don't have a contract for it, why in God's name should I be excluded? It makes no sense whatsoever.

This bill will ensure a free press, which is a cornerstone of our democracy.

NO
Sen. Dianne Feinstein, D-Calif.
Chairwoman, Senate Select Committee on Intelligence

From remarks before Senate Judiciary Committee meeting, Dec. 10, 2009

I've always believed that being a journalist carries with it certain responsibilities. Journalists are trained to at least try to cover an issue objectively and to search for truth. Established newspapers and broadcasters set journalistic standards for the reporters. They have editors, directors or producers who review the reporters' work and hold them to account. Under the new definition in this bill, none of these safeguards exist.

Under the definition that we proposed, the journalist worked as a salaried employee or independent contractor of an entity that disseminates information.

The current language makes anyone a journalist no matter how crazy, hateful or false the information they post.

Or let's say, hypothetically, that a neo-Nazi blogger obtained information from [another neo-Nazi] at an anti-immigration demonstration, and the authorities sought the identity of that [person] so they could identify the perpetrators of violent crimes. This neo-Nazi blogger would qualify as a journalist under this bill, and federal authorities would have to exhaust all reasonable alternatives [to a subpoena]. And the court would have to engage in analysis, applying a balancing test. . . . In my view, hate-mongers do not deserve the protection.

I'm concerned that if we keep the wide-open definition in the bill we will create a mechanism for a disgruntled person to leak slanted, incomplete or even deliberately false information to an ideologically sympathetic person, knowing that the person could then invoke the shield created by this bill to protect this ill-spirited source.

Even worse, we could create a regime where somebody could just make up a piece of information, and make up a source for it and then invoke the shield to cover up their own deception.

For those of us who have been around for a while and watched the change in journalism — a lot of it is very good. But there has always been a standard for legitimacy. Here, there is no standard for legitimacy. It's a hard one to come up with; I'm the first to admit it. But as I read the definition, it virtually applies to most of us. I could consider myself a journalist under this, and I'm not. I hope that this is a work in progress.

Senate passage would likely guarantee enactment. The House passed a version of the bill on a voice vote last March, and the bills are seen as relatively easy to reconcile. The Obama administration has endorsed the Senate bill.

"This legislation provides robust judicial protection for journalists' confidential sources," National Intelligence Director Dennis C. Blair and Attorney General Eric H. Holder Jr. wrote in a Nov. 4, 2009, letter to Senate Judiciary Committee Chairman Patrick J. Leahy, D-Vt., "while also enabling the Government to take measures necessary to protect national security and enforce our criminal laws."[59]

On the state front, Republican Texas Gov. Rick Perry signed a new state shield law last May. And shield legislation passed the Wisconsin Assembly and is pending in the state Senate.[60]

Subpoenaing Students

An unusual media-subpoena case under way in Chicago centers on a group of journalism students who are fighting subpoenas not for their sources — which are public — but for their grades.

The matter might sound relatively trivial, but it grows out of a homicide conviction and life sentence and the students' reinvestigation of the case.

The students were part of the Innocence Project at Northwestern University's Medill School. Since 1999, students in the program have conducted investigations that helped free 11 men from prison, five of them on death row.[61]

Last year, the students' digging succeeded in reopening the case of Anthony McKinney, convicted in 1981 in the killing of a security guard and imprisoned ever since. But the Cook County state attorney's office, which has cooperated with the Innocence Project in other cases, balked at cooperating in the McKinney case.[62]

State Attorney Anita Alvarez subpoenaed all of the students' notes and electronic communications in the case plus the grades they'd received and the grading criteria set by Project Director David Protess, a veteran journalist and criminal-justice researcher. As the case has developed, Alvarez and her colleagues have argued in court filings that in an effort to win good grades students paid two witnesses for their statements, and that a female student flirted with another witness to encourage him to talk.[63]

The alleged bribe centered on an alleged overpayment of $60 for a cab ride. And Protess and one of his woman students denied any use of flirting as a tactic. As to the suggestion that students' grades depend on acquiring evidence of innocence, a 2008 graduate said she'd gotten an A for work that proved one man's guilt.[64]

Beyond the factual issues is a link to the question that's preoccupying journalism-watchers and lawmakers elsewhere. "When I was a law student, I wasn't a lawyer," Alvarez said in an interview with *Chicago Magazine*, arguing that the journalism students aren't journalists — and hence ineligible for protection under the Illinois shield law.[65]

But, a coalition of 18 media companies and organizations countered in a friend of the court brief on behalf of the students, their work was clearly journalistic. And, a motion filed with the brief adds, "The use of student journalists is only likely to increase as news organizations face declining advertising revenues and shrinking newsroom staffs."

Freedom of Information

Press freedom involves more than protection from subpoenas. For decades, media organizations have been in the vanguard of campaigns for access to government documents and meetings and trials.

These guarantees, where they exist, apply to ordinary citizens, not just reporters. In practice, though, reporters make the greatest use of that access.

At a time when the media are short of time and money, some media-law experts worry that government officials are feeling less obliged to comply with reporters demanding access to meetings and records.

In Iowa, Democratic Gov. Chet Culver and the *Des Moines Register*, the state's leading newspaper, have been sparring for about a year over the paper's efforts to obtain internal documents concerning state supervision of facilities for disabled people.

State officials "may get sued yet," says Giudicessi, an attorney for the paper. "The statute of limitations hasn't run."

Culver's office argued a year ago that 50 e-mails between members of his staff concerning the 2008 death of a 26-year-old resident of the Glenwood Resource Center were exempt from disclosure under the state's open-records law because they are "draft documents."[66]

The newspaper reported that the law doesn't protect draft documents from public release. But the governor relies on an opinion by the state attorney general's office that the legislature never meant to include draft documents in the open-records law.[67]

Later in 2009, Culver's office began charging for document requests — not for standard photocopying costs but for the expense of staff analyzing the documents to decide if they could be released. For one set of documents involving state care for mentally retarded workers at another facility, the fee was $630. The newspaper turned down the arrangement on the grounds that it might be paying for documents it wasn't allowed to have.[68]

With both sides dug in, only courts can determine who is interpreting open-records law correctly. But, first, a news organization would have to bring the matter to court. And media lawyers worry that such lawsuits are becoming less common, as struggling news organizations tighten their belts.

"A lot of these acts — sunshine laws, public meetings laws, the Freedom of Information Act — are not self-executing," says Jones of Brigham Young University. "Without the mainstream media to act as the enforcement arm, some of these laws I really worry will be dead on the books."

OUTLOOK

Limited Resources

In late January *The New York Times* announced a fee system (to begin in 2011) for non-subscribers who want full Web access to the paper. "It was clear when consumer [circulation] revenues surpassed advertising revenues last year that *The New York Times* was going to come up with some kind of pay model," *Times* media columnist David Carr wrote."[69]

But, Carr acknowledged, "Every plan that could be conceived of heads into a large headwind, built up over years, that consumers do not expect to pay for content no matter where it comes from."

Meanwhile, think tanks are striving to develop plans to ensure that public-interest journalism survives, in some form.

At the University of Southern California, the Annenberg School's Center on Communication Leadership & Policy is proposing indirect public subsidies of the news

media. "The government has always supported the commercial news business. It does so today," argues a report by the center's director, Geoffrey Cowan, and David Westphal, a senior fellow, citing subsidized postal rates for mailed publications and special tax treatment for news businesses. "Unless the government takes affirmative action, though, the level of support is almost certain to decline at this important time in the history of journalism."[70]

The Pew Research Center's Project for Excellence in Journalism, meanwhile, devotes itself to analyzing trends rather than devising solutions to the business crisis. Where those trends are headed, acknowledges project director Rosenstiel, isn't exactly clear. "The analogy may be the early '20s and radio, when you're at the beginning of something, and the actual direction of the storm can be hard to determine."

One possible form the news universe may take is "a handful of national newspapers and a smaller number of metro newspapers, and an increase in the number of niche neighborhood sites," Rosenstiel says. "It may be that we have an ecosystem that is partly citizen- or amateur-based at a very local level, and more conventional and professional at a national level."

But will either model provide the resources for journalists — professional or amateur — to take on government officials who close off access or subpoena reporters' notes?

"My concern is that the only people who will be able to afford to wage those kinds of fights are people underwritten in one form or another by government subsidies," says *Des Moines Register* attorney Giudicessi. "If we go to a digital model, an iPod-Kindle model, I don't know where the money is going to come from to afford that watchdog element."

Web-based journalism operations funded by foundations and private donors offer a potential approach. The best-known of these is *ProPublica*, which was started two years ago with a three-year $30 million grant from husband-and-wife philanthropists Herbert and Marion Sandler and dedicated to nonpartisan, investigative journalism.[71]

Wasserman of Washington and Lee University argues the money might have been better spent in grants for investigative reporting by local newspapers, which is diminishing. "We are going to reap a year's worth of local and state corruption, because that's where the news cutbacks have been most numerous," he says. "God only knows what's happening in zoning and the provision of public works."

Jones of Brigham Young University Law School shares his grim outlook. She doubts that a legal battle for courtroom access that led to a 1980 Supreme Court victory by a Richmond, Va., newspaper company would happen today.[72] "That holding is not limited to newspapers," she says. "All of us as citizens are guaranteed access to criminal trials because newspapers had the resolve and dollars to litigate."

But at least in the near future, Jones continues, "unless some very creative solutions come into being quite quickly, I predict that at least initially we'll have a fairly significant void in this kind of democracy-enhancing litigation that newspapers have provided to us."

Still, Dalglish of the Reporters Committee says her organization and some big media companies remain capable of fighting free-press battles. As to the future, "I think the hemorrhaging of the mainstream media will have stabilized. I'm hoping that someone comes forward and figures out how to make journalism pay on the Internet."

NOTES

1. Christopher Elliott, "Full text of my subpoena from the Department of Homeland Security," *Elliott.org*, Dec. 29, 2009, www.elliott. org/blog/full-text-of-my-subpoena-from-the-department-of-homeland-security.

2. Larry Margasak and Corey Williams, "Search for answers, tighter security after attack," The Associated Press, Dec. 27, 2009; Richard Sisk *et al.*, "In An Upright Position," *Daily News* (New York), Dec. 27, 2009, p. 6.

3. Steven Frischling, "The Fallout From SD 1544-09-06: The Feds At My Door," Dec. 30, 2009, http://boardingarea.com/blogs/flyingwithfish/2009/12/30/the-fallout-from-sd-1544-09-06-the-feds-at-my-door/; Larry Margasak, "US ends journalist subpoenas over leaked memo," The Associated Press, Jan. 1, 2010, http://news.yahoo.com/s/ap_travel/20100101/ap_tr_ge/us_travel_brief_airliner_attack_tsa_subpoenas_1.

4. RonNell Andersen Jones, "Avalanche or Undue Alarm? An Empirical Study of Subpoenas Received by the News Media," *Minnesota Law Review*, 2008, p. 113, http://papers.ssrn.com/sol3/ papers.cfm?abstract_id=1125500.

5. Neil A. Lewis and Scott Shane, "Reporter Who Was Jailed Testifies in Libby Case," *The New York Times*, Jan. 31, 2007, p. A1.

6. Anne E. Kornblut and Michael A. Fletcher, "In Obama's decision-making, a wide range of influences," *The Washington Post*, Jan. 25, 2010, www.washingtonpost.com/wp-dyn/con tent/article/2010/01/24/AR2010012403014.html?hpid=topnews.

7. RonNell Andersen Jones, "Media Subpoenas: Impact, Perception, and Legal Protection in the Changing World of American Journalism," *Washington Law Review*, August 2009, p. 363, http://papers.ssrn.com/sol3/papers.cfm?abstract_id=1407105.

8. *Ibid.*, p. 144; and Jones, "Avalanche or Undue Alarm . . . ," *op. cit.*, p. 142.

9. David Westphal, "News Media in Crisis," in "Public Policy and Funding the News," University of Southern California, Annenberg Center on Communication Leadership & Policy, 2010, p. 5, www.fundingthenews.org/pdf/pub lic_policy_report.pdf.

10. David Lieberman, "Newspaper closings raise fear about industry," *USA Today*, March 19, 2009, www.usatoday.com/money/media/2009-03-17-newspapers-downturn_N.htm. Matea Gold, "CBS News staffers fret that layoffs will hamper newsgathering," *Los Angeles Times*, Company Town (blog), Feb. 2, 2010, http:// latimesblogs.latimes.com/entertainmentnews buzz/2010/02/cbs-news-staffers-fret-that-layoffs-will-hurt-newsgathering.html.

11. Video of Senate Judiciary Committee debate over the bill on Dec. 10, 2009, is available at "Full Committee, Executive Business Meeting," http://judiciary.senate.gov/resources/webcasts/index.cfm?t=m&d=12-2009&p=all.

12. "'New York Times' Begins Round of Newsroom Layoffs," The Associated Press (*Editor & Publisher*), Dec. 17, 2009, www.editorand publisher.com/eandp/news/article_display.jsp?vnu_content_id=1004054338;

Emma Heald, "Associated Press confirms total of 90 layoffs this week," editorsweblog.org, *World Editors Forum*, Nov. 20, 2009, /www.editorsweblog.org/ newspaper/2009/11/associated_press_confirms_ total_of_90_la.php; Paul Beebe, "Salt Lake Tribune owner files Chapter 11 reorganization," *Salt Lake Tribune*, Jan. 22, 2010, www.sltrib. com/business/ ci_14248521; Stephanie Clifford, "Time Inc. Layoffs Begin at Sports Illustrated," *The New York Times*, Media Decoder blog, Nov. 3, 2009, http:// mediadecoder.blogs.nytimes. com/2009/11/03/ time-inc-layoffs-begin-at-sports-illustrated/. Jeff Pijanowsky, "More than 15,000 People Have Lost Their Jobs in 2009 in the Newspaper Industry," *New Cycle* (blog), Dec. 14, 2009, http://news-cycle .blogspot.com/ 2009/12/more-than-15000-people- have-lost-their. html.

13. John Thornton, "A Note from Our Chairman," *The Texas Tribune*, Jan. 24, 2010, www. texastribune.org/ stories/2010/jan/25/note-chair man/; John Temple, "I'm moving to Honolulu to become the first editor of Peer News," *Temple Talk* (blog), Jan. 21, 2010, www.john temple.net/2010/01/im-moving-to-hono lulu-to-become-first.html; Bill Mitchell, "Nonprofit Connecticut Mirror Targets Gaps in Political Coverage and Data," *NewsPay* (blog), *Poynter Online*, Jan. 25, 2010, www.poynter.org/column.asp?id=131 &aid=176435

14. Michael Wolff, "Is a Tweet News?" *Off the Grid*, Jan. 25, 2010, www.newser.com/off-the-grid/post/382/is- a-tweet-news-and-is-murdoch-selling-his-papers.html.

15. David Shaw, "Do bloggers deserve basic journalistic protections?"*Los Angeles Times*, March 27, 2005, p. E14.

16. Garrett Graff, "Bloggers and Journalism," *echoditto*, March 23, 2005, www.echoditto.com/ node/619.

17. *Ibid.*

18. Adam Cohen, "The Latest Rumbling in the Blogosphere: Questions About Ethics," *The New York Times*, May 8, 2005, Sect. 4, p. 11.

19. Court decisions summarized in Mary-Rose Papandrea, "Citizen Journalism and the Reporter's Privilege," *Minnesota Law Review*, 2007, pp. 517-518, http://lsr .nellco.org/cgi/view content.cgi?article=1168& context=hc_lsfp.

20. *Ibid.*, p. 590.

21. *Ibid.*, p. 591.

22. Campbell Robertson and Bernie Becker, "Tampering at Senator's Office was 'Stunt,' Lawyer Says," *The New York Times*, Jan. 29, 2010, p. A16.

23. Statement from James O'Keefe, Jan. 29, 2010, http://bigjournalism.com/jokeefe/2010/01/29/ statement-from-james-okeefe/#more-14542.

24. Josh Levin, "Rather Serious," *Slate*, Sept. 10, 2004, www.slate.com/id/2106553/.

25. "The Times and Iraq," *The New York Times*, May 26, 2004, p. A1.

26. Zachary M. Seward, "Top 15 newspaper sites of 2008," Nieman Journalism Lab, Feb. 17, 2009; "The State of the News Media 2009," *op. cit.*, p. 12. "Site profile, nytimes.com," as of Feb. 1, 2010, http://siteanalytics.compete. com/nytimes.com/.

27. Perry Bacon Jr., "ACORN video creates new conser- vative star," *The Washington Post*, Oct. 31, 2009, www.washingtonpost.com/wp-dyn/content/article/ 2009/10/30/AR2009103003737_pf.html.

28. Except where otherwise indicated, this subsection draws on Alex S. Jones, *Losing the News: The Future of the News That Feeds Democracy* (2009). For back- ground, see Kenneth Jost, "Free-Press Disputes," *CQ Researcher*, April 8, 2005, pp. 293-316.

29. Both quoted in Jones, *ibid.*

30. "U.S. Espionage Act, 15 June 1917," firstworldwar .com, www.firstworldwar.com/source/ espionageact .htm.

31. *Gitlow v. New York*, 268 U.S. 652 (1925).

32. *Near v. Minnesota*, 283 U.S. 697 (1931).

33. Except where otherwise indicated, this subsection is drawn from Michael Emery and Edwin Emery, *The Press and America: An Interpretive History of the Mass Media* (6th ed., 1988), pp. 216-217.

34. Quoted in Michael Schudson, "The objectivity norm in American journalism," *Journalism*, 2001, jou.sagepub.com/cgi/content/abstract/ 2/2/149.

35. Quoted in *ibid.*

36. Edwin R. Bayley, *Joe McCarthy and the Press* (1981).

37. Quoted in *ibid.*, p. 216.

38. Except where otherwise indicated, this subsection is drawn from Emery and Emery, *op. cit.*

39. For 1960 statistic, "Facts for Features," U.S. Census Bureau, March 11, 2004, www.census. gov/Press-Release/www/releases/archives/facts_ for_features_special_editions/001702.html.

40. Peter Braestrup, *The Big Story: How the American Press and Television Reported and Interpreted the Crisis of Tet 1968 in Vietnam and Washington* (1994).

41. Jones, "Media Subpoenas," *op. cit.*, p. 319.

42. *New York Times Co. v. Sullivan*, 376 U.S. 254 (1964).

43. The case is *New York Times v. United States*, 403 U.S. 713 (1971).

44. *Branzburg v. Hayes*, 408 U.S. 665 (1972).

45. Jones, "Media Subpoenas," *op. cit.*, p. 346.

46. *McKevitt v. Pallasch*, 339 F.3d 530 (7th Cir. 2003), quoted in Jones, "Media Subpoenas," *op. cit.*, p. 347 (footnote 118). For the legal ambiguity of Powell's opinion, see Adam Liptak, "Courts Grow Increasingly Skeptical of Any Special Protections for the Press," *The New York Times*, June 28, 2005, p. A1.

47. Carol D. Leonnig and Amy Goldstein, "Libby Given 2-1/2-Year Prison Term," *The Washington Post*, June 6, 2007, www.washingtonpost. com/wp-dyn/content/article/2007/06/05/AR 2007060500150.html; Neil A. Lewis and Scott Shane, "Reporter Who Was Jailed Testifies in Libby Case," *The New York Times*, Jan. 31, 2007, p. A1.

48. David Kravetz, "Freelance journalist is freed after spending record time in jail," The Associated Press, April 4, 2007.

49. "Press Accuracy Rating Hits Two Decade Low," Pew Research Center for People and the Press, Sept. 13, 2009, http://people-press. org/report/543/.

50. Jim Puzzanghera, "Democrats speak out for Fairness Doctrine," *Los Angeles Times*, July 23, 2007, p. C1.

51. David Carr and Tim Arango, "A Fox Chief at the Pinnacle of Media and Politics," *The New York Times,* Jan. 9, 2010, www.nytimes. com/2010/01/10/business/media/10ailes.html?scp=1&sq=RogerAiles&st=cse.

52. Ian Masters, "Media Monopolies Have Muzzled Dissent," *Los Angeles Times*, May 1, 2003, Part 2, p. 15.

53. Steve Carney, "The message of Air America's end," *Los Angeles Times*, Jan. 23, 2010, www. latimes.com/entertainment/news/la-et-air-america 23-2010 jan23,0,1604003.story.

54. Quoted in Marlene Cimons, "Some See Internet Coming of Age During Clinton Troubles," *Los Angeles Times*, Feb. 2, 1998, p. A5; "Newsweek Kills Story on White House Intern," Jan. 17, 1998, www .drudgereportarchives.com/data/2002/01/17/ 20020117_175502_ml.htm; David Plotz, "A Slate Timeline," June 19, 2006, www.slate.com/id/214 3235/; Site profile: slate.com, siteanalytics.com pete .com/slate.com.

55. Quoted in Charles Piller, "Web News Sites Fail to Click," *Los Angeles Times*, Aug. 18, 2000, p. A1.

56. Matthew Klam, "Fear and Laptops on the Campaign Tra—," *The New York Times Magazine*, Sept. 26, 2004, p. 43.

57. Josh Levin, "Rather Serious," *Slate*, Sept. 10, 2004, www.slate.com/id/2106553/.

58. "Full Committee, Executive Business Meeting," webcast, *op. cit.* O'Reilly quoted in Brian Stelter, "Liberal Radio, Even Without Air America," *The New York Times*, Jan. 24, 2010, www.nytimes .com/2010/01/25/arts/25radio.html?scp=1&sq=aira merica&st=cse.

59. Blair and Holder to Leahy, Nov. 4, 2009, www.rcfp .org/newsitems/docs/20091105_155125_letter.pdf.

60. Kelly Shannon, "Texas Governor Signs Shield Law to Protect Journos," The Associated Press (*Editor and Publisher*) May 14, 2009, www. editorandpublisher. com/eandp/news/article_ display.jsp?vnu_content_id=1003973183; Stacy Forster and Patrick Marley, "Shield law for reporters gets OK," *Milwaukee Journal Sentinel*, Sept. 23, 2009, p. B3.

61. "Medill Innocence Project" Web site, /www. medillinnocenceproject.org.

62. Bryan Smith, "The Professor and the Prosecutor: Anita Alvarez's office turns up the heat on David Protess' Medill Innocence Project," *Chicago Magazine*, February 2010, www. chicagomag.com/Chicago-Magazine/February-2010/Anita-Alvarez-turns-up-the-heat-in-her- battle-with-Northwesterns-David-Protess-and-his-Medill-Innocence-Project/.

63. *Ibid.*; Karen Hawkins, "Prosecutors claim students paid 2 witnesses," The Associated Press, Nov. 11, 2009.

64. Smith, *ibid.*

65. Quoted in *ibid.*

66. Quoted in Clark Kauffman, "E-mail 'drafts' on Glenwood death kept secret," *Des Moines Register*, Jan. 8, 2009, p. B1.

67. *Ibid.*

68. Clark Kauffman, "Consultant's report not ready for public, governor's office says," *Des Moines Register*, Sept. 4, 2009.

69. David Carr, "Dialing in a Plan: The Times Installs a Meter on its Future," *Media Decoder* (blog), Jan. 20, 2010, http://mediadecoder. blogs.nytimes.com/2010/01/20/dialing-in-a-plan-the-times-installs-a-meter-on-its-future/.

70. Geoffrey Cowan and David Westphal, "Public Policy and Funding the News," Center on Communication Leadership and Policy, Jan. 28, 2010, p. 14.

71. Joe Nocera, "Self-Made Philanthropists," *The New York Times Magazine*, March 9, 2008, p. 58.

72. *Richmond Newspapers, Inc. v. Virginia*, 448 U.S. 555 (1980). For background, see Jost, *op. cit.*

BIBLIOGRAPHY

Books

Bollinger, Lee C., *Uninhibited, Robust, and Wide-Open: A Free Press for a New Century*, Oxford University Press, 2010.
The president of Columbia University calls for making press freedom a priority in domestic and international affairs.

Jones, Alex S., *Losing the News: The Future of the News That Feeds Democracy*, Oxford University Press, 2009.
Combining personal memories with recent history, a veteran journalist who directs the Joan Shorenstein Center for the Press, Politics and Public Policy at Harvard University's Kennedy School of Government analyzes the collapse of the old business model and explores possible new directions.

Sanford, Bruce W., *Don't Shoot the Messenger: How Our Growing Hatred of the Media Threatens Free Speech For All of Us*, Rowman & Littlefield, 2001.
A veteran First Amendment lawyer examines the reasons why public esteem for the media began plummeting.

Articles

"Nonprofits and Journalism: An Interview with Mark Jurkowitz," *The Nonprofit Quarterly*, Sept. 21, 2009, www.nonprofitquarterly.org/index.php?option=com_con tent&view=article&id=1611:nonprofits-and-journalism-an-interview-with-mark-jurko witz&catid=154:current-issue.
The associate director of the Project for Excellence in Journalism discusses the growth of foundation-financed journalism.

Breitbart, Andrew, "Media does matter for America," *The Daily Caller*, Jan. 11, 2010, http://dailycaller.com/2010/ 01/11/media-does-matter-for-america/.
A conservative Web publisher hails Internet-enabled competition with what he calls the false objectivity of the mainstream media.

Kauffman, Clark, "State withholds another Glenwood document," *Des Moines Register*, Dec. 5, 2009, p. B1.
Iowa's leading newspaper reports on its latest attempt to access state documents concerning state institutions for disabled people.

Mutter, Alan D., "Putting bite back in newspapers," *Reflections of a Newsosaur* (blog), Dec. 15, 2009, http://newso saur.blogspot.com/2009/12/putting-bite-back-in-news papers.html.
An adjunct journalism professor at the University of California says more point of view in newspaper articles might bring back readers.

Yusuf, Huma, "Rise in lawsuits against bloggers," *The Christian Science Monitor*, July 16, 2008, www.csmon itor. com/Innovation/Tech-Culture/2008/0716/rise-in-lawsuits-against-bloggers.
The potential legal pitfalls of blog journalism got early attention in an old-line newspaper that switched entirely to the Web in 2009.

Reports and Studies

"Press Accuracy Rating Hits Two Decade Low," Pew Research Center for the People & the Press, Sept. 13, 2009, http://people-press.org/report/543/.
A nonpartisan survey finds continued diminution of public confidence in the media.

"The State of the News Media: An Annual Report on American Journalism," Project for Excellence in Journalism, 2009, www.stateofthemedia.org/2009/index.htm.
An in-depth analysis shows the extent of crisis in traditional news organizations.

Cowan, Geoffrey, and David Westphal, "Public Policy and Funding the News," Center on Communication Leadership & Policy, USC Annenberg School for Communication & Journalism, January 2010, http://fundingthenews.org/.
Leaders of a journalism think tank argue for increasing indirect public financing of the media.

Downie, Leonard Jr., and Michael Schudson, "The Reconstruction of American Journalism," *Columbia Journalism Review*, Oct. 19, 2009, www.cjr.org/recon struction/the_ reconstruction_of_american.php.
Universities, foundations and other institutions should help fill the gap left by the continuing collapse of traditional news media, a former *Washington Post* editor and longtime journalism professor conclude.

Gajda, Amy, "Judging Journalism: The Turn Toward Privacy and Judicial Regulation of the Press," *California Law Review*, August 2009, http://papers.ssrn.com/sol3/papers. cfm?abstract_id=1103248##.
A journalist-turned-lawyer points to perils for reporters in public and judicial reactions to privacy erosion in the Internet Age.

Jones, RonNell Andersen, "Media Subpoenas: Impact, Perception, and Legal Protection in the Changing World of American Journalism," *Washington Law Review*, August 2009, http://papers.ssrn.com/sol3/papers .cfm? abstract_id=1407105.
A nationwide survey shows editors feel under siege legally as well as financially.

For More Information

Big Journalism, http://bigjournalism.com. Site founded by conservative Web publisher Andrew Breitbart for criticism of mainstream media; published the undercover ACORN videos of James O'Keefe.

Citizen Media Law Project, Berkman Center for Internet & Society, Harvard Law School, 23 Everett St., Second Floor, Cambridge, MA 02138; (617) 495-7547; www.citmedialaw.org/about/citizen-media-law-project. Also affiliated with Arizona State University-based Center for Citizen Media, the Project focuses on promoting and defending citizen journalism and related activities.

Joan Shorenstein Center on the Press, Politics, and Public Policy, John F. Kennedy School of Government, Harvard University, 79 JFK St., Cambridge, MA 02138; (617) 495-8269; www.hks.harvard.edu/presspo. Fosters contact between journalists and academic experts.

The Poynter Institute, 801 Third St South, St. Petersburg, FL 33701; (888) 769-6837; www.poynter.org. Nonprofit journalism-training organization whose Web site includes Jim Romenesko's popular industry-news site.

Project for Excellence in Journalism, 1615 L St., N.W., Washington, DC 20036; (202) 419-3650; www.journal ism.org. Researches trends in the news business, including the rise of Web-based media.

The Reporters Committee for Freedom of the Press, 1101 Wilson Blvd., Suite 1100, Arlington, VA 22209; (703) 807-2100; www.rcfp.org/. Provides free legal representation for reporters, researches free-press issues and advocates free-press legislation.